No Sleep 'til Sudbury

Adventures in 80s Hard Rock and Metal Deconstruction

Brent Jensen

EDWARDS PRESS COMPANY
TORONTO

Copyright © 2014 Brent Jensen
All rights reserved.
ISBN: 0987715909
ISBN-13: 978-0987715906

For Tegan

Acknowledgements
Take a Bow

Love and gratitude to tolerant wifey Alison Jensen for never, ever changing the station.

A few people were avid and encouraging readers of sample chapters: childhood pal Bryan Sloss, Larissa Moffatt, Brad 'Jammer' Jemmett, and Kent 'Blaze' Bailey. I very sincerely appreciate every insight and kind word you offered.

Thanks to my high school English teacher Mr. Don Stos for making a difference by taking the time to challenge me on everything, including the consideration of long hair as a social trapping. His words were wise and inspiring, and always provided without quarter. In my mind I can still see his red ink impression on one of my essays: *"Bullshit baffles brains, but remember that some of us carry shovels"*.

Thanks also to David 'The Wealthy Barber' Chilton for providing valuable information and guidance, inspiration, and his phone number, and to Martin Popoff for always immediately responding to my inane emails and telling me that my *Chinese Democracy* article was the best he'd read on the topic.

Many thanks to Jason Gross at Perfect Sound Forever, Patrick Schabe at PopMatters, Tony Anselmo, Dr. Liam Ennis, Steve 'Crystal' Flemming, James Wylie, Kevin 'Wyatt' Reid, to absent friends, and to everyone else who provided encouragement and stimulation along the way.

Special thanks to my brother-in-law Craig Sutoski, who encouraged endless hours of dialogue on the myriad reasons why Van Halen trumps Van Hagar, why Alice Cooper's *Billion Dollar Babies* is mostly brilliant, and why it's fundamentally important to appreciate Rose Tattoo if you call yourself a hard rock fan. This book is for you, pal.

Contents

Prologue
A Shout Out to the Devil...ix

Chapter One
Papertown 1

Chapter Two
First KISS 5

Chapter Three
No Sleep 'til Sudbury.. 19

Chapter Four
Frankie Goes to Hollywood... 31

Chapter Five
Metallica, Slayer, Raven, and...*Dokken*? 45

Chapter Six
Living on a Thrash Metal Prayer 59

Chapter Seven
Tony's Record Store... 75

Chapter Eight
Kerrang!... 91

Chapter Nine
Gunter Glieben Glauchen Globen 103

Chapter Ten
Achtung Rabies 119

Chapter Eleven
Former Things Passed Away..................................... 129

Chapter Twelve
The Pit 147

Chapter Thirteen
Everybody Wants To Go To Heaven,
But Nobody Wants To Die 157

Chapter Fourteen
Heavy Metal or Hard Rock? 173

Chapter Fifteen
Hard Rock is Dead, Long Live Hard Rock 189

Chapter Sixteen
The Pointlessness of Debate 201

Chapter Seventeen
The Church of Axl 205

Chapter Eighteen
Jammed 221

Chapter Nineteen
Canuck Metal 223

Chapter Twenty
I Don't Trust People Who Don't Drink 245

Chapter Twenty-One
Dreaming of a Black (Sabbath) Christmas 253

Chapter Twenty-Two
Fear and Consumption 269

Chapter Twenty-Three
White Sabbath 279

Chapter Twenty-Four
So Much For Hollywood 283

About the Author 295

Prologue
A Shout Out to the Devil

A few things compelled me to write this book, some more important than others.

I've read way too many rock books that were just versions of the same. Maybe a new morsel of information I didn't already know inserted here or there, but otherwise just a sterile retelling of history. Bookstore shelves are loaded with these books.

I wanted to write a book that touched more on the personal aspect of how music is received and experienced, because that's really the whole point. I wanted to talk about what music means to an individual. How music *feels* to the listener as a result of how it sounds and looks.

I knew back in 1983 that Motley Crue's *Shout at the Devil* was no *Born to Run*, and I didn't care. What I did care about was how tremendously alive *Shout at the Devil* made me feel. In that sense, *Shout at the Devil* actually was my personal *Born to Run*.

Later on in life when I listened back to *Shout* and all of those other records from my teen years, I considered the enormous impact that this music had on my adolescence. It was clear that the power of these records really came from a desire to connect and to identify - regardless of any lack of artistic substance, musical quality, or even relevance. The type or quality of the music didn't matter at all. It was the experience that mattered. And I thought quite a lot about that.

Then I wrote it all down and published it.

One
Papertown

As reluctant as I am to contribute to the growth of Gene Simmons' ego any further beyond its already gargantuan size, I can certainly credit KISS for being partially responsible for my love of hard rock and heavy metal.

I started buying KISS records when I was eight or nine, and I think *KISS Alive II* was my first one. I remember holding it in my hands and being transfixed by that headshot of Simmons on the back cover with the fake blood caked on his face and dripping with sweat, morbidly cast in gloomy stage lighting while stoically gazing upward like some sort of ghastly warrior. I bought the record at Wally's Music in Espanola - my glum little hometown in northern Ontario, about four hours northwest of Toronto.

Espanola's primary industry in the 70s and 80s was the E.B. Eddy paper mill, an undeniable monolith that belched grey smoke as it loomed large over town. Most of Espanola's 3,500 or so population worked there, but that was only if you were fortunate enough to have a relative who could get you in. The Espy Life Plan was simple – get your grade twelve, get on at the mill, and wait for death. No worries in between. You had it made, and you had everything you would need. There was no point in leaving town to attempt to further your education at university or anything like that. In fact, there was no need to leave at all. Higher education wasn't talked about a lot in Espanola. When it was, it was framed as something that existed on some other plane, somewhere else. There was no need to leave the comfortably lax, familiar confines of Espanola to try to make a living somewhere else. No need to be different. The prospect of life beyond Espanola was met with mumbled sentences that trailed off before they finished. No point. Don't try.

In the process of manufacturing its products, the paper mill used to emit chemicals into the air via its smokestacks that made Espanola smell of rotten eggs. This fact was not lost on those who lived in neighbouring areas, or those who had traveled through Espanola at any point. The town had a reputation for smelling badly. To this day, people will still raise this point when I tell them I grew up there. The thing about it though is that, like most other peculiarities that went down in Espy, no one really thought of it as unusual. It was just *there*, and you went about your business in spite of it. You just accepted it as a matter of course. It was normal. Just like the two signs on the town's main watering hole – 'NO ILLEGAL DRUGS', handwritten and posted beside the front entrance of the dilapidated building. Twice.

After a while, I didn't really even notice the smell most of the time. I was desensitized, much in the same way that I suppose most small town people are within the confines of their small towns. The sleepiness of Espy lent itself to the communally trancelike environment that floated its citizens through their lives there. Stimulus would have come at a premium if it had come at all. Cloudy weather was just that much more punishingly grey somehow, and time was all you really had. People rushed to look out their windows when a siren was heard – police car, ambulance, or fire truck each carried mildly varying propensities for tabooed titillation. Or at the very least, something to talk about. When there were no sirens, no one really talked much about anything outside of the typical circular conversation about the weather or what they saw on television recently. After that chat had run its course, people talked about each other. Facts were malleable, and stories metamorphosed as convenience required. It wasn't that the telephone was broken necessarily. It was more that reality was massaged into something that matched desired condition, and desired outcome.

There were no (openly) gay people in Espanola when I was growing up there. There was the inevitable speculation of its potentially homosexual citizens, and it got discussed. Not a lot of ethnicity in town. There was one black family whose patriarch was one of the medical doctors at Espanola General Hospital. There was also one Chinese family, the Engs. They operated the Arena Grill restaurant, which also served as the local Greyhound bus depot. The Arena Grill had the best fries and gravy in the entire North Shore. One of the family's sons, Bernard Eng, who seemed eighteen for the duration of my own teenage years, was a gifted tennis player. He acknowledged the younger kids at the town courts by letting us play with him and his friends when the courts were busy, which made him even more larger than life than he already was for his tennis skills. The only other visible minority in Espanola was a group of Vietnamese refugees who did not speak English and were referred to as the 'Boat People'. The oldest male member of this group used to amble slowly around town every night, leaning deliberately from right to left and left to right as he walked, his hands clasped behind his back and with a big, bright smile beaming from his face, waving enthusiastically to everyone he encountered in his travels. I can still see his smiling face in my mind.

Much of what I learned about the world in my youth back in Espanola was gleaned through the television screen, and my appetite stemmed from what I consumed with my eyes from the TV. This made growing up in Espanola difficult in a sense. While I could see what was available out there through the TV window, I resigned myself to the fact that most of it was not at my immediate disposal. As a kid, seeing the commercials that came in from the Toronto and American networks for Taco Bell and Cookie Crisp cereal felt like a mild form of waterboarding back then. Reason number forty-six to leave Espy when the time was right.

The closest city to Espanola was Sudbury, a city situated about 45 minutes east with a population of roughly 100,000 people at the time

I guess. Sudbury was the closest place to Espanola with a McDonald's, and before any of my friends and I were sixteen and had access to a car we would pay people with a driver's license to pick up Big Macs and McChickens for us if they happened to be going into the city. Though I myself didn't ever do so, it wasn't out of the question for some people to order four or five McChickens and refrigerate the uneaten ones for later. That was part of growing up in Espy back in those days. A McDonald's and a Dairy Queen finally came to town around 1993, but I was long gone by then.

Two

First KISS

So - this record shop where I bought my music was the only one in town. It was called Wally's Music and owned, believe it or not, by a guy named Wally.

Wally had all the accoutrements of an aging 70s rocker. He had long, thick hair and a huge, bushy moustache that challenged my preteen mind to consider how he ate or drank. I was just slightly too naïve to consider his dealings with the fairer sex at that point. He wore clothes that clarified his alternative position in our town as a bona fide rock and roller. Wally stood out in a crowd, because almost everyone else in town looked more or less exactly the same. In Espanola, everyone seemed to try to maintain a cumulative *sameness* to complement the sociology that they subconsciously foster as a member of an isolated, reclusive community. Same hairstyle. Same clothes. Same shoes. Same vocal inflection. Same ideas. Same perceptions. The funny thing is that people actually look like versions of each other if you take a good look. These days, my wife Alison and I go back up to Espanola every now and again and we always notice how the older women, my mom included, all seem to be about the same height, have the exact same hair style and colour, the same short-sleeve light collared shirt (typically white), the same pants of the same dark colour, and the same moccasin-type footwear. Sameness is comfortable and safe in Espanola. Things that will differ are preferences in National Hockey League teams and beer brand preferences, two rudimentary foundations upon which a good number of Espanola residents build their individual identities.

The records in Wally's shop were crazy expensive because he capitalized on the monopoly he enjoyed as the town's only music vendor. But to Wally's credit, this was possibly also because of the cost involved in getting the records all the way up to Espy. He used to sell them for anywhere between $19.98 and $21.98, and he would put a second little sticker on the albums right above the one that contained the price. This second sticker showed a figure that was a couple bucks higher, usually $24.98, and it would have a pen stroke through it. I always thought that this was Wally's attempt to impress upon me, and all the other hapless suckers in town, that we were supposedly getting some kind of a deal when purchasing his records. Little did I know at that time that these same records could be purchased for less in Sudbury. This was of little meaning to me at the time, however. Didn't care. I had to have the KISS records at any cost.

To an unspoiled lump of male pre-adolescent clay presented with musical options like Loretta Lynn, Donna Summer, Seals & Crofts, Steely Dan, or KISS, the latter was the way obvious choice in 1977. What it really boils down to is that KISS closed the gap between my interest in comic book superheroes and my developing interest in music. They used the very powerful element of fantasy to lure me in like a musical Venus flytrap. KISS got to me when I was at my most impressionable. As I type this, I envision an image of Gene Simmons rubbing his hands together and laughing fiendishly against a backdrop of a huge pile of money. I would assume he does this a couple of times a day. Throughout a few phases of my life since the 70s, I'd fostered a tumultuous love-hate relationship with Simmons and KISS. It's not a tremendous point of consideration anymore, but I had my moments.

Before the first musical note was even audible, KISS' image was like a visual blitzkrieg in my mind. They sent a message through their pictures that they had bombast, flash, and colour. They had *power*. One of the first times I think I ever actually saw KISS before I bought *KISS*

Alive II was on the cover of their *Hotter than Hell* record that a friend had brought over to my house. I was nonplussed at first, because the cover had an awkward Asian motif that was more of a peculiarity than something cool for a kid to look at. I found out later that the pictures on the sleeve were taken during a shoot wherein singer and guitarist Paul Stanley was drunk, which was allegedly a unique circumstance as it was one of only a very small handful of times that he'd ever been intoxicated. Truth? Who knows. I do know that the sleeve design would make more sense to me if Stanley had been drunk during the approval process of it.

As far as KISS album covers go, the band only hit their stride later on with their 1976 breakout record *Destroyer*, which was finally a hand-in-glove fit with their whole image dynamic. Their first three record covers were actually pretty pedestrian, with the exception of maybe *Dressed to Kill*. The *KISS Alive* cover is too posed to be cool. The new direction KISS took on *Destroyer* with painted, pseudo-cartoon-KISS-members-as-demigods concept would take KISS to cult level status. The *Dressed to Kill* cover did give fans a more feasible alternative to mimicking them come Halloween time though. It was much easier to come across a crappy suit at The Salvation Army as a complement to the makeup you wore resembling your favourite KISS member than it was to try to replicate those crazy costumes using tin foil and sequins, and looking like a complete dick. Most fans likely know what I'm talking about.

Back then KISS was a radical departure from the Bay City Rollers, my previous favourite band. All the fantastical, ethereal, sinister earmarks were there to draw a curious youngster in. Blood, fire, glitter, you name it. Of course, the most intriguing element was the full makeup, and this was because it bred anonymity and implied distance. This made KISS unattainable and thus that much more desirable. As an eight-year-old kid, I played right into KISS' hands because of that cartoonish fantasy element. Almost to the point where, in line with the larger-than-life theatrics, I knew they were regular human beings but...a very small part of me kinda wanted to believe that they weren't. And this is what the entire foundation of hard rock and heavy metal is based upon, really – fantasy, and a requisite need for escapism; for reality reconfiguration. KISS' (and metal's) real *coup de grace* was built on a simple supply-and-demand principle – the natural hunger of stimulus-deprived fans that craved this outlet in the hopes of considering themselves as part of something very, very different from the reality that was currently theirs.

I dove headlong into the KISS fantasy, brandishing the requisite face paint on Halloween, wearing the KISS t-shirts to school, and grabbing anything else related to KISS that I could get my hands on, or rather that my mom would shell out for. Growing up in a remote area didn't make for a great experience in terms of exposure to the KISS phenomenon. Most if not all of my connection was through the recorded product. But like I said, I was much more into KISS' look than I was their music initially.

However, the impressionable were easily converted into KISS music fans through simple conditioned association. The music is what it is. It's devoid of any real dimension, but it's requisitely catchy. And because we didn't have decent cable and I had no other tangible line of sight into KISS from my small northern Ontario town back then, their songs would default as my prime connection to the KISS mystique. And just as Simmons had planned, I got hooked like a junkie to smack. The important thing to note though is that although KISS' music in the 70s was more or less considered a secondary implement, once you were converted this is where the *real* taste for heavy metal came from. Motley Crue and other facsimiles would further the process six or seven years later. For their part, KISS was like headbanger kindergarten for me.

KISS' actual music only served as the soundtrack to the electric vaudeville act that took place before my eyes in their pictures, or during that time when I managed to see them on The Mike Douglas Show. The guys in KISS have in fact admitted that the music isn't anything special. In one of the 50 million articles I'd read as a rabid KISS fan over the years, Simmons referred to it as "big, dumb, rock". He and Paul Stanley have also admitted that they "borrowed" from other bands - specifically, creating the main "Deuce" riff from the Rolling Stones' "Bitch" by inverting the chords, and fashioning "Hotter Than Hell" from Free's "All Right Now". And those are just the ones they admitted to. There are loads of additional thefts if you listen closely. "Makin' Love" is unquestionably lifted from Aerosmith's "Toys in the Attic", and on and on and on. When talking about the musical prowess of KISS, Simmons once actually referred to the band as a "heavy metal Beatles". This is of course ludicrous, but it's in keeping with the image maintenance the band used in interviews as a branding flanker to The KISS Fantasy, in which I was fully engrained as a young KISS fan. And the residue was long lasting: back in university late one night on a bender, I actually tried to call Ace Frehley's residence by dialing 411 and asking for Connecticut directory assistance. Not proud of that, but it's true.

Despite the larger-than-life bombast, the KISS personalities are more or less transferable to those in average society. Stanley was that guy you knew that always dressed with tacky flamboyance, was outspoken and cocky, and reminded you a bit of Bea Arthur for some reason. Simmons shared similar traits, but was much more chauvinistic and Donald Trump boorish, full of bullshit bravado for every pretty girl within a five mile radius. Drummer Peter Criss was the insecure loner who drew caricatures of his teachers with exaggerated facial features and undersized erections alongside big pictures of flaming spliffs on his textbooks, but that was only when he wasn't enjoying one in the school john. And lead guitarist Ace Frehley was the quiet, mysterious type who moved through the place speaking more with his vibe than with his mouth, projecting the same brand of cool that Val Kilmer's Doc Holliday did in *Tombstone* when he wasn't falling-down wasted. Which for either of these guys, wasn't often.

Frehley was my favourite KISS member by a very wide margin. He was probably the favourite of most KISS fans primarily because he played the coolest instrument in rock - lead guitar - thus inspiring legions of next-generation guitar heroes ranging from Pantera's Dimebag Darrell (RIP) to Skid Row's Snake Sabo. But the real reason Frehley was so attractive to KISS fans was because, of the four original members of KISS, Frehley was the only member to actualize what KISS in fact sought to be – mysterious, bigger than life and, well...*cool*. The irony is that Frehley, despite a non-leadership role in KISS, stole the show without even trying just by being his distant, taciturn self. This is because the wispy androgyny that made Frehley's character so intriguing was directly attributable to his natural tendencies underneath the makeup. He was believable because he was really just playing a more decorated, amped-up extension of himself - a legitimate, organic rock and roll guitar player in the Joe Perry / Keith Richards vein. He was the most real, and the most believable of the KISS members.

This is why his 1978 solo record sold the most copies. It wasn't just because of the "New York Groove" cover song. It was because Frehley's sound, vibe, and authentic rock and roll swagger was what KISS fans, primarily as 70s hard rock fans at large, felt they should be listening to. This was how KISS fans felt KISS should really sound. When I first got into KISS as a kid, what made Frehley the most interesting member to me was what he *didn't* show me. In addition to being the coolest looking member, his real mystique came from his character's reserved apathy. It made me want to know more about him. I would find out later that the irony of his character affiliation within KISS – a spacey mystic from another planet – was that it served as a metaphor for Frehley's real life detachment as a foil for his insecurities, and also because he spaced himself out regularly with booze and drugs to deal with his hang-ups.

Anybody who knows anything about Frehley knows that he drank himself into oblivion nightly for years and years and years. After the KISS heyday was over, I attended a few KISS conventions in Toronto and bought up all of the VHS bootlegged live footage of him playing with KISS in San Francisco in 1974, Cobo Hall in 1976, both nights in Houston in 1978 (containing footage of a clearly wasted Ace Frehley going to a wrong chord during his performance of "Shock Me" and then looking over his right shoulder with raised eyebrows at a disapproving Gene Simmons[1]). However, the best find among those bootlegs was that legendary Tom Snyder interview from 1979, a priceless gem

---

[1] *This clip was one of the highlights of a compilation videotape I crudely spliced together using two VCRs back in the early 90s. It contained all of my favourite Frehley moments from all of the bootlegs, and I called it "Frehleyvision". I know, right?*

wherein Frehley is absolutely blasted, stopping just short of getting his ass beaten by the visibly irate Simmons and Stanley, who were desperately trying to hold the interview together.

This interview took place during the *Dynasty* era, which was the beginning of the disintegration of classic KISS as we knew it. Peter Criss, apparently also on the sauce during that interview but yet much quieter, would be booted from the band before the next record was released. Frehley would follow shortly afterwards. Both of them were out for the same reason though it wasn't directly addressed until much later, not surprisingly as "substance abuse issues". The first time I saw the Snyder video I felt like I was seeing something I wasn't supposed to see. Frehley was completely out of control, way beyond the typical choreographed KISS interview. And for the first time, KISS had a visible and tangible realness. I had first seen this video long after the actual interview, around 1995 during a period of 'rediscovering' KISS as a nostalgic totem. KISS' initial grip on me had loosened by the time *Creatures of the Night* was released, and while I had paid a lot less attention to the glittery shimmer of the KISS franchise after that record (I still bought KISS' records up to 1985's *Asylum*, which marked the end of the road after my first listen), I still kept a periodic eye on my man Frehley.

Up to the point where he would eventually reunite with KISS the following year, Frehley still drank legendarily. He seemed like a slightly tragic figure to me at this point. In fact, I always thought he shared stark similarities with the main character Thomas Newton in Walter Tevis' 1963 novel *The Man Who Fell To Earth*. Both Frehley and Newton are from another planet (Newton is an alien seeking help on Earth for the dying people of his planet Anthea, and Frehley claimed to be from planet "Jendell"). Both become increasingly wealthy on Earth. Both develop a fondness for alcohol that gives rise to instability (duh). Both would also have their real identities revealed (Newton's by the CIA, Frehley after KISS took off the makeup). Both would be unsuccessful in their primary goals (Newton to save his people, Frehley to save his career post-KISS). And finally, both would try to remain stoic in spite of failure (Newton creating a recording to send to his people to say goodbye, Frehley releasing a solo recording recently for his fans that more or less says the same).

I have to admit that I was very much enraptured with the concept of Ace Frehley for a significant portion of my life. In my deluded mind, my overall perception of Frehley could almost be likened to an after-school special spanning almost twenty years in which I vicariously participated, in the following sense. I had initially seen him in this messianic light as an impressionable kid. Then as a young adult, I saw him as this glamorously tragic figure that I tended to pattern my drinking sprees after, using him as an emblem that ultimately represented some sort of identification issue I must have been having at that point in my life. I even started drinking Stoli after hearing it was a favoured drink of his. In denouement, Frehley and I both stopped drinking so heavily and lived, more or less, happily ever after. Frehley stopped drinking heavily because his life most likely depended on it, and I stopped just because I wised up. And because I hate wasting entire Sundays dealing with a massive hangover when I have a full-time career that requires my alarm clock to sound at 6am every weekday morning.

I doubt I was much different from most other KISS fans that had a favourite member they idolized. For some, it may have been Paul Stanley. I myself could have never been into Paul Stanley that way. Just not my thing. I like him, and I think he did a great job as a performer and a frontman (also, props for his *Phantom of the Opera* run in Toronto). And I've never seen Stanley phone it in once in all the times I've seen KISS live. He clearly prided himself on putting on a good show. His persona was just a bit too much for me, that's all. Great entertainer, it just came across as a bit too cheesy for my taste. Maybe a bit overdone.

Peter Criss? He had a fantastic rock and roll voice, but I always thought the cat motif was a bit sketch. It wasn't anything I could get into. And, he was back behind the drums. It's almost impossible to make an impression from back there when you're competing against a demon that spits blood and breathes fire, a lead guitarist whose guitar smokes and levitates up and away into the darkness of the rafters, and a preening, strutting asexual banshee with big red lips. Really.

Gene Simmons' image as The Demon was the obvious choice as favourite in theory, but that's why I didn't buy it. It seemed *too* obvious for me. Too aggressive, almost too geared towards getting attention. The reason Simmons wasn't my favourite KISS persona is the same reason why I typically skip the first track when I'm listening to CDs. I prefer latent to active. The first track on most albums is placed there in an attempt to blatantly draw attention, and this compels me to dismiss it. Any quality it might have is likely usurped by the connotation because I feel like it's almost like a commercial for the album in that sense. So, in the same way that I now skip through television commercials with my PVR I often skip the first song on a record, especially Bon Jovi's "Lay Your Hands On Me" from *New Jersey*, "Fast as a Shark" from Accept's *Restless and Wild*, "Breaking the Law" from Judas Priest's *British Steel*, and "1984" from Van Halen's *1984* (and "Jump" too, for that matter). Not ironically, "Detroit Rock City" from KISS' *Destroyer* also falls under this category. However, some records do negate this concept because their leadoff songs work well with the remainder of the material as a cohesive contribution to the record. Like "Night Songs" from Cinderella's debut record of the same name, Whitesnake's "Slide It In" likewise from their record of the same name, and Aerosmith's "Back in the Saddle", an excellent one-two punch tandem with subsequent track "Last Child" from *Rocks*. Of course, Judas Priest's "The Hellion" and "Electric Eye" can't be left off of this list. Anyway, the point is that Simmons is kinda like the KISS advertisement for me, so I tend to look past him for what's on the inside.

This isn't to say that Simmons didn't get my attention when it counted, because he certainly did. I spent a lot of time by myself as a kid, and much of that time was in turn spent listening to music. I used to sit in my basement listening to KISS records in particular, establishing a connection to the band through the lyrics I heard. Of all of the KISS songs I listened to, I was especially preoccupied by "Great

Expectations" from the *Destroyer* album, wherein Simmons pontificates about the role he plays as a rock star, establishing further distance between the KISS fantasy and fan reality. I keyed into one of the lines in that song every time it played – *"in the din it seems that I'm a million miles away"*. I guess it was because I felt particularly distant in my isolated little town. Music, and I think hard rock and heavy metal in particular, will always be an obvious compensatory vehicle for kids who may not realize how lonely they are.

Turns out I met Simmons at a book signing in Toronto twenty-six years later, and it was a funny, gratifying experience. I thought it would be cool to shake hands with the God of Thunder, after having spent a lot of time thinking about the impact KISS had on me up to that point. So I went down to the bookstore and waited for a few hours in a line that snaked through the store's shelves. While I progressed through the queue, I tried to think of something half-decently relevant to say to him other than garden-variety fare like *"KISS fuckin' rules, dude!"*. So, after considering my fascination with KISS as a kid in rural northern Ontario, and being about five people away from finally having my book signed, I suddenly remembered the "Great Expectations" lyric and its impression on me back then. I thought it would be worthwhile to try to frame it in some quick chat somehow, instead of the regular blathering that I could hear Simmons getting from people in front of me. Christ, the guy in front of me was fucking *crying*.

In a few moments, I would stand face-to-Kabuki-face with Gene Simmons. Man. I almost felt like I already knew him somehow. Then I started to freak myself out. What exactly would I say? What would *he* say?!? My heart was pounding as I got closer.

I was next. Because there were so many people there to see him, his handlers whisked us along allowing for maybe fifteen to twenty seconds of gushing, tops. After some consideration, I had prepared my idea of what I wanted to say. I wanted to try to say something a bit more meaningful. Now, don't get me wrong. I'm a sap just like the rest of these poor goddamn saps standing in line for almost half a day in exchange for twenty seconds of exposure. As a matter of fact, at this point I was wondering if I was going to be able to muster anything at all, because I was actually getting nervous! All of the images and memories of a band I had spent so much of my childhood focused on ran through my head. I was really into it now. And this was my chance to make a connection. I took a deep breath, exhaled, and stepped forward.

GENE: (*dryly*) How you doing, boss?
ME: (*gulp*) I'm doing great, Gene. How are you?
GENE: Good. How are they treating you in line?
ME: Fine.

I may as well have been eight years old again. He's sitting on a raised platform and I'm standing, so our faces are lined up eye-to-eye about two and a half feet from each other's. His face: sinister, wry smile. My face: perverse wonderment.

My book's been signed, and one of Simmons' monkeys opens the next guy's book and is in the process of sliding it down the table to Simmons. Here comes my bit.

ME: Y'know Gene, '*In the din it seemed that you were a million miles away*', but not today. I can't tell you how great it is to meet you after twenty-five years of being a fan. You just made my world a lot smaller.

The monkey looks at me like I have three heads. Most people would be thinking that I was some kind of meth addict for saying that. I wondered too after I heard myself say it, actually. But since that lyric best represented that visceral point of connection I had with KISS in my mind, I thought it was the most *apropos* thing to say.

GENE: (*laughing*) I wish I could come up with something as profound, but it's been a long night.

Dang. He didn't realize that I was quoting one of his songs. I shouldn't have been surprised, as he did write "Great Expectations" twenty-odd years previous around 1976, and it would have been considered filler on a record like *Destroyer*. I chose not to try to jog Gene's memory, as I could feel his handler's cut-eye burning a hole in the side of my face urging me to move it along. Time for me to finish up. Simmons offered his hand, and I shook it. I surprised myself a bit with what I did next, but it was just reflexive. I wanted to make some sort of impression but instead I defaulted to my childhood fandom.

ME: Gene, thanks for making me feel the way you did for all those years (*what the fuck did I just say that for?!?!*).
GENE: You're welcome. Thank *you*.

Then I put my left hand on top of our clasped hands and said...

ME: *Love you, man!*

Gaaaaahh! As hard as I tried, I couldn't help it. I completely regressed.

But really, I couldn't be blamed. There's meaning in this regression. The regression was a function of the premise of what enjoying rock and roll is really all about. Not being at all preoccupied with doing what you or anyone else thinks is right – just doing what naturally feels right to *you*.

As a kid, I sought out stronger sensations. The importance of experiencing these stronger sensations was linked to how profoundly I considered them over the course of experiencing them, and these impressions played an indelible role in my development and in my self-identification. So, I really couldn't be blamed for regression during an in-person exchange with someone who had made such a significant contribution to experiences that had so much impact on my formative years.

As such, I realized after a while that it wasn't necessary to hack on Simmons and KISS so hard for their commercial enthusiasms. At one point, Simmons' open preoccupation with money actually compelled me to make a point of *not* contributing any further to the KISS Commerce Machine. No more concerts and certainly no more purchases of recorded product. When their 2009 record *Sonic Boom* was branded as a return to the *Rock and Roll Over*-era of KISS I almost choked with laughter, especially after having read a Paul Stanley interview a few years back in which he said that he couldn't write another "Love Gun" with a real gun pointed at his head. The idea that hired hands Eric Singer and Tommy Thayer now wore the original member KISS makeup was blasphemous to me. I snickered when I watched Simmons and Stanley in live interviews trying to escape from holes they'd previously dug for themselves with outlandish non-sequiturs based on contradictions they'd offered to past interviewers. They were always much better spin-doctors than musicians. In fact, The Spin Doctors should have called themselves something else, and KISS should have called themselves The Spin Doctors. Above all, I was embarrassed to have been such an enthusiastic KISS fan at this point.

I scoffed at KISS for becoming bloated, greedy shadows of their former selves, but I eventually realized that not much had changed. KISS had always been greedy, and with no disrespect intended, Simmons had almost always been a bit bloated (an affinity for cake will do that for you).

The real source of my resentment towards KISS was rooted in the fact that I couldn't see, and didn't *want* to see, the fact that KISS wasn't primarily about satisfying my personal fandom. KISS always was a business, this just became more blatantly obvious as a) I grew older and more reflective, and b) KISS grew older and more desperate to sustain a humongous KISS franchise by upping the ante with more creative product like KISS Kondoms, and KISS Koffins. All part of the KISS Master Plan.

At the end of the day, I simply had to reconcile my childhood impressions of KISS against what KISS actually was. The merchandising bothered me because it compromises the innocent circumstances under which I 'learned' KISS. But you have to enjoy things for what they are. It was interesting to me that KISS was able to almost hurt my feelings in such a way, because this validates the significance of the emotional contribution I made to what KISS meant to me as a kid. And really, this is something I should be suitably appreciative of considering the level of enjoyment I took away from my childhood KISS fan period, as sad as that may be.

In true Gene Simmons tradition, we can look at this from a position of economy. In exchange for my purchase of thirteen KISS records, three cassettes, nineteen CDs, three books, one VHS tape (*KISS Exposed*, not a bootleg like the others I bought at conventions), six posters, one board game, three highly overpriced concert t-shirts, one Mego Ace Frehley action figure (oops, bootlegged from a convention), and six concert tickets, all at the suggested retail price, KISS provided me with sensations strong enough to last a lifetime. Fair deal?

I guess so, even if this is how I compensate for my ultimate disappointment in Simmons' consideration of KISS fans being his personal ATMs.

✷ Three ✷
No Sleep 'til Sudbury

The first time I had ever heard of Iron Maiden was back around the time when their album *The Number of the Beast* was released in 1982. Quite honestly, I was a bit intimidated initially by the imagery of the band, particularly band mascot Eddie wielding that hatchet and the whole fire-and-brimstone thing on the album cover. Not in a frightening way but instead more in an off-putting, mildly irritating way. Like when someone turns the channel to a UFC program on TV. The *Number of the Beast* album cover pitted Eddie against what I assumed was the devil, battling on a cliff in some post-apocalyptic hell-type setting. Several smaller, less fortunate silhouetted figures could be seen below in the background, also fighting and carrying on along the fiery landscape. It wasn't until I looked very closely at these figures that I noticed a few of them sported male genitalia, some of it in fact erect. As a young man of twelve, I was perplexed by the purpose of this. So many questions filled my pre-pubescent small town brain. Of course, the most important of these questions was, *"What must this music sound like?"*

Fearing the worst, I didn't shell out the money for this peculiarity at the time even though I was nonetheless as intrigued as I could possibly be. I was a bit of a stray dog as a kid. I carried a lot of fair-weather friendships, most of these being spontaneous and based on geographic and situational availability. I must say that I made some poor decisions relative to my friend selection, sometimes hanging out in some less-than-savoury social circles. I do sometimes wonder though had it not been for this lapse in judgment, if I would have ever come to experience the sheer joy that was listening to Iron Maiden.

    I don't remember how any of these frivolous friendships even started, nor do I remember the endings of them. But when you're that young, there's practically zero responsibility or accountability invested or even expected in relationships of any sort. Even the smallest of towns subscribe to a social class system, and while my 'best' friends in Espanola were the ones who were in my class at school, whose houses I was able to sleep over at, and with whom I tended to fraternize with in most social settings, I do remember having friends when I was around the age of twelve that were peripheral to my previously established social niche. I suppose I hung out with them when no one else was around. I'm not sure why, but I just kinda opened it right up socially. I think that in Espy, friendship was essentially about self-involved gain more than anything else at that age. Consideration and consequential thinking were lax. There weren't really many 'real' genuine friendships that I witnessed or participated in that could be validated by core values like sincerity, honesty, or loyalty. My memory tells me that the idea of friendship for most of us in Espanola was approached from a mercenarial tack. You took what you needed to satisfy yourself first and you moved around as you saw fit, without having any real allegiance to anyone.

    Man, it seems crazy to me now that I would even set foot in some of the houses I did back then. But set foot I did, and listen to the first strains of *The Number of the Beast* record I did as well. I was captivated by the lightning-in-a-bottle anarchy of the whole thing, the sinister ferocity of it. It was much different than anything I had heard before. Eventually I was so into *The Number of the Beast* that me and this other guy would pretend we were in the band when we listened to it, using props like pool cues and broomsticks to ape my newfound heroes. The beauty of make-believe was perpetuated in the fact that you could be whichever band member you wanted at the time, based on whether there was a great drum riff or series of fills, or a guitar line that you wanted to 'play'. You were any and every band member at any time as you saw fit. I would mostly be the singer with a pool cue. We would both play the lead guitar parts, because you couldn't just stand there and do nothing during the lead break. We established a stage in front of the stereo and took our positions as needle made contact with vinyl, the metal riffs that poured out of the speakers serving as a malignant outlet for our misplaced, adolescent small town angst. The sheer freedom and wanton self-involvedness was the immediate order of the moment. And it was bloody *glorious*.

And so it was, my blossoming courtship with Iron Maiden. When I got to high school, I found out very quickly that the parameters of social demarcation were even more clearly defined. Being a metal fan unfortunately meant you were looked upon as a lowlife. This was a branding that obviously thwarted any significant socialization opportunities outside limited social circles. Not that I was the overly gregarious type anyway, but I kinda saw myself as more of a multi-dimensional type. I didn't really completely fit into one category. I didn't want to. I wasn't a card-carrying, denim n' leather clad metalhead, but I *loved* heavy metal. I wasn't a phony preppy but I dressed like one most of the time. I wasn't a jock but I held a first-line position on most of the sports teams I belonged to (though this was not at all a major achievement in Espy at the time). And, I wasn't a nerd but I was very interested in learning. I loved English Literature and I'd periodically flip through the dictionary just to learn new words. Despite the tacky cliché, I suppose I was a much less romanticized version of John Cusack's character in *Say Anything*. Socially chameleonic but clumsily so. Always looking to relate, but at my own accord. Looking for myself in the lyrics of my favourite songs and using those lyrics as validations for who I thought I was or should be, though I really had no idea. Drawing associations between my own personal situations and song lyrics enhanced the intensity of the experience and added pretended grandiosity to my boring small town life. I was bright enough and maybe just barely good-looking enough to stay ahead of the lowlife tag, always just looking for a place to happen. But on my own terms. And all the while, living in my own little world of self-delusive happy goodness.

In my first year of high school I made fast friends with a guy named Bryan Sloss. We shared the same inclinations and we were pretty similar. We both had longish hair that conceded socially somewhat by looking more Steven Adler than Axl Rose. We had an appreciation for the arts as much as you could where we were from. And we both loved heavy metal, Iron Maiden in particular. We read Hit Parader, Circus, and Creem, and listened closely when Maiden brought in their new drummer Nicko McBrain for *Piece of Mind*, the follow up to *The Number of the Beast*. I bought the record right away and phoned Bryan from another friend's house to discuss Nicko's cred and how good he sounded, I distinctly remember that. Girls called each other to blather about boys, makeup, and shoes, and I blathered about Iron Maiden.

Even though this was the case, I couldn't really be considered a *headbanger*. At least not in the same way the guys in metal shop were. But who knows? Maybe I was. Maybe I didn't want to come to grips with the fact that I refused to put all my identity eggs in one basket because I would be missing something or limiting myself to a stereotype. Especially one so reviled by the girlies I was trying to get with during that time. So shamefully fragile in character was I.

Iron Maiden had become massively popular by the time their next record, *Powerslave*, came out in 1984. Inexplicably, their tour to support *Powerslave* would bring them to...Sudbury!?!

So Iron Maiden was coming (close) to my hometown. I was running around the room and jumping on the furniture like Ed Grimley when I found out. I couldn't figure out why they would come to Sudbury because they were *huge*, and bands of their stature didn't bother coming any closer to Sudbury than Toronto, which was four hours south. As a young kid, I would read the tickets-for-sale section of *The Toronto Star* classifieds to find out which bands were playing down there. Looking back on that now, it seems more sado-masochistic than interesting. But, as much as I hated seeing Motley Crue tickets for sale for their show at Maple Leaf Gardens, it somehow felt like that was the closest I could get to being part of the action, and as close as I would get to my favourite bands. Toronto may as well have been in another solar system for me at that time. When I found out Maiden was coming to Sudbury - after I came to the realization that it wasn't some sort of error, misrepresentation, or cruel joke - I almost peed myself with anxiety. I was fourteen, and this would be my first-ever live concert.

My new metal pal Sloss and I set about trying to organize our plan to make this happen for ourselves. Ticket acquisition was primitive back then. You could either buy the tickets from the arena or from the local record stores in person. No Internet, no TicketMaster. The show was general admission, so wherever you planted yourself in six-thousand-seater Sudbury Arena was your own business. If you wanted to be up front, you could work your way up there. There was no scalping for front-row or floors. I don't think I'd even heard the term 'scalping' yet at that point. If I had, I probably would have tried to work it in to the conversation somehow, thinking I would raise my cred with edgy-sounding slang without even really knowing what it meant. Most of us did that in Espanola.

I don't remember exactly how we did get the tickets, because I doubt that we would have been able to make two trips to the city for that. Sloss used to have access to his parents' car, but not with any regularity. Christ, I don't even remember how we got to the actual show itself, to be honest. Must have taken the Greyhound.

I do remember being in Sudbury fairly early that day and hanging out in the malls, hitting all the record shops and really soaking it all up. There was a small gang of Espy boys there to see the concert. I also remember that out in front of the City Centre Mall in downtown Sudbury, three of us were asked by a reporter from *The Sudbury Star* newspaper if we wanted to answer a question for a feature they were doing on the new cable channels that had just been made available to us in northern Ontario. Back in 1984, we were just getting that big brown rectangular Jerrold box that was still connected to the television with a cord, and it had buttons on it that went *ka-chik* very loudly when you changed channels. And that was a big development. *"Holy crap, we don't have to get up to change the channel anymore!"*

I think the reporter's question had to do with the perceived value of the new channels. Did John Q. Public think the channels were worth the money that would be charged for them, something like that. I'm still not really sure why he was posing this question to three fourteen-year-old longhaired punks dressed in metal getups. At any rate, I remember giving a half-decently credible answer, and I remember that Sloss also provided a thoughtful response. I'm not sure if the third guy perhaps didn't clearly hear or understand the question, or if he may have been nervous or something, but the answer he gave was a bit stupid. After the reporter noted our comments, names, and ages he took our pictures, thanked us for our time, and told us the feature would run the following day. So, there I was, all fucking proud of myself for being in *The Sudbury Star*. Mullet, fake leather jacket with a Flying V pin in it, Iron Maiden *Killers* three-quarter length sleeve baseball t-shirt and all. When I picked up the paper the next day, I was mortified to discover that the knuckleheaded comment the third guy provided was inserted under *my* name and picture, and *my* comment was under *his* picture. Christ.

There was a lot of nervous giddiness before this concert. We were more like little schoolgirls than tough metal guys at this time. Someone in general proximity said that they heard that Iron Maiden lead singer Bruce Dickinson was spotted at the health food store in the City Centre, and we went goddamn *nuclear*. The delta that existed between a gaggle of small town hicks and a seemingly pseudo-mythical being like Dickinson was unfathomable when you're one of the small town hicks. It didn't seem possible that he would move among us in our pedestrian spaces. And to be honest, for the sake of pure fantastical entertainment (which was really a key fundamental of my obsession with heavy metal in the first place) I didn't really *want* to believe that he would. That may have spoiled the fun. Whether or not I would admit it at the time,

I knew that heavy metal was specious escapism for me. And it still is, really. I just happen to be a lot wiser and more enlightened in my consideration of its scale these days.

I could have been considered a serious Iron Maiden fan back in 1984. I wouldn't say that I was a *diehard*, because I didn't care for the non-Dickinson, pre-*The Number of the Beast* Iron Maiden albums yet (Bruce Dickinson had just joined Maiden prior to *The Number of the Beast*). There was such a dichotomy between Dickinson's more metal, operatic, human air-raid siren vocal approach and that of previous frontman Paul Dianno's punkish-inflected delivery that I just couldn't get into Maiden's first two records, *Iron Maiden* and *Killers*. I actually didn't until just recently. And it's a shame, because they're fantastic records. I did, however, devour everything that Maiden subsequently released after *The Number of the Beast*. I bought *Piece of Mind* and *Powerslave* the minute they were available, in addition to all of the 12-inch singles, B-sides, posters, T-shirts, all of it. With the concept of band mascot Eddie and his countless reinvented machinations adding a whole new dimension to the band's fan draw, it was an exhilarating feeling to be part of the momentum that was building. The band had a distinct identity, with a history and an exciting future that seemed as though it would be never ending. Not that I gave endings any thought as a fourteen-year-old. It was just goddamn exciting to be directly in the middle of it.

This is a principle point of difference in music then and now. Back then, and dating further back to the 70s with bands like Deep Purple and Led Zeppelin, there was an opportunity for sustained continuity for artists. The artist had a couple of chances with their first and second records, and if they didn't necessarily light the world on fire with those, they could make a third record, and maybe a few more. Bands had time to develop. There was no pressure to knock it out of the park the first time and every time after that. Def Leppard, Whitesnake, and even U2 come to mind as great examples. But as the music business becomes more about business and less about music, everything is so front-loaded that any real substance that existed before is long gone.

But back to the Maiden concert. It's *showtime*.

Twisted Sister was the opener, a popular band at the time based on the success of their singles "We're Not Gonna Take It" and "I Wanna Rock" with MTV-friendly video accompaniments. This live performance, however, was anything but friendly. Dee Snider could have been jailed for his vulgarity during their set. I'm definitely no stranger to the Fuck-bomb (like it's even really that shocking anymore), but there were some younger kids there to see Twisted Sister with their parents. Man, were they in for a shock. There was a woman off to my left with her young son, and I can still see the image of her mortified face in my mind. I'm not sure what she expected to see and hear, but Snider used all of George Carlin's *seven-words-you-can't-say-on-television* a couple of times each plus a few others to boot. Snider probably swore so much to try to offset that glitzy MTV sheen. But no matter how menacing Twisted Sister wanted to appear, they still came across as endearing in spite of themselves.

The 80s had to be a weird and challenging time for bands like Twisted Sister, who formed in the early 70s and slogged it out on the New York club circuit for ten years or so before breaking through. And I always admired them for that.

Anyway, Dee Snider and Twisted Sister ploughed their way through the set that night in Sudbury.

And now, the mighty Iron Maiden would finally tread the boards. I had been able to tape the "Aces High" video from some Canadian music video show one night after scrambling to find a blank VHS tape to shove into the colossal VCR we just purchased the previous year during the video show's commercial break: "*New videos from Duran Duran, Spandau Ballet and Iron Maiden after these messages!*". The video was basically live footage of the band performing the song, so I had a general idea of what I was about to see live. Sudbury Arena was no Madison Square Garden though, and a scaled-back version of the *Powerslave* set was being erected right before my eyes. I remember wondering what it would be like to see this show at MSG, or even at the Gardens in Toronto. It was beyond unfathomable at that time.

The lights eventually went down, and I may have wet myself a little bit as Churchill's intro speech to "Aces High" came over the PA. The Maiden boys sprinted onto the stage, and I was in another world. My face felt like it was stuck in awestruck-wonderment place. As the set list progressed through "Two Minutes to Midnight" and "The Trooper" I didn't know where to look. I wanted to see everything at the same time. I tended to mostly watch Dickinson, and guitarists Dave Murray and Adrian Smith when they soloed. As the songs moved through their crescendos, especially from the breakdown in "Two Minutes to Midnight" powering back into the main riff (one of the finest moments in the history of heavy metal by my estimation), I could feel that tingling swell in my torso and a smile so bright on my lips that my face could have easily served as an additional spotlight.

As my initial excitement levelled out after the opening numbers, I began to broaden my scope of attention to include the more detailed aspects of the production - the activities of the stage hands just off in the wings, what went on between numbers, and what Dickinson was doing when he wasn't singing. As a first-time concertgoer, these little nuances were very interesting to me. I noticed that Dickinson would retreat to the drum riser periodically to drink from a Solo cup and to blow his nose. He announced later that he had a cold. He must have really enjoyed being in sub-zero Sudbury in December given that was the case.

Later on in the show he asked the crowd, *"Sudbury, do you mind if we come back to see you next year?"* Being a young, gullible optimist I was delighted, though I couldn't imagine why they'd want to come back up to Sudbury. Or why they'd even come in the first place really. Unless, I thought, Maiden was impressed by the rabid enthusiasm of the rural metal-starved crowd. Yeah, that had to be it. So *when* they came back, not *if*, because Bruce Dickinson himself said they would, I would be there for sure. Closer to the stage next time. Of course, Maiden would not return to Sudbury on the following *Somewhere in Time* tour. Or ever again for that matter to my knowledge, a fact I remember being mildly bitter about. I felt as though I'd been had slightly. My concert virginity had been taken away, with the suggestion that there would be future liaisons, but with nothing materializing from that cruel innuendo. I was the jilted cheerleader to Iron Maiden's high school quarterback. Woe was me.

And much like the newly deflowered cheerleader whose love was unrequited, my crush remained for some time after. Iron Maiden's star was as high in the sky as it had ever been in 1985, and the release of their next studio record *Somewhere in Time* instilled the standard giddiness that the release of a new album does in a serious fan.

But things were changing.

While the album kickoff track "Somewhere in Time" and single "Wasted Years" were solid, it felt like there was a bit more filler on the rest of the album. It was clear that Iron Maiden was going in a new direction. The album sounded very polished, almost synthetic. Filler tunes like "Alexander the Great" and "The Loneliness of the Long Distance Runner" alienated me a bit. The loneliness of the long distance runner? What was *this*? This song reminded me a bit of *Piece of Mind's* "Quest for Fire", a peculiar inclusion on an otherwise strong record. At least *Powerslave*'s lengthy epic "Rime of the Ancient Mariner" had shades of malevolence. But a long distance runner? Jeez.

I remember feeling like my favourite band was changing and that I didn't completely understand them anymore. When the next record, *Seventh Son of a Seventh Son*, came out in 1988, it marked the first time in five years that I didn't buy a Maiden record immediately on the date of release. In fact, I only just bought that record in 2007. The fact that it was a full-fledged concept record led me to believe at the time that Iron Maiden may have jumped the shark. Before long, Adrian Smith and then Bruce Dickinson would both walk away from the band.

During this same time, the intensity that I had once felt as an Iron Maiden fan had faded to a glimmer. Maiden's career arc at this point coincided with my graduation from high school and my experience of the culture shock of leaving home for my first year of post-secondary education. Even though Laurentian University was in Sudbury, I lived in dorm there and my life would transform into something completely different. I still cherished metal, but I would never have the same relationship with it again in lieu of all the radical newness of university life and the end of my teenage years.

I could not have left Espanola behind with any more entirety. Though initially a bit reluctant, I was fully reinvented by my new life in dorm. New stimuli. New friends. New perspectives. New direction. I got so caught up in the new version of me that I even lost sight of my dear friend Bryan Sloss, and pretty much any other Espanola friends that I had. I was gone.

In 1989 I stood at the crossroads of new beginnings, and Iron Maiden felt like that childhood friend whose family had put their house up for sale and moved away.

Or maybe it was the other way around. More on this topic later.

Four
Frankie Goes to Hollywood

Motley Crue was only successful for two reasons. One, because young people are so willingly prone to give in to their basest instincts as human animals. And two, because Nikki Sixx knows this.

Nikki Sixx is a concept created by alter ego Frank Feranna. It's not real, and neither was Motley Crue. Motley was a visual production accompanied by a musical soundtrack, all cobbled together and helmed by young Frankie. Essentially a proto-KISS regurgitation based on what he absorbed from them and other acts that placed an equal or greater emphasis on image as they did musical content. I'm speaking in the past tense to emphasize focus on Motley's 80s days, in line with what most Motley fans are focused on.

If this sounds negative at all, it's not intended to. Motley Crue was a very important part of my indoctrination into hard rock and heavy metal fandom. Frank Feranna (more appropriately referred to as Nikki Sixx from here on in) indelibly coloured my adolescent imagination. Later on he impressed me with his resilience and tenacity. I cherish my experiences as a teenaged Cruehead, and *Shout at the Devil* will always be one of my top five favourite hard rock and metal records of all time, even if it is artificial. That never mattered, because being a Motley Crue fan was really about inserting yourself as far as you could into the Motley Crue *experience*. As with KISS, the music was purely supplementary.

After drifting around the country as an adolescent, Sixx rooted himself in Los Angeles at age seventeen. Legend holds that he stole a bass guitar from a music store by asking the guy at the counter for a job application, sending him into the back and allowing Sixx to abscond with the instrument. Even before leading the Crue, his wiliness was evident.

Sixx auditioned unsuccessfully for the Randy Rhoads-version of Quiet Riot and for Blackie Lawless' early band Sister. He temporarily positioned himself as the bass player in a band he formed with guitarist Lizzie Grey called London, popular only for featuring musicians who would later graduate to bands who achieved some form of fame, like Fred Coury from Cinderella, Bobby Marks from Keel, Lawless from W.A.S.P., and Izzy Stradlin and even (albeit for a very short period) Slash from Guns N' Roses.

Sixx wasn't stupid. In fact, he was an astute observer of all that transpired around him. He understood that image was a propulsive element that didn't even need to be paired with musical skill. He was also a hardened punk who wasn't afraid to step up and take charge as a leader. In a short time he would leave London to start Motley Crue, and in doing so, Sixx was essentially an architect who set about building a mechanism that could make him famous. I don't think there was anything terribly musical about this, given the fact that Sixx was described by many, including Geffen A&R guy Tom Zutaut, as someone who could barely even play his instrument. It was more about Sixx's aptitude in studying the variables involved in his heroes' ascent to fame, and how he could apply those variables to his own situation to join them.

Motley Crue's realness was most obviously betrayed by the assembly of the band as coordinated by Sixx. The fact that this group was quite literally a 'motley crew' was no accident. Sixx recruited teenage drummer Tommy Lee from his Sunset Strip band Suite 19, and while Lee would probably be the best musician in Motley, Sixx may have wanted him in the group more so because of Lee's flashy stick-twirl playing and for hitting cymbals so hard that he actually broke them regularly.

As his guitar player, Sixx brought in a guy named Bob Deal, self-reinvented in 1981 as Mick Mars. Mars was the oddest fixture of this band because not only did he stand apart from other more androgynous-looking Sunset Strip types by resembling a member of The Munsters, he had also just turned thirty around the time the band formed, making him a full eleven years older than Tommy Lee. That's a major age difference at that point in life, a nineteen-year-old playing with a thirty-year-old. But Sixx got an experienced Mars when he was desperate, after having already been around the block for the last decade as the guitar player in mediocre bands like White Horse.

Sixx's next choice to round out the Motley lineup still confuses me to this day, but that's only because Nikki and I evidently have two completely separate schools of thought where lead singers are concerned. Tommy Lee knew Vince Neil from high school and from his goofily-named band Rockandi, and apparently because Neil a) looked good and b) did a great Robin Zander according to Lee, it was decided that he would get the frontman job in the Crue. I laughed out loud when I read Neil's bit in *The Dirt* where he had the audacity to say that Motley Crue got him when he "was weak". Vince Neil was easily one of the worst singers and performers in all of hair metal, on par with Stephen Pearcy from Ratt and just slightly better than the guy from Pretty Boy Floyd. But in Motley Crue, talent wasn't necessarily the order of the day. It was more about getting people's attention in the same way the New York Dolls and KISS did before them. Motley would figure the rest out later.

David Bowie once said that if you look like a rock star and act like a rock star, you might actually *become* a rock star. Nikki Sixx was listening. David Bowie didn't mention anything about being musically talented, or even musically inclined - that was something that could eventually be sorted out. Creating a stir with image came first. It didn't hurt that Sixx was one of the coolest looking guys in hard rock and metal. The genius behind his look was a blend of androgyny and comic book super villain, almost a unique mix of the two most intriguing figures in KISS. Sixx had the detachment of Ace Frehley by hiding his eyes from view underneath a shock of blue-black hair, but he also deployed that manic clenched-teeth presence and blood-n-guts stage swashbuckling that Gene Simmons did. A near perfect balance between *Rocky Horror Picture Show* and *Mad Max*.

A certain type of look was rudimentary in 80s hard rock, but there were a handful of guys who stood out from the rest based on a combination of their physical attractiveness and their swagger in the same way that Frehley and Aerosmith's Joe Perry did in the 70s. Part of the job description in hard rock and metal is to achieve a certain level of visual coolness. It was expected. Despite any ironic clichés, a lot of guys were successful in nailing that image – Slash, David Lee Roth and his understudy Marq Torien of the BulletBoys, Dokken's George Lynch, Vince Neil, Tommy Lee. Beyond them, there were a handful of guys like Matthias Jabs of Scorpions, Randy Rhoads, Accept's Wolf Hoffman, Tommy Keifer of Cinderella, and Warren DiMartini from Ratt who just had that special look that set them apart and allowed them to extend their coolness beyond the requisite level. And Nikki Sixx was at the vanguard of that group.

The Motley Crue fantasy was an escapist production not at all unlike a Broadway show, complete with compelling actors filling the roles of what were perceived initially as heavy metal musicians, at least based on the imagery involved. Tommy Lee was the best actor of all because he didn't even know he was acting until much later, around the time when the Methods of Mayhem project came about.

This collection of rock and roll thespians hooked me in 1983 during the first act of their show with a full-page advertisement in *Creem* magazine to announce the release of *Shout at the Devil*. I was standing outside the Pinto convenience store on the main drag in Espanola when I first saw it, and it stopped me in my tracks. It jumped right off the page at me. Black and red colour scheme. Fire. Big hair. Makeup. Pentagram. Leather and studs. Nothing was missing. I honestly remember thinking that this may be a new and improved KISS for teenagers, and I was right. I ripped the ad out of the magazine and put it up in my high school locker, because it was the coolest thing I'd seen since Ace Frehley circa 1978.

Motley Crue essentially was a rite of passage for post-graduate KISS fans that were fourteen in 1983. This is where Frank Feranna's concept squarely hit the bullseye. As a KISS fan himself, Sixx knew it was a tried-and-true formula that just required some tweaking for a new generation. Simmons breathed fire; Sixx lit his legs on fire. Simmons spit blood; Mars drooled blood. Having a smoking guitar that lit up was not in the budget, so Neil beheaded mannequins with a chainsaw instead.

When I got *Shout at the Devil*, it was like a weirdly compelling musical horror movie. I got to know every sonic nook and cranny of it - every cymbal crash, every drum fill, every pick scrape, every lyric. I even still wonder who it is that says *"yeah"* at 0:38 into the title track (though I suspect it's Sixx). *Shout at the Devil* was one of my absolute favourite records, one that I viewed as a cornerstone of my collection in the years after I bought it in 1983.

Whenever I hear the opening strains of "In The Beginning", it takes me back a couple of lifetimes to the only place where that sort of an album introduction was actually cool. Which is kinda retrospectively cool in itself. The beauty of listening to this record now is in the recollection of the sheer bliss I felt when I listened to it as a fourteen-year-old.

I didn't listen critically, at least not in the same way that I do now. Any 'critical listening' took place on a very superficial scale, and really only existed to distinguish bands that sucked from bands that didn't suck. Bands that 'sucked' most often didn't really suck for legitimate reasons, of course. It was just that their material placed them out of favour based on guidelines governed by either established metal covenants (Stryper sucked because Christian metal was an oxymoron), or because the idea of the band ran counter to my own underdeveloped socio-personal dogmas (Stryper sucked because Christian metal was 'gay').

Where Stryper, Motley Crue, and virtually every other hard rock and metal band were concerned, compositional standards were set nice and low, and any exceptional virtuosity I may have perceived was outlined in metal apologist discourse I used in trying to sell non-metalheads on the fact that "metal is not for the mindless". I actually wrote that exact quote in a note to a girl in 1987 in striving to prove Metallica's intellectual sophistication as demonstrated in their lyrics for "Creeping Death". Jesus.

Of course back then, I was talking out of my ass on several fronts. I didn't really notice a lot of things. Like for example that Neil's voice was nasal. Or that Lee's drumming was sublime. Or, that Sixx inserted Aerosmith lyrical references like *'just a punk in the street'* from "Last Child" into his own song "Too Young To Fall In Love", or that he copped the *'seasons of wither'* bit of the "Shout at the Devil" lyric *'through the seasons of wither we stand and deliver'* from Aerosmith's song "Seasons of Wither". Even if I had been an Aerosmith fan back then, I wouldn't have noticed based on Neil's delivery anyway. I couldn't understand a goddamn word he was singing. But that was part of the glory of experiencing *Shout at the Devil* as a teenager – none of this mattered. The best thing about being young is that you're afforded the liberty of being stupid, and the best thing about *Shout at the Devil* is that it's a stupid record for stupid young people.

My second favourite Motley Crue record is *Shout at the Devil*'s predecessor, 1981's *Too Fast For Love*. I love that the production of this record is so spare. Not much is done in the way of trying to thicken Neil's thin voice, and Lee's snare drum actually sounds normal and not like the typical 80s cracking-of-a-whip snare. It lends authenticity to the record. *Too Fast For Love* actually has a seminal proto-punk feel that comes across as genuine even in spite of Sixx's cleverness. Mars' guitar is a thick slab of fat, delicious distortion. He experimented a lot with his tone with different gear from album to album, with varying results - his tone on *Too Fast For Love* is killer, and he achieves a near-perfect metal tone on *Shout at the Devil*. Unfortunately it all went sideways after that for poor Mick.

Tommy Lee's drums sound like a barrage of artillery exploding around your head. And yet, he still found time to make creative use of the cowbell. Bless that man. His playing really adds dimension to this record, and his finest moment starts at 3:40 of album closer "On With The Show", when he adds all those extra kicks in the song's final chorus. I had a personal email address of Tommy's about ten years ago, and I sent him an email letting him know that I was fond of this particular drum piece. Didn't expect a response. He responded the next day, and when I sent something back saying that I thought it was cool that he actually responded, he replied again! Then I sent him a stupid email about listening to one of my demo CDs I was passing around at the time. He did not respond to that email.

The song "Take Me to the Top" from *Too Fast For Love* reminds me of that weak-ass choreography the band did at the US Festival in 1983 during the song's passage right before the verses. If you've seen footage from the show you'll know what I mean. You'll also know what I mean when I say that Neil was unbelievably terrible during that entire very critical US Festival performance. He was clearly wasted and missed keys like crazy, so much so that Lee (who with Mars actually salvaged the show) allegedly cried after their set because he thought the dream was over. It should have been Neil doing the crying, especially after that idiotic rambling stage rap that opened "Piece of Your Action" about some chick the band had all done at the same time. Instead of crying though, after the set Neil found solace in banging Tom Zutaut's girlfriend backstage. And this is what made Motley Crue kings of the hair metal frontier - they stuffed the holes where they were lacking with obnoxious sideshow dressing that dared us not to look. But look we did.

After he got the attention he sought with *Shout at the Devil*, Nikki Sixx tried his hand at Bowie's game of perpetual reinvention and donned a polka-dotted jumpsuit for follow up record *Theatre of Pain*. The characters-as-musicians fantasy element is best demonstrated in the intro of the "Home Sweet Home" video, with each Motley member typecast in their stereotyped role – Neil as the blond surfer dude, Mars as the dark, creepy goth, Lee at a beachfront house party surrounded by fellow stoners, and Sixx sitting at the bar of some live music booze can, blasted out of his mind. Remember - that's characters-as-musicians, not the other way around.

Sixx's masterstroke during the *Theatre of Pain* era was indeed the "Home Sweet Home" video. It was fashioned to be a Motley Crue mini-documentary romanticizing Sixx's sex, drugs, and rock and roll vision years before Poison's "Every Rose Has Its Thorn" video did (and even before Bon Jovi's "Wanted Dead or Alive" vid, though Jon and Bret cleverly raised the ante by doing their videos in black-and-white to attempt *film noir* dramatics). The "Home Sweet Home" video microcosmically represented what Sixx wanted us to believe Motley Crue embodied. It was all there in dramatic slow motion - live concert footage of Neil and a female fan sharing his microphone to sing to each other, another female fan lifting her shirt for the camera, Sixx wincing in faux-pain and plugging his ears with his fingers while succumbing to the madness that is a Motley Crue concert, and the obligatory footage of the bus moving through its long and weary slog along an endless highway.

Sigh.

I always wondered what happened to Vince Neil's hair when I saw that video. It looked like someone had crudely cut off his bangs. Probably a Tommy Lee gag after Neil passed out somewhere other than in his tour bus bunk.

As a fan, I distinctly remember the thoughts that went through my head after having bought the *Theatre of Pain* LP (LP because my family had a basement recreation room with a record player as part of the stereo and I would just record LPs onto blank Maxells for my Walkman – I felt like I missed out on the album artwork after buying the *Shout at the Devil* cassette). I sat in front of the stereo and stared at the mauve coloured album cover compelled by thoughts that Motley Crue was something else now. Neil was wearing lace and Sixx was in a polka-dot jumpsuit. WTF? As a kid, the logic of why Sixx would have taken the band in this direction was lost on me.

As far as the material went, Brownsville Station cover "Smokin' in the Boys' Room" seemed like cheeky fodder used to endear Motley to an expanded audience that might have included non-metal fans like my sister, along with obvious single "Home Sweet Home". The rest of the record contains spit-shined leftover *Shout* riffs and fake-Aerosmith outtakes like "City Boy Blues". *Theatre of Pain* proved a lot of things, but above all it proved that Motley Crue was not the metal band it purported to be with *Shout at the Devil*.

For the record, it's clear that Motley Crue is not a metal band at all. If you joined the Motley Crue circus as a result of the experience *Shout at the Devil* provided, then it was an honest mistake. But *Shout at the Devil* only sounded the way that it did to get your attention, and also to provide a metallic backdrop to the image that Sixx lifted from his old London bandmate and later W.A.S.P. frontman Blackie Lawless. It wasn't a real metal record any more than Motley was a real metal band. Motley Crue was a shape-shifting musical menagerie that evolved by the estimations of what Sixx deemed necessary to achieve and maintain stardom. Period. Sixx used his influences as a starting point – *Too Fast For Love* was angry Sweet and T.Rex, right down to the handclaps in the initially unreleased track "Toast of the Town". *Shout at the Devil* was the edgier sonic equivalent of what KISS probably looked like through Sixx's eyes. *Shout at the Devil* is no more metal than KISS' *Creatures of the Night*, and it employs the same devices. The only diffcrence is that in KISS' case, *Creatures of the Night* was overcompensation for their soft concept album *Music For The Elder*.

Theatre of Pain aspired to achieve a Bowie *Hunky Dory / Ziggy Stardust* musical coup, at least as well as Motley could muster. And Aerosmith's influence always loomed in the background until *Girls, Girls, Girls* and *Dr. Feelgood* brought it right up front after the fame hurdle was out of the way and overtly heavy metal and glitzy glam get-ups were no longer necessary. None of these records are metal. They're just dressed up to be, some more than others.

Nikki Sixx was an angry, disenfranchised kid that would do whatever it took to make it, and he just had a greater sense of how to do that than most of his peers. Sixx's old London band mate Lizzie Grey has said in interviews that Sixx understood how to hustle, how to turn image into money. This was the key difference between Sixx and Motley Crue and other bands that didn't "make it". According to Grey, Sixx used the initial *Shout at the Devil* heavy metal image as a 'checkmate' against Blackie Lawless for getting kicked out of Sister, Lawless' late 70s band that looked like an early version of W.A.S.P.. Grey also said that after Sixx and Lawless got famous, they didn't want to be around anyone who reminded them of what they were like before they were rock stars. This has always been the most fascinating aspect of fame for me – that very prominent and yet very imaginary dividing line that separates the non-famous from the famous. Or rather, the real from the make-believe.

Today, fame is practically a misnomer. With all of the supplementary mass communications implements we have at our disposal, fame is virtually ordinary. The simple, artificial brand of fame manufactured by *American Idol* and other similar shows is proof. 'Fame' doesn't carry the same heft it used to because it barely means anything anymore. Before the advent of technology like Twitter, we had 'celebutantes', people like Paris Hilton who were inexplicably famous without being tied to any particular talent or achievement. This type of artificial fame was manufactured by our own self-interpretation, because a person like Hilton is perceived as the glamorous end state of the aspirations of millions of young girls. A public figure is selected based on what we see or want to see of ourselves in this figure, and the figure is lionized by our motivation to realize our goals of 'becoming' them through an increased preoccupation. This type of fame is completely different from the more classic type that features respect and adulation for some form of tangible achievement. It's more self-serving on both sides of the equation, because it's based on superficial status and greed.

In this way, Nikki Sixx was a pioneering Paris Hilton of the movement that people would later call "glam metal". He manufactured an identity for himself using the influences and tools available to him and invented a world-famous brand, inspiring thousands of kids who were looking for answers within themselves to continue the cycle. And in turn, *this* was his tangible achievement. All of the music that would come later was simply by-product.

When you look at Nikki Sixx and Motley Crue in this way, it makes the consideration of Matthew Trippe even more interesting. Trippe was that guy who claimed to have been approached by the Motley Crue management team of Doug Thaler and Doc McGhee to 'stand in' as Nikki Sixx from July1983 to April 1984, after Frank Feranna crashed his car and was allegedly unable to perform, potentially ruining the ascent to fame that Thaler and McGhee anticipated for Motley.

It's a crazy story. According to Trippe, he moved to Los Angeles from Erie, Pennsylvania and befriended Mick Mars one night at the Troubadour. Mars asked him if he could play bass, and explained that his band's bass player was in a car accident (Trippe said he had never heard of Motley Crue before this conversation), and that there may be an opening in the band as a result. Trippe said that Mars brought him into the McGhee Entertainment offices after hours to meet with Thaler, McGhee, Tommy Lee, and others to 'audition'. He claimed to have played "Danger" and some other song with a stupid title, and he was then asked to sign four contracts without being allowed to take the time to read them. He was asked to sign them 'Nikki Sixx', not Matthew Trippe.

Once he was 'in the band', Trippe claims he was whisked into Cherokee Studios and that he 'cleaned up' songs the band had already written, saying that they were weak and that he 'spiced them up' by adding new arrangements and satanic references. He also says that he toured with Motley Crue while they opened for KISS and Ozzy, noting that he had a 'falling out' with Osbourne. Trippe was adamant that he wrote "Wild Side", "Girls, Girls, Girls", "You're All I Need", "City Boy Blues", "Danger", and "Knock 'Em Dead Kid". Hell, he claims to have written all of *Theatre of Pain* except "Smokin' in the Boys Room" and "Home Sweet Home" (because he 'wouldn't write a wimpy song like that' - according to him, he wanted to do a cover of "Mississippi Queen" instead). In addition to all of this, Trippe says that he: 'felt like a faggot' wearing the spandex from the *Theatre of Pain* era but had to because it was Doc McGhee's suggestion; was thrilled when a fan supposedly told him Neil died in the crash that actually killed Hanoi Rocks drummer Nicholas 'Razzle' Dingley (*"I loved it! It was about time that little bastard died!"*); and that he personally invited Hanoi singer Mike Monroe to replace Neil as Motley's singer and that Monroe was interested, but that McGhee kyboshed the idea.

Trippe goes on to say that he was removed from the band because of an armed robbery he committed (nice) that led to a small jail stretch in 1985. He stipulated that he hired private investigators that were holding the copyrights for the songs he wrote, and that 'ink and paper analysis' was being conducted (!). He claims that he wasn't paid at all, but that it didn't matter because he was 'only in it for the chicks, the booze, the drugs, and the fun'. However, years later when he launched this bizarre story, he claimed that he had assembled a legal team to bring the case before the courts, and he refused to settle out of court because his case was so strong.

An American journalist named Ed Esposito interviewed Trippe in 1988 and submitted the piece to *Kerrang!* magazine. Upon reading it, it's clear that Trippe isn't exactly a Mensa candidate, and that the laughable details he discloses about his allegedly being in the band for almost a year are inconsistent, unrealistic, and stupid. For example, Trippe claims to have met Mick Mars in June 1983, joined Motley Crue and went into the studio to write and record *Shout at the Devil* in July 1983. The band had already played the *Shout at the Devil* material at the US Festival on May 29, 1983.

Trippe is most likely just some lying dirtbag, but there are some aspects of the story that were questionable enough to give rise to a smallish conspiracy theory. Trippe presented some photos that are allegedly of him as Nikki Sixx on the *Theatre of Pain* tour, and they actually look more like him than they do Frank Feranna when you look really closely at the features. One of these pictures is of him with Motley Crue tour manager Richard Fisher, which is a bit peculiar. The other unusual aspect of this story is that the publishing credits on the records change from Nikki Sixx Music to Sikki Nixx Music for no apparent reason. Trippe claimed this was done to distinguish between songs that he wrote and songs that Feranna wrote. I've always wondered about that.

There's not much on the Internet about any of this, except a story about an old bandmate of Trippe's that came forward saying that he didn't know if the whole story was true or not for a number of reasons. One of those reasons being that he had seen official Library of Congress copyright documents with Matthew Trippe's social security number showing beside the name Nikki Sixx, alongside the other band members' stage names, birth names and social security numbers. He also said he had heard that Trippe had been awarded an out of court settlement from Motley Crue, which may explain the fact that this bizarre story didn't really have an ending, and why Motley Crue nor their management have said very little about any of it to this day.

My personal assessment of this bizarre story is that if there *is* any truth to it, it's an extremely small amount. If Doc McGhee and Doug Thaler did actually see fit to substitute someone in for Frank Feranna so as not to lose any momentum leading up to the *Shout at the Devil* release, it would have most likely been for a very brief period of time, maybe during a few key moments, and with much less exposure than Trippe describes. It makes sense that they would have inserted someone who was as intellectually challenged and easily manipulated as Trippe evidently is. If any substitution was indeed made, it certainly wasn't carried out on the same scale that Trippe describes.

Trippe's version of the story is a series of bad lies as told by a bad liar. His account is consistently seasoned with small details peripheral to the main story that could be true but couldn't really be validated by anyone, and provided in an attempt to build some sort of artificial credibility. The same shtick psychics use when they take you through all of their bullshit. Trippe's story is transparent in the same way. When I met Frank Feranna at the Toronto stop of his *Heroin Diaries* book signing a few years back I considered asking him for some insight on this topic, though I suspect he would have been none too pleased to have this question posed to him.

Anyway, regardless of the amount of truth involved the Matthew Trippe incident actually validates the idea that Nikki Sixx is really only a manufactured concept in the same way that Motley Crue is. Nikki Sixx was an artificial persona created and propelled towards a goal of fame and fortune by a real person, Frank Feranna, and Motley Crue is a collection of these personae as assembled by Feranna. In theory, once this creation is up and running, the presumption is that real people other than Frank Feranna could keep it moving. If you believe the Matthew Trippe theory in any capacity, it lends even more credence to the fact that Motley Crue is a group of role-playing characters no different from the man behind that curtain in *The Wizard of Oz*. We all know that Vince Neil isn't *really* a singer; he just plays one in Motley Crue.

Because I see Frank Feranna and Nikki Sixx for what they really are doesn't mean I love Motley Crue any less. I just enjoy them in the same way that I would enjoy a movie – as fiction. Feranna is a smart, resilient mofo and I tip my hat to him, because despite Motley Crue's record sales and established position in hard rock history, Frank Feranna's real achievement was his ability to sell his dream to the world, in turn selling our own dreams back to us.

✪ Five ✪
Metallica, Slayer, Raven, and...*Dokken?*

It was in the late summer of 1984, at the age of fifteen and on vacation with my family traveling through the southern United States in a wood-paneled station wagon that I cut my heavy metal teeth on thrash metal.

I had never heard anything this heavy. Prior to this, I had been getting into heavier metal without even really realizing it by gravitating towards the albums in the record store rock bins that were more aggressively themed and more interesting looking. Black leather, blood, and fire always got my attention. Natural transgression from the KISS years. I was really attracted to that glamorous malevolence that KISS sought and that *Shout at the Devil*-era Motley Crue brought, along with other bands that incorporated a visual element into their art - the Maidens, the W.A.S.P.s, the Judas Priests, the Lizzy Bordens, and so on.

As much as imagery caught my eye and held my attention as a kid, I usually did fairly well in being able to separate the wheat from the chaff when it came to determining which records were worth buying and which were not. This isn't to say that I didn't make my fair share of errors of course. Being able to sample songs in iTunes would have been like having a superpower when I was a teenager, but sadly it wasn't available to prevent me from throwing away money on records like Living Death's *Metal Revolution*, Rage's *Execution Guaranteed*, and Dogs D'Amour's *In The Dynamite Jet Saloon*.

Back then, there were hundreds of brand new metal records on the racks competing for my very limited amount of record-buying dollars. I closely scrutinized all of the visual variables on the sleeve of any record that piqued my initial interest. The visual cues I thought were important were things like artwork, song titles, logo fonts, notes, and that sort of thing. I believed this stuff was indicative of what the bands where about, what their music might sound like, and whether or not I would be into them.

I guess a parallel could have been drawn between my level of musical interest and the concept of dating. Because my love for music was such a substantial force in my life, I was looking for bands that I could really get into, beyond just their music. For me, the songs were only one component (albeit the most important) of a group's overall package. Metaphorically, I guess I wasn't looking for just a disposable musical one-night stand. Not most of the time anyway.

Every now and again songs were 'used' for quickie musical entertainment. I had no plans of developing any further interest in the bands that wrote them. Something like say, Autograph's "Turn Up the Radio". I listened to this song with the same disposable intent a casual music listener might put on something to serve as 'background music'. It's a matter of convenience and there's no attachment. There were plenty of bands that released catchy singles that had little semblance to the remainder of their song catalogue or their collective band identity. One-hit wonder groups like Madness or Wall of Voodoo or Jetboy. All ripe for cheap musical flings.

But I was really looking for *investment*. Something I could sink my teeth into. I wanted to get involved. I was looking for groups that were emblematic of the same things I thought that I was, or wanted to be. I was looking for identification and connectivity, something that I could get inside and be a part of. Something I could call my own. Lots of psychological devices at work here to be sure, but I would think the same is evident in most teenage motivations where music is concerned. Especially at the age of fourteen or fifteen when impressionability is practically combustible, and there's really not much else going on.

As far as album artwork went, I paid a lot of attention to the overall message a band was trying to convey. I evaluated that message based on what I thought their perception of themselves was *vis-à-vis* this message, and if I could identify with that. If a band used cheesy, cliché-ridden artwork with lousy fonts and an amateurish approach, it was an indication of the band's musical limitation to me. The chances that their music was going to suck were likely. On the other hand, if a band didn't seem as though they were trying too hard to get your attention with a bunch of stupid gimmickry, and they presented the artwork with a sense of confidence or even aloofness, it made me more interested. Again, just like high school dating, really. There were clear demarcation points that existed along the way in forming relationships. And if the litmus test yielded a significant failure at any point, the show was over. There was no time to fuck around.

Heavy Metal as a genre is inherently cheesy. This is no secret. Everyone knows it. But there are varying degrees of *fromage*, which most self-respecting metalheads also know. There exists an acceptable level of schlock, an expected amount that just comes with the territory, the kind that makes metal what it is. In fact, metal wouldn't be metal without it. There's no formal gauge by which to measure it, it's just something that's evaluated instinctually. And anything beyond this level is unacceptable.

Take band logos for example. Band logos are a very important facet of hard rock and metal (that logic is cheesy in itself, isn't it?). With the proliferation of the logo patch-encrusted denim jacket in the early 80s, a lot of effort went into band logo design as an immediate identifier of the band, not to mention all of the symbolism that went along with it. There are some great, instantly recognizable font types – AC/DC, Iron Maiden, Judas Priest, Scorpions, and Metallica for starters. I have to admit that even Dokken's logo is cool, actually. There are also some pretty cheesy ones, and they can compromise a band's chances of being heard. Silly but true.

Any text on a record sleeve was also part of my album evaluation process. Song titles are often a dead giveaway of the intellectual capacity involved, and that the songs themselves may potentially be piffle. But then again I didn't want *too* much intellectual capacity, because it was heavy metal after all. So, I made plenty of allowances in this area because it was necessary. Within the genres of hard rock and metal, we have to accept the fact that a good percentage of song titles will be representative of the token established lifestyle trappings of groupie banging, chemical adventure, and general chaos and rebellion. In keeping with this theme, song titles like "Slide It In", "Let Me Put My Love Into You", and "Push, Push" will be prevalent. No worries there. I didn't, however, have a lot of time for titles that lazily deployed single letters in the place of whole words ("Shoot U Full Of Love", "U Got It"), or numbers ("2 Late 4 Love"), or gratuitous use of the letter *z* ("EZ Come EZ Go", "Squeezin' Pleazin'"), because they were reminiscent of an approach to titling songs that Prince had taken. I had initially overlooked Tesla in the 80s mainly because of their cover of "Signs", but had I known they used song titles like "2 Late 4 Love" and "EZ Come EZ Go" (both from their debut record *Mechanical Resonance*), I would have been doubly repulsed.

Sometimes there were written communications or quotes on a record sleeve that may have impacted whether or not I thought I would like a new band. For me back then, the more cryptic and mysterious the better. Bands that used mythical, mystical imagery as their theme typically deployed grandiose Latin-based messages that had to do with vanquishing the enemy or something along those lines. This was neither here nor there in my mind. It fell into line with the overall motif of the band, so it didn't really impact whether or not I would buy the record. It wasn't really quite giving me enough to work with, mostly because it was almost expected.

Bands like Stryper would plaster their records inside and out with quotes from the bible, which were met with an instant rejection from me. I could never really figure Stryper out. I always thought Stryper was a lot like that really-really-good-looking-but-really-really-knows-it girl that we've all known. At first blush, there's an interest based on physical attributes and visual stimulus. These elements are compelling enough to initiate further scrutiny. And then, the good-looking girl opens her mouth. Turns out she's an annoyingly vain, empty-headed, self-centred fool. And it's over. Any initial attraction is negated. In Stryper's case, their boldly colourful look, compelling image and even initial sound may get them past the initial smell test, but as soon as they open their mouths, all of the religiosity comes out. And they're done. That's a real shame in Stryper's case, because the band seemingly did have the tools to be a pretty good group. They just needed to relax a little bit. Go down to the pub, have a drink. Have a few laughs. Get laid. But I guess we all have our crosses to bear, hardy har har.

Anyway, back in 1984 the aggregate of all of these evaluation factors and maybe a few others culminated in the decision as to whether or not I would buy a record. Still do, to a degree. So on a stop at a mall in Atlanta, I was in a record store looking through the cassette bins and there were plenty of exciting things to see. This was around the time when the New Wave of British Heavy Metal was flaming out and the west coast scene had just launched its first wave of hair bands post-Van Halen. At about the same time, really heavy stuff was just coming available through Megaforce and Metal Blade, and the Bay Area thrash scene was really revving up. I sifted through all kinds of new releases from bands I'd never heard of.

One of the first records I picked up was by a band named Oz called *Fire in the Brain*. The front cover employed the requisite metal colour scheme of black backdrop and red logo font, with leather & spikes, skulls, fire, blood, and general evil. Good show so far. While the blood on the hand holding the fiery skull (*can you really get much more metal than this?*) was of the disappointingly thin bright red, obviously-food-colouring variety, it was noted that all the preliminary artwork bases were pretty much covered at least. The record made it out of the bin and up into my hot little hands for further analysis. The band logo and font of the album title were amateurish, the title font remotely resembling Greek alphabet lettering. At this point, my position on this record was that the music might have suffered from being overly clichéd, even for metal.

On to the back cover and the song titles. Most of them were predictable. Some of the others were mildly intriguing though considering the overall theme of the record. I remember that there was one song called "Gambler", and another one called "Megalomaniac". It seemed like more of a Whitesnake theme was afoot here as opposed to the obvious black metal overtones. This was interesting. The "Megalomaniac" title struck me as atypical too, even if Black Sabbath did use a similar title in "Megalomania".

In the end, the funny thing was that I put the record back in the bin. I might be mistaken because it happened more than twenty-five years ago, but I'm pretty sure I put the record down because there was an off-putting picture of a bald guy on the back. I think I may have been under the impression that he was "Oz", and I didn't like something about that. Probably swayed my overall perception of this record and I ended up passing on it. But that's how I bought my records back then. Instinct. Of course today, a much more informed decision is possible through the Internet via reviews, blogs, iTunes, illegal downloads, et cetera. In fact, with the help of the World Wide Web, I'm seeing now that *Fire in the Brain* was lauded as a Scandinavian power metal tour de force, and this resurrects my interest. I'm surprised to find *Fire in the Brain* on iTunes and I sample it, realizing that it actually sounds like something I definitely would have been into back then. So much for my intuitive perception.

After I walked away from the Oz record that day, I looked at another record that caught my eye by a band called The Rods, but I didn't have a good feeling about it either. Ditto Abattoir, Impaler, and Venom. Pass, pass, and pass. I'm not at all proud of this, but I ended up deciding to buy an album because of the picture of drummer Rob "Wacko" Hunter wearing a hockey helmet on the back of the album sleeve. That wasn't the only reason, but it may have been an impacting factor.

That album, Raven's *All For One,* pretty much had everything a young hard rocker was looking for. Singer / bassist John Gallagher's screech could have likely shattered panes of glass, guitarist brother Mark bludgeoned with riff after nimble yet crushing riff, and the aforementioned Hunter absolutely pummelled his poor drum kit.

No Sleep 'til Sudbury

I still listen to this record regularly (I upgraded to Japanese-import CD from Megaforce cassette in the late 90s). The remarkable thing about *All For One* is that, while the hockey helmet doesn't at all seem like an unreasonable accoutrement for these weirdoes, the musical finesse and control Raven actually demonstrates is surprising. The songs are thoughtfully arranged and cohesive, and the musicality is much better than one might expect. Strike two for instinct.

The ace in the hole for Raven was obviously guitarist Mark Gallagher. The riffs were colourful and yet very powerful, and his playing in general was unique and inventive on *All For One*. His chugging power metal rhythms remind me a bit of Deep Purple's "Burn" ratcheted up to a speedcore intensity - almost. And therein lies the beauty in this record. The thing I love about it the most is that, despite the lawless insanity Raven may have you believe permeates from the very fibre of their collective being, the songs themselves aren't compromised by the same goofy logic. They stop just short of thrash metal extremism, harnessing intensity and retaining pulverizing power without falling into that abyss of foolishness that so many bands of their ilk did. There is some silliness on this record, particularly in the CD's bonus track "The Ballad of Marshall Stack", but it's more deliberate than unintended.

Unfortunately all of the fantastic riffing, thoughtfully written and arranged songs, and the singing that smacked of the testicles being mercilessly squeezed in a vice (yet without the contrivance of Justin Hawkins of The Darkness), would make *All For One* the exclusive pinnacle of Raven's career. The band was later signed by a major label (Atlantic), and went on to release a couple of ill-advised albums that were such sellouts that they were almost vomit inducing. One of those, *The Pack is Back*, featured a cover of the Spencer Davis Group's "Gimme Good Lovin'" complete with a horns section complement that also figured into a couple of other songs on the record. Coming from a band like Raven, it sounded so tremendously horrible that I barely stopped short of smashing the cassette on my bedroom floor after the first (and last) listen. Very disappointing. I did buy *Live at the Inferno* before that back in 1984, but when my tape player ate it I didn't bother to replace it because I was so bitter about those goddamn horns.

Back in the record store of the Atlanta mall, my roving eyes spied another album cover that featured all the commensurate metal trappings, including demonic eye makeup and upside-down crosses on the back cover. In fact, it was that back cover that sold me on my second selection of the day. The front cover was dodgy, featuring a clownish little Minotaur-type character wearing a cape and brandishing a sword, looking a bit like it may have been a direct transfer of the scrawled doodling from one of the band members' high school textbooks. This album was called *Show No Mercy*, and it was Slayer's debut.

As is the message conveyed by guitarist Kerry King's full forearm leather armband barely seen for all of the six-inch nails jutting out of it in all directions, *Show No Mercy* clearly states that Slayer does not fuck around. Opening track "Evil Has No Boundaries" gives the listener a pretty good idea of what's to come twelve seconds in with frontman and bassist Tom Araya's pitchy falsetto shriek to kick off the proceedings – ten songs of crude, raised-middle-finger-in-your-squinting-face thrash metal. But that's not all. As far as thrash metal goes, the material on *Show No Mercy* is actually digestible, not just full-blast cacophonous foolishness. "The Antichrist" actually deploys a groove-laden riff that makes me wonder what the song would sound like slowed down, with a tempo change in the middle eight that suggests some thought went into these compositions rather than just an attempt to out-thrash other bands (though that may not have been such a formidable feat around the time of the release of this record). Besides the speed, the most compelling aspect of *Show No Mercy* is its overtly satanic lyrics. No vague references here. We're talking *get ready to offer up your entrails at the altar of your almighty master Satan* stuff here, before King Diamond commoditized the angle. And it didn't feel like a gimmick.

The opening riff for "Fight Till Death" is the best one on the record, and the song is the speediest yet. But that's what I like about *Show No Mercy*. It doesn't ever get quite *too* stupid. Where thrash (or subsequently developed *black*) metal peers Venom just offered tuneless silliness, Slayer played fast and heavy songs that were built around imaginative, tuneful riffs on *Show No Mercy*. The band always did have that capacity, though it was demonstrated only periodically later in songs like "Angel of Death" and "Seasons of the Abyss".

Side two of *Show No Mercy* opens with "Black Magic" beginning with that creepy gradual fade-in that you just don't hear anymore, like an army coming in the distance, gradually getting closer and closer with the intent of bashing your head in. Though the production doesn't necessarily do him any favours, skinsman Dave Lombardo is the driving force behind Slayer, widely recognized as the best drummer in thrash metal with very good reason. Tracks like "The Final Command" and "Show No Mercy" make you break a sweat just listening to the guy play. The intro for "The Final Command" is vividly reminiscent of the first two Maiden records, until the beats per minute are ratcheted up through the roof at 0:28. Guitarists Kerry King and Jeff Hanneman are no slouches on this record either, even if their scale vocabularies limit their lead playing somewhat. But that doesn't matter. The nimble, precise riffing on *Show No Mercy* is what made Slayer more interesting than most of their contemporaries.

After I developed an affinity for this record as a kid Slayer lost me with their subsequent releases because, with the exception of the odd standout track like "Angel of Death", every song sounded the same to me. Araya's general singing style always reminded me of that cantankerous old man in your neighbourhood who shouted threats and general vitriol at pesky kids who wouldn't stay off his lawn. Which was fine, because that was Slayer. I did pay attention to the highlights of *Reign in Blood*, *South of Heaven*, and *Seasons in the Abyss*, but I didn't own any of those albums and still don't.

A few years ago I bought *God Hates Us All* on a lark, but I played it and shelved it. I *want* to like Slayer completely, but I just can't. *Show*

No Mercy finds its way into my player once a year or so and I still enjoy it, but there never seemed to be enough variance in the newer compositions to make them really interesting. It was just layer after layer of dull bludgeoning sludge with nothing inside. There was always this intended resistance with Slayer, and in a sense I respect them for it because like AC/DC, they stuck to their guns and it worked in their favour in the long run. But I couldn't hear enough of the colour Slayer displayed on *Show No Mercy* in their subsequent records to ever call myself a real fan.

Slayer peers Megadeth also alienated me somewhat, but for different reasons. I always thought that Megadeth's records would be much more listenable if it weren't for Dave Mustaine's unnecessarily unorthodox vocal delivery. At first glance, Megadeth is a thrash metal dream – thunderous double bass kick drums, skillful and agile riffing galore, imaginative songwriting, and a great balanced sound. I just never understood Mustaine's insistence on singing in weird, garbled voices the way he did on songs like *Countdown to Extinction*'s "Sweating Bullets".

It is noted that after getting tossed out of Metallica for excessive drinking and drug use (kicked out of Metallica for excessive drinking? Isn't that like getting kicked out of Al-Qaeda for being too mean?), Mustaine looked for a singer for the first six months of forming Megadeth but, like previous Metallica bandmate and fellow guitarist James Hetfield, he eventually just took on the vocal duties himself. In this case, I could be more inclined to give Mustaine credit for singing and playing those crazy riffs at the same time. But "Sweating Bullets" also exemplifies another reason I could never fully get into Megadeth... the lyrics. In this song, Mustaine is having some sort of peculiar dialogue with himself - *"Hello me, meet the real me"* and *"Hello me, it's nice talking to myself"*, all sung in that grating voice. The worst lyrical example may be "A Tout le Monde", wherein the chorus is sung in French. Why?

I always thought Mustaine's (metal) heart was in the right place. He was a tragic figure with some legitimate personal problems. My issue with Mustaine and Megadeth was that even as the band became more and more successful after the release of their 1986 breakthrough record *Peace Sells...But Who's Buying?* (which I thought was a decent record, Willie Dixon's "I Ain't Superstitious" cover and all), Mustaine's sour grapes lamenting just seemed to get more and more toxic and it compromised the music to the point where I became disinterested. An apples-to-apples comparison of Megadeth's music against Metallica's legitimized Mustaine's inferiority complex and made him seem whiny. Sure, there was lots of pressure living in the shadow of Metallica. But it wasn't like Mustaine fell into some sort of Pete Best-like obscurity and had to go off and work in a factory or something. Megadeth is considered a musical pioneer, a respected member of the original thrash metal Big Four that still does brisk business today. Megadeth's bass player David Ellefson said it himself recently in the press – without Metallica, there would be no Megadeth.

My mindset on Mustaine's position back then was that if he deserved any empathy at all, it was because while his overt bitterness was the main propulsive element behind Megadeth's ascent to fame, the material he intended to be venomous and malevolent more often than not just came across as juvenile. After I read Mustaine's recent autobiography, I changed my mind a bit. More on Mustaine later.

I didn't pick up any Anthrax product that day in Atlanta. I did buy their *Fistful of Metal* debut on vinyl shortly after this trip however, either despite or because of the fact that the cover was adorned by an image of a spike-laden fist exiting someone's head via their mouth as the result of being punched in the back of their head. And it sounded like it looked. The only interesting (or tragic) thing about the record was that it marked the first time I'd heard Alice Cooper's "I'm Eighteen".

I only picked up Anthrax's next full-length release, *Spreading the Disease*, after seeing the video for "Madhouse". It sold me on the power and the energy of the band, and *Spreading The Disease* demonstrated songwriting depth and impressive musicianship (in addition to being a highly skilled drummer, Charlie Benante was also an accomplished lead guitar player). Most importantly though, the record positioned Anthrax in an interesting light as a thrash metal band during this period.

It provided glimpses of their sense of humour, and it demonstrated the band's multi-dimensional character.

This was a curious aspect at a time when thrash metal was barely five years old. The genre was heavily predicated on dark and ultra-aggressive themes of warfare, violence, isolation, and Satanism. Humour and irony were devices that seemed an unlikely and unwelcome fit. Yet Anthrax made them work somehow, while at the same time delivering songs like "Medusa" and "Aftershock" that featured riffs that were as punishing as anything Slayer was offering. In fact, onward through subsequent Anthrax releases *Among The Living*, *State of Euphoria*, and particularly with the recording of their jokey rap-infused "I'm the Man" single in 1987 and 1991 duo with none other than Public Enemy on "Bring the Noise", Anthrax would represent the polarized thrash metal version of Slayer. And as a listener I came for the power, but stayed for the character.

At some point during that afternoon in Atlanta I picked up a record with a title that read *Kill 'Em All*, from a band whose name immediately struck me as cool - Metallica. It was perfect. The cover had the obligatory red-on-black, blood and violence theme and when I flipped it over I saw four haggard, hung over-looking dudes. Drummer Lars Ulrich looked like a Scottish mechanic, and for a second I thought singer and rhythm guitarist James Hetfield might have been that guy Malachai from *The Children of the Corn* movie. Cliff Burton and Kirk Hammett both looked like they really smelled. But, the band name and song names ("Seek and Destroy", "Phantom Lord" "Metal Militia", "Motorbreath") scored high marks. I decided right away that this record would be coming back to Canada with me.

I had money for this cassette and three others that day. After some careful consideration of several other new releases, including Exodus' *Bonded By Blood* and Canuck thrashers Exciter's sophomore effort *Violence and Force*, I went with *Kill 'Em All*, *Show No Mercy*, *All For*

One, and Dokken's *Breaking the Chains.* Yep - one of these things does not belong, to be sure. I don't remember why I bought that Dokken cassette. Must have been the logo.

I can tell you, however, that Dokken's cassette didn't get nearly as much airtime as the first three did in my yellow Sports Walkman on the long ride back home to Espanola. Things would never be quite the same. My poor mother was mortified.

✲ Six ✲
Living on a Thrash Metal Prayer

As a young new metal fan, the most exciting thing about heavy metal for me was the vicious ferocity of the guitar riffs. It was for this reason that Metallica's *Kill 'Em All* quickly became my favourite of these four cassettes that I had just bought. Listening to riffs like the one in the interlude of "Seek and Destroy" filled me with absolute glee. Without question, James Hetfield wrote some of the most blistering heavy metal riffs ever recorded, all of those being on Metallica's first three records. At the risk of sounding like a geezer, riffs like them just don't get written, played, or recorded like that at all today, son. Period.

Kill 'Em All is essentially a massive treasure trove of superb metal riffage. Most of the songs on the record contain more than one riff, and have an expanded middle eight section that introduces a completely new riff (or three). It didn't occur to me at the time that these songs could have been cobbled together from leftover pieces, and I didn't care. New bands can do this with all of the material they've amassed before doing their first and maybe second record. It's obvious that some songs on *Kill 'Em All*, like "Jump in the Fire" for instance, are the result of a merging of several different riffs of various tempos. Because each riff is so frenetic and inventive however (and because it's metal), any tempo fragmentation in the overall song composition is overlooked. But it's all good.

Metallica were keen students of Black Sabbath and the important bands involved with the NWOBHM movement, but also of bands like Lynyrd Skynyrd and The Allman Brothers. The band's heightened degree of musical sensibility allowed them to infuse subtly composed melody into their gritty, speedy, crunchy power and offer something a bit more substantial. Metallica's debut effort barely seems amateurish when compared to what would follow in *Ride the Lightning* and *Master of Puppets*. Metallica was unmatched among even the more popular acts that comprised the still relatively neophytic thrash metal scene. Venom and peers like Hellhammer barely warrant mention. Slayer had tremendous instrumental skill, as mentioned earlier in the uncanny speed-with-accuracy playing of drummer Dave Lombardo and acrobatic riffing of Kerry King and Jeff Hanneman, but they weren't quite at Metallica's calibre in terms of crafting really substantial *songs*. But this was by choice. While Slayer and Metallica were still sizing each other up during their progression through the underground thrash metal scene, Slayer chose to pursue the speedier, more Black Metal route while Metallica moved in the opposite direction by deliberately removing the satanic overtones on their second album. Ian Christe provides some really interesting details on this subject in his book *The History of Metal*, discussing how the "Big Four" thrash metal bands - Metallica, Megadeth, Slayer, and Anthrax – all interacted with each other in their early days. It's a great read, check it out.

James Hetfield made a lasting impression on me as I became more and more intrigued by Metallica as the 80s progressed. I identified him as the figurehead of the band (sorry Lars), and my entire high school locker door was covered in Hetfield-only full-page pictures collected from *Circus* and *Hit Parader*. Also stuck up there was the cover of *Kerrang!* issue number 120 that featured Hetfield playing live wearing that black Damage Inc. sweatshirt. As Nikki Sixx metamorphosed away from his *Shout at the Devil* leather look and into polka dotted ubiquity, Hetfield took over full command of my attention. With Hetfield, it wasn't so much his look *per se*; it was his intensity. He didn't deliberately strike rock star poses. In fact, he hunched over his guitar

No Sleep 'til Sudbury

to the point where it made my back hurt just watching him do it. He just seemed to personify the coolest version of calamitous mayhem. With his Gibson Explorer (later ESP) cranking out bonecrushing riffs, and hair whipping around everywhere at full speed in headbanging abandon, he looked like a perfectly authentic representation of how Metallica's music sounded.

Watching Hetfield play guitar was riveting. His picking hand was ridiculously accurate, all downstrokes, even as he sang and played simultaneously. His fretting hand was super fast, index and pinky fingers outstretched in opposite directions as they moved through each note of each riff. Above all with Hetfield, I was amazed at how proficiently he could still play while he sang. And drank! It's no secret that James was buzzed during most of the 80s. He's humbly said in the past that the studio is a forgiving atmosphere in terms of mistakes and that his playing may not have been as good as is depicted on recordings, but he's been impressive in any live environment I've seen him in, even way back then.

I had found out much later that Hetfield only became the singer of Metallica by default, because they couldn't find anyone else they liked – John Bush of Armored Saint (and later Anthrax) fame was asked to join but he declined. Of course, it's hard to imagine what the band would have sounded like with someone else as the lead singer. Though he didn't get a ton of accolades as a vocalist, I always thought Hetfield's naturally raw approach was perfect for the music. It's funny, because he was regarded as more of a guitar player than a vocalist back then, if he was even regarded as a vocalist at all. In the earliest incarnations of the band, Hetfield had initially intended to only sing and not play guitar. I never really gave any consideration to the fact that most metal bands in the 80s had definitive singers whose roles, whether deliberately intended or not, added sensationalism to the material with higher register histrionics - guys like Rob Halford, Geoff Tate, and Lizzy Borden. Even in the speed / thrash / black metal genres there were screamers like Hades' Alan Tecchio, Mercyful Fate's King Diamond, and Helloween's Michael Kiske. Incidentally, before the addition of Kiske,

Helloween's founding guitarist Kai Hansen was the band's singer but he had difficulty singing and playing at the same time.

I caught Metallica live in the metropolis that is Sudbury when they were touring the *Master of Puppets* record in 1986. They headlined this show, an off-date from their opening slot on Ozzy's *The Ultimate Sin* tour, with Metal Church and a Canadian hard rock band called Kick Axe opening. The Sudbury Arena probably held about five thousand people, and I think it was about half full.

Kick Axe came and went. The three recollections I have of them are that 1) the drummer had these unusually long, tubular drums in his Ayotte kit, 2) the band played a smashing cover of Humble Pie's "Thirty Days in the Hole", and 3) the singer's name was George.

Metal Church was second on the bill. I had bought their debut album way before this show, but I actually didn't care for it very much then. I liked the songs "Hitman" and "My Favorite Nightmare", but I wasn't big on much else the record had to offer. It seemed a bit dull to me, and the "Highway Star" cover version at the end was noticeably out of place compared to the rest of the track list. The production wasn't so lively and I pretty much overlooked the whole record. The lyrics in "Hitman" were well suited for young passive-aggressive headbanger fantasy engagement, dumb fantasy akin to those old Chuck Norris movies like *The Octagon* that featured ninjas and throwing stars and loads of improbable action. The same base dynamic was deployed - a manufactured outlet through which to channel the aggression of youth in a healthy, non-Columbine way.

While this fantasy element is one of the most attractive aspects of metal in general for young teens, it's also one that has been manipulated to the point where it's become pejorative. This topic is fodder for all kinds of stupid debates, all of which unnecessary. Because really, the controlling factor is common sense. Pure and simple. The difference between me listening to AC/DC's "Night Prowler" and enjoying it as a form of entertainment, and Richard Ramirez listening to it and going out and killing people because he said the song compelled him to do so, is *common sense* - common sense of course being the active element of mental stability and the ability to reason. I had my share of rage to channel as a teen, as most teens do. But I did so through more rational means. Sports. Other related activities. I didn't go out and fucking *kill* people for chrissakes. And I certainly didn't even remotely consider snuffing it when I listened to Ozzy's "Suicide Solution" or Judas Priest's "Beyond The Realms Of Death". Things like that don't even cross the mind of the rational person. It's ludicrous to think that you can blame that sort of behaviour on music. Of course, wading into these waters means opening up the floodgates of myriad debates, including organized religion and free speech, and maybe even euthanasia in the case of that one kid who misfired during his suicide attempt while listening to Judas Priest and lived, despite blowing most of his face off. Debating these topics (like debating most other topics, really) is pointless. If you're willing to take your own life at the perceived suggestion of a lyric in a song, your problems are deeply rooted and far-reaching, and those problems were percolating long before the play button was pressed.

Anyway, it wasn't until I bought Metal Church's second record *The Dark* that I really opened my eyes (and ears) to the band, but that was only after seeing them at this Sudbury show. My friend Johnny and I were like giddy schoolgirls after watching the band rip through "Ton Of Bricks" and "Psycho". I needed to get my hands on *The Dark* after seeing that. When the record was finally in my hot little mitts, I noticed that it had placed quite a lot of distance between itself and the first album. It was slickly produced, almost too much so with respect to the drum tracks. They almost bore an electronic sound. In this sense, the record seemed to have a slightly commercial flavour. It almost seemed like the two albums came from different bands. Record companies refer to this as 'artistic growth'. Regardless, I liked *The Dark*, and when I went back to check out the first record again I really dug it as well. I listen to it a fair bit these days in fact. I had picked up Metal Church's third album,

Blessing In Disguise, on CD after I had left for university but I flipped it at a buy-and-sell shop shortly after. Just couldn't get into it.

I remember that this Sudbury show was played under somewhat unusual circumstances, wherein guitarist Kirk Arrington had very recently broken his arm and couldn't play the gig. He was standing off in the wings and some other guy, maybe his guitar tech, was filling in for him. The tech was also standing back there, not out on stage with the rest of the band for some unknown reason. The other guitar player, Kurdt Vanderhoof, was a fucking mental case on stage that night, running around and banging his head like a lunatic. I remember thinking that he resembled John Hinckley Jr. a little bit.

Metallica took the stage after Metal Church, and it was a raw, deafeningly loud show. I was paralyzed with giddiness that James Hetfield and Metallica had come to my remote little corner of the universe. In addition to my memory of actually feeling the crack of the snare drum in my shins from the floor in front of the stage when the drum tech was checking it beforehand, I also remember a lot of spitting. Hetfield and Ulrich were constantly spitting during their set. Ulrich's saliva projectiles looped up over his kit and came down to the front of the stage often just missing Hetfield, who himself must have expectorated at least three or four times per song. Hetfield remarked between songs that he loved Canadian beer, toasted the crowd and gulped from his plastic cup (Sudbury's by-laws sadly but wisely prevented the sale of alcohol in the Sudbury Arena). I also remember that he substituted the word 'Sudbury' for 'the city' when he sang the first line of "Seek and Destroy" – *'scanning the scene in Sudbury tonight'*. I'm sure Hetfield did this during the previous and next night's shows in other cities, but I still got a charge out of it. Just as I did when he asked the crowd during the "Seek and Destroy" intro if we had the *Kill 'Em All* record. A resounding *'yes!'* response resulted, to which Hetfield earnestly asked, "*Can I borrow it?*".

I always thought that was funny back then because it was all part of the sneering, defiantly juvenile joy that I immersed myself in as a teenage Metallica fan. I still have the ticket stub for that concert. I had ticket number 16. The date on it reads Wednesday, December 10, 1986. Admission was $15.50.

○○○

When Metallica's second album *Ride the Lightning* came out, I was pleasantly surprised. As a metal kid, you want your favourite bands to just keep making the same record over and over, because anything billed as 'artistic growth' always translated as 'selling out by whoring under the demands of the record company suits'. At least that's how I saw it as a teenager, especially when seemingly legitimate and perfectly likeable new metal bands like Icon followed up excellent debut records with disappointingly wayward keyboard-saturated, desperate-for-airplay piles of fucking crap.

Metallica actually did 'grow' with *Ride the Lightning*. This album is probably my favourite Metallica record just because it retains the band's still-fresh naïveté and youthful aggression while demonstrating their sophisticated musicality, a factor that was unparalleled by the remainder of the Big Four or any other thrash metal outfit. The band would 'grow' yet again with their next release *Master of Puppets*, defining themselves as an absolute metal superpower.

Master of Puppets was essentially a more or less perfect thrash metal record, boasting equal parts unbridled skull-bashing intensity and smart, atmospheric depth in composition delivered at a master class skill level. With the recognition that this record would bring, Metallica began the very first steps of that bittersweet and imminent traverse into the dreaded Mainstream, a journey that brings great rewards but sadly also renders the purity of a band's beginnings practically indistinguishable. I've always viewed this transition in a band's career as a painfully ambivalent one, because greatness undoubtedly and deservedly garners the spoils of success. But, certain legitimacies are unfortunately either obscured or completely lost when this happens.

While it wasn't a bad record, Metallica's next release *...And Justice For All* positioned the band closer to mainstream success, but also just past that pivotal point where the band began to move in the opposite direction. I have a theory on this topic. I guess it's actually more of a metaphor as a vehicle to support a theory, but I liken a band's change in direction to the Earth's solstitial changes and the concept of daylight savings time, which lengthens and shortens days based on hours of daylight.

I look at it this way. Legitimate bands' careers start out from nothing, which could be equated to the shortest day of the year (or longest night) and progress from there. The band moves forward, moves forward, moves forward...and then, for just a brief instant, stands still, at the absolute apex of its legitimacy as an artist. At the height of a band's legitimacy, they reach the summer solstice, the longest, brightest day of the year. Then, in only a brief moment in time, the band's axis reaches a point where its legitimacy begins to work against it in the face of mainstream success and momentum is reversed. It slowly begins to move backwards, descending again. Back against all of the legitimacy it demonstrated through its forward ascension. This is *not* measured from a commercial success standpoint, but rather from one of artist legitimacy. It can rack up all the gold records and money imaginable, but the band's motion is changing direction and falling away from its point of greatest strength – the defining moment it reached at its zenith as a pure musical artist. From that moment, the artist will never be the same, and the downturn towards the end of its career begins, each day getting shorter and shorter.

Conceptually, this parallel can be applied to any band's career when you step back and look at the big picture. It even works in tandem with the "jumping the shark" idiom, which occurs after the longest day of the band's career when drastic changes are made after it's been noted that the longest day of its career has indeed passed, in the hopes of reliving that day. Even though the jumping the shark concept lends itself more to revitalization of commercial success and not artist legitimacy, we all know you can't turn back time. Even with the addition of Ted McGinley to the band's lineup.

Every artist is susceptible to the solstice measurement. It's a forgone conclusion that talented bands have no choice but to move through this equation, even if it is less pronounced today through approaches like using the Internet to bypass the record business in ardent attempts to retain underground status and indie cred. It still happens, because people will always be greedy and hungry to consume more and more once we have a taste. Even when artists die before the longest day of their legitimacy solstice, the moment of their death would thus be considered that day and the commercialization that ensues to sate our greed with unreleased material and any other available scraps will always be a certainty.

Metallica, despite their grit, is no exception to this theory. Their longest day did come sometime in late 1987 with the release of *The $5.98 EP - Garage Days Re-Revisited*. This move would almost seem like an attempt on the part of the band to mitigate the trajectory in their ascension towards commercial success. The release was a mini-album of cover songs performed by the band, allegedly jammed mostly in the garage of Ulrich's new house in El Cerrito. It ran directly counter to industry inclinations - as indicated in the cassette liner and on the cassette itself, the album was "not very produced" by Metallica, and it featured an adamant insistence in the album artwork and title that it be sold for no more than five dollars and ninety-eight cents. It's a fun little record, because it holds true to its claim of basically being a sloppy, drunken garage jam of some of the band's favourite songs. For me it just made Metallica more endearing as a band, and it intensified my connection to them and their legitimacy as musical artists. But change is imminent.

As Metallica's ascent to eventual world domination continued, *The $5.98 EP - Garage Days Re-Revisited* was actually discontinued only to be repackaged eleven years later in 1998 along with previous *Kill 'Em All* add-ons "Am I Evil?" and "Blitzkrieg" (considered the original *Garage Days Revisited* material) and other covers on a release called *Garage Inc.*. The album cheekily features the original cover photo of *The $5.98 EP – Garage Days Re-Revisited* on the back cover, but with the band members' faces covered with updated photos of them from 1998 – tidily shorn and mockingly reminiscent of the journey they'd made through the seasons of their career.

None of this should be perceived as a slight against Metallica, because it's certainly not. It's completely obvious that bands could not possibly continue to move forward endlessly through their ascension periods. One of the key ingredients in the legitimacy of a band's early material is that special fire that only youth and inexperience can bring. Of course, this fire exists in a finite capacity and like youth, it can't be sustained forever. The problems come when this rationale is juxtaposed against the built-in intensity of more extreme musical disciplines, like thrash metal.

A while ago I read an excerpt from thrash metal-cum-Trans Siberian Orchestra guitar virtuoso Alex Skolnick's blog. I was a mild Testament fan in the 80s, but the reason why I clicked on the link was because it was entitled, "Testament's Alex Skolnick Reveals His Guilty Pleasure". Did I open this up to find out about a peculiar sexual proclivity or eating disorder of Skolnick's? Nope. I had a feeling it was about a metalhead professing an interest in a musical genre that was decidedly anti-metal, and I was more or less right. It turned out an old-school thrash metal headbanger sang along to Bon Jovi's "Livin' on a Prayer", in public.

The reason why I say I was *more or less* right is because, while Skolnick openly admits that he and other members of heavier metal acts were in a tour bus together singing along to one of Jon Bon's cheesier anthems at the tops of their lungs, he is quick to clarify it was purely circumstantial, heat of the moment stuff. He also states that he is not a fan, does not own any Bon Jovi records, and doesn't need Bon Jovi's music 'in his life'. Skolnick goes on to make some interesting points in the blog about how the initial antithesis of Metallica and Bon Jovi in the 80s was altered by their eventual connection through producer Bob Rock, how Metallica only achieved significant commercial success after Bob's work on Metallica's pivotal *Black Album*, and so on. As I read, it occurred to me that the most interesting aspect of this topic is the displacement resulting from that schism between the metalhead's vehement death-before-dishonour approach to wearing the heavy metal genre like a badge, and the eventual coda that sees the aging headbanger gradually shape-shift beyond the genre.

We've seen all kinds of cases of this, but one of the best examples is definitely Metallica. The most important dynamic in Metallica's early successes as an uncompromising underground thrash metal phenomenon was that intense aggression, particularly that of James Hetfield. But, that's only important because it was juxtaposed against equal parts vision and innate musicality. Every thrash metal band is obviously aggressive. The real magic comes when the raw aggression is tempered by said musical wherewithal and vice versa. Aggression served as the impetus behind *Kill 'Em All,* and had you tried to suggest a connection between Metallica and Bon Jovi to Hetfield back then, you would have likely suffered a concussion.

Looking at Metallica's ascension to mega-stardom, you witness a delicate balance coming into its own over the next two records that would follow *Kill 'Em All.* An acoustic guitar piece introduces opening track "Fight Fire with Fire" on *Ride the Lightning.* It doesn't last more than 35 seconds before the bludgeoning intensity kicks in to full-throttle after that. It's these subtleties that add depth and dimension to the songs, and provide hints that Metallica had the ability to propel themselves beyond the thrash metal pale. A year later *Master of Puppets* would also open with an acoustic passage, a flamenco-ish guitar piece to boot, tastefully translating into the skull-splitting leadoff track "Battery". *Master of Puppets* clearly delivered the message that Metallica were peerless in the thrash metal genre, and were taking the movement to new heights. I remember reading in *Metal Hammer* magazine that Lars Ulrich said Hetfield was singing three part harmonies at that point. I didn't know exactly what that meant at the time, but it was clear to me that Metallica was miles ahead of the rest of The Big Four and younger thrash metal upstarts like Death Angel and Flotsam and Jetsam. Knowing today how Ulrich handles the media, I'm guessing he slipped that in about Hetfield just to add further distance to the gap.

With the release of *...And Justice for All* in 1988, Metallica reached out to the MTV generation, eschewing their 'underground' label. Their next record, referred to somewhat ironically as the *Black Album,* would see Metallica become a household name. This is something I really never, ever thought I would see. At this point, the aforementioned balance that had given fire to Metallica's first three records was no longer there. The vision and musicality were still present, perhaps even more so at this point, but that initial angst was spent.

Again, I'm not saying this is wrong. It's not. It's logical and it's imminent. Metallica's fury was impossible to sustain really, and it's unreasonable to think that any band could carry on at that pace for more than two or three records. But it's always been interesting to me that the metal mindset appears to be that you can and must continue in this way, or your status as a 'legitimate' metalhead will be compromised. And that includes denouncing all non-metal musical genres, especially glam metal. As a raging headbanger, one of your prime agendas is to defy mainstream commercial success not just by ignoring it, but also rather by outwardly and aggressively rising up in the face of it. That's what headbangers do. They're outwardly angry, rebellious, lawless scourges by definition. At least that's how they start out.

The reason anyone is attracted to heavy metal in the first place is because it's perceived as being oppositional and recklessly aggressive. And because, as I mentioned earlier, it offers stronger sensations. Young people look for outlets through which to project themselves, and the natural tendency is to seek security and connectivity through commonality. On a much broader scope, if we recognize music as a fulfilling behavioural outlet, we self-identify as pre-pubescent kids with the route on which we think we 'fit', almost like a restaurant patron looking at a menu. Pop music satisfies the energetic, aggression-free diet and progresses from there. If you have a taste for some mild rebellion that rock and roll in general represents, then maybe some classic Springsteen is your thing. Angry enough to bash someone's head in at the slightest provocation? One large order of thrash metal, please.

Psychopathy notwithstanding, the noteworthy aspect here is that as powerful as the hurricane is, it always blows itself out. And as the aggression seeps away, so does that magic X factor that makes metal albums like *Kill 'Em All* and *Ride the Lightning* so extraordinary. Yes, other variables like fame and the music industry are also influential.

But this general principle applies to any form of art impacted by the youthful ideal. And in the case of heavier metal, extreme polarities make the ramifications seem that much more radical.

When we heard Metallica do Lynyrd Skynyrd's' "Tuesday's Gone" on 1998's *Garage Inc*, the unyielding headbanger was placed in a disenfranchising situation. A great pioneer had seemingly shed its thrash metal skin. Of course, before this moment we had already watched Metallica evolve away from their grassroots beginnings through the 90s, but "Tuesday's Gone", featuring guys like John Popper on harmonica, may have been a watershed moment in terms of what some probably considered a "sellout". However, it's apparent that with this particular choice of ballad and Metallica's aforementioned musicality a broad musical appreciation was really there all along on their part, albeit thoroughly eclipsed by the overt aggression of their youth. And they're not the only ones.

So then, the question is: as a card-carrying fan of Heavy Metal and all of its thrash/speed/death et cetera permutations, is it necessary to be so myopically metalheaded?

The answer is yes *and* no.

On one hand, the angst of youth is the precipitator of such an initially fierce stance and it powers a pure, innocent passion that's absolutely glorious. On the other hand, after the youthful mystique is gone, it leaves behind a shell of what formerly was. That spark of angst is no longer there, but the pressures of stereotyping remain.

The notion behind metal, especially thrash metal, is that the very essence of what makes the genre pure is an unrelenting resistance against the mainstream. Metalheads, the kind who actually refer to themselves as metalheads, are musical nihilists. Real-deal headbangers evaluate themselves and each other as such, or they risk being labeled as 'poseurs' as a basic tenet of metal culture. The more extreme your metal preference, the more adamant your stance. This proves problematic for older metalheads, because young aggression and heavy metal have a symbiotic relationship - metal being a mechanism by which to burn through the aggression, while young aggression ensures integrity of musical output. Conversely, older musicians and metal simply have a causal relationship, the metal being a by-product of whatever effort is put in. Without the naïveté of teenage angst, the results vary. Don't get me wrong, it's not quite a 'jumping the shark' philosophy (though I suppose it can be). Artists have produced some great metal later in their careers, but it just ain't the same. It's been said that rock and roll is a young man's game, and heavier metal is even more so.

There's no question that thrash metal classics like Metallica's first three records wouldn't exist without an intense metal mentality. And if we're seeing things for what they are, their brilliance is made possible largely by the exacerbated adolescent rage of James Hetfield in particular. Hetfield himself has admitted that his strict Christian Science upbringing and broken home childhood manifested themselves in severe alcohol abuse and a tendency towards violence. Much has been made of the *Some Kind of Monster* documentary wherein Hetfield returns from rehab and suggests that work on the *St. Anger* record end each day at 4pm so that he could spend time with his family. I'm personally happy for James for getting it together and putting his issues behind him, because really, that's what *should* have happened. Otherwise, Hetfield is a character in an Aronofsky movie played by Mickey Rourke. I do have to say though, maybe hypocritically, that as pleased as I am for Hetfield, the 'monster' that his crappy upbringing created was responsible for some of the best moments in the history of heavy metal. If that tells us something about the genre and what it's about, then so be it.

Metallica was my last line of defence against the world in 1984, long before everyone else gathered to collectively suckle at the "Enter Sandman" teat. And if we're being honest, I admit that it's hard to hear "Until It Sleeps" at the gym and see people getting all revved up when it comes on. But the fact of the matter is that while Metallica's early career magic came from the purity of raw, young aggression, you can't hang on to this stuff forever. And it can't be manufactured. Scopes broaden as time wears on, and most people evolve. They get wiser as they get older, and they do what they need to do. This is why it's completely absurd when people say things like Metallica's *Death Magnetic* is "Metallica's return to *Master of Puppets* form"[2]. They only say that because they *want* it to be. Not because it actually is, or even can be.

And, of course, this is also why it's okay for Alex Skolnick to sing along to Bon Jovi songs in public, as loud as he wants.

---

[2] *It's also very fucking absurd when your wife tells you that one of the teenaged characters on her favourite soap opera* The Young & The Restless *said to another teenaged character, 'I listen to Metallica. Not new Metallica, though – only the old stuff'. Come on.*

⊛ Seven ⊛
Tony's Record Store

Tony's record store was called Records on Wheels, a franchise in name only. Whenever I made it into Sudbury as a kid, I would try to hit three or four record stores that were in the general geographical proximity of what the trip to the city was centred around – a visit to the dentist and then clothes shopping. Mom was pretty militant when it came to sticking to the plan. There wouldn't be any deviations from the pre-established course so that I could go off and buy Venom records. Not that I would have ever bought one of those. But through Mom's eyes and ears, anything that was hard rock or heavy metal may as well have been Venom.

I had sourced out four or five decent record shops on previous trips to Sudbury. Luckily almost all of them were in malls, allowing me to spend time perusing them while the rest of my family shopped for whatever in Bonimart and Towers. I always asked for an estimate of time spent at malls that housed more than one record store beforehand, so I knew how much time I was able to spend in each store and consider how I wanted to spend my time in each. I had the trip down to a very organized stratagem. As I became more familiar with the stores and what I liked and disliked about them, I would maximize on my opportunities.

The mall stores were all franchise names, pretty commercial and homogenized. The New Sudbury Shopping Centre in the east end had Sam the Record Man, A&A Records, and The Record Stop, and there was another A&A Records in the City Centre mall downtown along with some other record store whose name I don't remember. Something with the word 'disc' in it. Doesn't matter. That store was run by this slick-looking chap with a porn moustache. He sold bootleg videos in the store that he most likely recorded and re-recorded himself, and when the place started to take a bit of a dive in the early 90s he sold hockey jerseys and glossy "autographed" celebrity photos, and other stuff like that.

There was also a small record store at the other end of the City Centre before this disc place opened that sold the three-quarter length sleeve black-and-white rock shirts, featuring every hard rock and metal band on them that you could name. I bought way too many of these shirts. I had Ozzy, Maiden, Priest, Motley, Scorps, Van Halen, and a bunch of others. And I proudly wore each of them to school when I was in grade nine. Maybe I *was* a metalhead during that period. I even had an Asia shirt because I thought that the album cover with the serpent, which was featured on the shirt, looked cool. Christ.

My favourite stop on the Sudbury record store circuit was Records on Wheels. This place was in a standalone building downtown just a couple of steps down the street from the City Centre, run by a guy named Tony Anselmo. It was the kind of place that was a cultural hub not only for music fans, but for anyone who wanted to shoot the bull about why the local junior hockey team was losing so much lately, which city councillors actually got the job done and which ones needed the sack, or pretty much whatever current event you cared to bring up. It was a very warm, vibey environment. Not at all like the other stores, which were too much like...well, *stores*. Being at Records on Wheels was like being at Tony's house, as Tony's guest. There was this sense of community within. I realize now when I think back on the time I spent there just how much great music he had packed into that smallish space, sandwiched between the mall and a Hakim Optical outlet.

Back then I was only focused on the metal, and I didn't have time to fool around with anything else. I made the most of my minutes in there. There was plenty of stuff with which to occupy a young headbanger, none of which could be found at the franchises. European 12-inches with obscure B-sides by W.A.S.P., Maiden, and various NWOBHM bands. Unique posters. Studded leather belts and wristbands. And a British magazine that I would develop a mild addiction for in my teens called *Kerrang!*. More on that in the next chapter.

What Tony didn't have in the hallowed space of Records on Wheels, he would order for me. When I couldn't find Exciter's *Unveiling the Wicked* anywhere, he could produce it in a few weeks. I think that my fondness for being a 'regular' customer at any given establishment may have developed at Records on Wheels. I'm one of those people that likes being able to have a *place*. A *guy* or *girl* for pretty much everything - local drinking hole, waitress at a favourite diner, hair stylist, mechanic, whatever. When I find these things, I try to hold on to them. I'm a traditionalist. A sentimental creature of habit. And Tony's was my habit as a kid. Going to his store was like an event to look forward to for me.

Somewhere along the way Tony brought in the guy who used to work across town at The Record Stop. The Record Stop was a newer place that operated predominantly as a shop that sold hard rock and metal records. They featured all the newest releases right up front and played them over the store's system. Back in the early 80s heavy metal was not at all mainstream and still relatively low-key stuff. To imagine Metallica being played on the radio back then was absolutely fucking crazy, at least in the Sudbury area.

But The Record Stop featured lots of brand new metal in the 'Now Playing' capacity, and this is how I discovered German speed metal band Helloween. "Murderer" was blaring out of the speakers when I walked in one day. I looked over at the 'Now Playing' display that featured the EP album and picked up my own copy on cassette, excited that I had found a unique new band that I couldn't wait to learn more about. A year or so earlier I had discovered Lizzy Borden after hearing *Love You to Pieces* in the same way, over The Record Stop stereo system.

It really was exciting to experience this crazy maelstrom of all kinds of new metal bands from around the world, even if it was on a somewhat smaller scale in a more remote area like Sudbury. The early-to-mid 80s was the one truly glorious time for hard rock and heavy metal.

Anyway, I remembered Derek from The Record Stop, because he *looked* like a metal guy. He actually looked like guitarist Dave Pritchard (RIP) from Armored Saint. When The Record Stop closed down to become a Randy River and he defected to Records on Wheels, I chatted him up a bit. His knowledge of hard rock and metal was fascinating, and soon he would introduce me to all sorts of stuff I'd never heard of in the way of lesser-known European bands. It turned out that he lived outside Sudbury, closer to Espanola in an even smaller town with a population of about five hundred people called McKerrow. He was living there with a relative or something.

So, whenever I went into Records on Wheels there was a lot of easy chat, and I really liked that. I felt at home in there. Every time I left I looked forward to the next time I could go back. Derek was probably about twelve years older than me so it was still a bit intimidating, but goddamn cool for a kid my age.

I don't remember how it came about, but through my ordering of albums from Records on Wheels we got to talking about Derek's personal metal collection, and it was like this whole new uncharted vortex of happy musical goodness for me. I remember talking to him on the phone and he would play me parts of songs and I would say whether I liked them or not. If I did like them, he would give a description of the band, including who was in the band along with other assorted details in the same way a baseball enthusiast might run through a player's stats, or a mechanic would describe an engine's composition.

These days it strikes me as a bit strange that this guy, who was much older than I was, was discussing music with me over the phone. But dude had a girlfriend, and I don't remember who called who or why, or many other details of how all that stuff went down. Wasn't weird at all at the time for me. I didn't even give it any thought. In hindsight, he probably just wanted to feed his ego a bit with someone who would actually listen to all of his chat. Probably the same way I do now with my brother-in-law, poor guy. Derek lived in fucking *McKerrow*, for crissakes. Who else was he going to talk to? I wasn't privy to his social situation or any of those details. I wasn't paying attention to any of that. Didn't care. At the time I just thought it was cool that someone older and more knowledgeable than me would take the time to engage me in conversations about my favourite music.

My memory is sketchy and I don't remember all of the details, but as I moved through the final years of high school in the late 80s my perception of Derek changed somewhat. He left Records on Wheels and got a job in Espanola at a video store. I'm not sure why this happened or what the deal was. He had said that he wanted to open his own place, but I couldn't really figure out why he would take a step that was seemingly backwards. From Sudbury to Espy was definitely not a forward step.

At the time, I was about sixteen and working at a department store called The Met after school and on Saturdays for some extra record buying scratch. I had to dress presentably as an employee of this store, so I would wear these Le Chateau shaker-knit sweaters, a polo shirt underneath with the collar popped, wool pants, lace-up dress shoes, and a Le Chateau overcoat that was super bloody preppy. Like I said before, I was a bit of a stray dog socially. My fashion sense changed as the wind blew. I used to walk to work because I didn't have the luxury of owning a car, and I had to walk right by the video store Derek worked at. I remember trying to take alternate routes to avoid him so that he wouldn't see how I was dressed. I remember the first time he did see me there. We bumped into each other, and he just kinda looked me up and down with a peculiar look on his face. Awkward. After that, I completely avoided him. It was very strange. Almost like he was getting too close to compromising my personal space. I think I did it as a defensive measure. Maybe I saw him as a role player in some sort of alternate version of reality I was trying to assemble for myself or something, I don't know. Nonetheless, his role was getting invasive so I decided that I needed to scale it back a little.

I've always been a fairly private person. My personality lends itself to a jack-of-all-trades-master-of-none social construct, and different people who've come into my life are placed into categories based on what they represent in my eyes based on the terms of how we met - musical interests, geographic proximity, social circumstance, sports interests, or work relationships. While I've gotten much better at not compartmentalizing people over the years, I still don't like to mix associations by trying to inter-mingle acquaintances from two completely different social milieus. It just doesn't work for me. The last time I tried it failed abominably and resulted in one of the worst nights of my life.

I traveled to Montreal with my girlfriend at the time and a university friend I used to live with in dorm. This was fine, since we all knew each other well. I knew a few people in Montreal and normally I would split my time between these people in separate visits, but I figured that this time I would see if we could all do something together. I'm not going to use the real names of these individuals in the recounting of this story. But since there are several of them to keep track of, and I don't want to use initials or names like Person X and Person Y, let's stick with the theme and use heavy metal pseudonyms for them instead. I'll even fashion them after individuals they're similar to in image and personality type. Just because I'm an idiot and I think this sort of thing is funny.

So, my girlfriend Lita Ford (*cough, cough*) and my dorm friend, Marc Storace of Krokus fame, travel up to Montreal intending to visit Queensryche's Geoff Tate, another dorm friend who previously lived with Marc and I. Geoff is a guy I had more of a cerebral relationship with, complete with plenty of sharp verbal jousting, quid pro quo and meaningful insight. My relationship with Marc was the opposite. The only thing we really had in common was our dependency on alcohol and a shared interest in hockey. I had other friends in town that I hadn't seen for some time and I was tempted to look them up. One of them was my hometown high school pal Lee Aaron, who was an upstanding citizen by day. By night, she was one of the most notorious drunks I've ever experienced. And I've experienced several. Also in Montreal was Nikki Sixx, a charismatic sociopath I became friends with when he moved into dorm two years after Geoff and Marc moved away. Nikki is a renowned boozer as well. But we all were back then, really. It was all in how you carried yourself and what kind of a drunk you were. Nikki was one of those guys who never lost his edge despite drinking most everyone else around him under the table. He was my personal Satan. The guy could talk me into anything.

All of these people had met each other at some point in the past very briefly, mostly through me. After I made the requisite calls to everyone, it was agreed that we would all meet at Geoff's place for some drinks and then we'd hit the bars. Someone had the bright idea of bringing magic mushrooms to this little rendezvous. I had already had a couple of drinks and didn't care so much about my responsibilities as a social moderator in this United Nations-like amalgam of personalities anymore. Fuck it. I was tired of being anxious and just wanted to kick back and rip it up a bit. We all took the mushrooms and drank while we waited for the fun to begin.

It started with Lita. She and Lee were well on their way to being throttled already. They were in the bathroom together with the door closed and locked, refusing to let anyone in. We were in an apartment and this was the only bathroom. So we're not off to a good start.

Finally after much pleading, the ladies opened the door so the rest of us could use the facilities. During this time Marc, who tended to be shy and withdrawn while sober but was a consistently sloppy drunk, was complaining that his mushrooms were not working and he was getting obnoxious about it. I began to think about how Marc had not been great with holding his liquor sometimes (most of the time), and how many of his evenings ended in the same way. Someone would have to look after him to ensure he avoided situations in which he endangered himself or others because he would get so ka-bombed that he couldn't function. He typically way overdid it with the booze. Often he would bring up his booze with the rest of his stomach's contents after a night of drinking, and that bothered me somewhat. I'm not saying I didn't ever spew from drinking, because I have. But that was back in school, when it was funny. Hell, it was *expected*. I was in my late twenties at the time of this story, and I guess I just wondered how someone couldn't figure out how to keep the drinking under control enough to avoid puking all over themselves routinely. Maybe it's in the genes. I drank to enhance my outings. I drank quite a lot, but I always tried to keep my edge and I knew my limits. I needed to be aware of my surroundings and have a handle on my faculties at that point in my life. It seemed strange to me at that time that he didn't have similar concerns.

While the ladies were transitioning into the happy-joy phase of their buzz, we decided it would be a good time to head out to the bars. Geoff, feeling the effects of the mushrooms but remaining lucid and mellow, preferred to use his chemical adventures as a means to expand his mind. Not in a weird way, and without any hippie allusion. He was just a mellow drunk, and liked to study his surroundings so as to gain some increased measure of world perspective. He was easily irritated by messy drunks like Marc. I could see the early warning signs of a disaster coming as Marc arrived at that silent stage you hit when you're way too loaded. His mushrooms were just kicking in, and he had already crushed several beers in lieu. The mushrooms were coming on for me as well. It was probably about nine o'clock. Nikki was his charming, malevolent self.

Off we went into the night.

When we got to the first bar, Marc was having difficulty standing upright. He had that distant and mildly pained look on his face, like his world was moving in slow motion and he was studying it intently. You know the one. He stared at the floor like he was surveying a spot to throw up on. The ladies were off somewhere dancing and talking in unnecessarily high volumes. Geoff pulled me aside, physically, which kinda freaked me out given the effects of the mushrooms. He told me that he had just seen Nikki exchange money with someone for what looked like a packet of cocaine.

Here's where things start to go off the rails. Everybody in the group was feeling the full effects of these mushrooms now. I was starting to get a bit freaky because Geoff was telling me that Nikki was on coke. He made a convincing argument, as Nikki was no stranger to nefarious behaviour. In our friend group cocaine was a pretty major deal. I've never done it. It seems to exist just on the other side of that drug boundary I'd established for myself long ago that also excluded heroin, ketamine, meth, ecstasy, and all of those other fucking crazy narcotics that intimidate the hell out of me. I've never even done acid. Came close once, but yellowed out.

So now the 'shrooms were making me paranoid. I was suspicious of Nikki, but also suspicious of Geoff. I didn't want to believe his claims, and I knew that Geoff has been put off by Nikki just because of the way Nikki carried himself. Maybe Geoff misinterpreted whatever he saw. My brain was working way too hard on this.

At any rate, Geoff wanted us all to leave the bar. Lita was completely drunk off her ass and could hardly walk. She needed to go home, but that was the last thing she wanted to hear. It was also the last thing I wanted to consider. It was only maybe ten-thirty, and we had a long way to go yet. It wasn't uncommon to carry on until six or seven in the morning back then, just because I never wanted the party to end. I was just getting started.

Meanwhile, Marc had just begun to wrap up his evening by gracing the floor with a pancake of vomit. Geoff told me that Marc took twice the amount of mushrooms the rest of us did because they weren't kicking in fast enough. He was done.

Nikki reappeared, eyes glazed, with several rounds of shots and a wad of cash in his hand. He was pounding through the booze like the real Nikki Sixx, almost as if it was giving him some kind of crazy superpower. His functioning actually seemed ameliorated, like on that episode of WKRP where Johnny Fever participates in the drunk driving demonstration to prove that reaction time diminishes with each shot of liquor, but Fever's actually improves as he drinks more. Nikki definitely had a little bit of Johnny Fever in him.

The night had begun to come undone. I started to get a bit hazy myself at this point, and that familiar chaotic swirl of loud pounding music, crowded bar, and dulled senses started to set in. Time slowed down. Calm insularity was prevalent. People's movements left smallish hints of vapour trails. I guess it was much later when I looked around to find that Lita, Marc, and Geoff had all gone. I didn't know where. At this point in the evening, this situation is not unusual or fearsome at all. It just happens. To a degree, those kinds of drinking sprees were mercenarial. All the social etiquette goes out the window, and the splintering begins. This was the time when chemical bravura gives way to new adventures taking shape, and they were welcomed wholeheartedly back then.

I found myself at another bar with Nikki and Lee. More of a dance club, dark with thick bass that pounded like an earthquake. A new member had joined our group. This guy didn't say much to me, but he and Nikki had some hushed exchanges that seemed a bit suspect. The guy was just too *on*. He just exuded a drug dealer vibe and the mushrooms didn't help me to try to rationalize an alternate explanation. The two of them were just standing there with sadistic smiles, smug as two secret service agents. They surveyed the scene with dead looks in their eyes and contempt in their faces. Lee was in fuck-all land, spilling her drinks on the floor and yelling things at random people. I was actually surprised she was still in the picture. The drinks kept coming and coming, compliments of that wad of money in Nikki's hand.

Being on a really serious bender is a lot like dreaming. Consciousness and reality are obscured to the point where things that normally seem improbable or even impossible happen readily, without seeming out of the ordinary. Completely separate scenarios blend into one another without warning, twisting and turning but somehow not unusually. Any pre-established rule or taboo falls to the wayside. People you would typically not acknowledge, or that would not acknowledge you, come into your life and become your best mates in the entire world during the bender. Encumbrances of any kind are completely stripped away. And it all makes *perfect sense* at the time! And, like a dream, when you wake up the next morning and try to remember everything that happened, your mind often isn't willing to cooperate. On a previous trip to Ottawa I was out drinking with Geoff at a bar, but after many shots I ended up across the provincial border in Hull, Quebec eating donairs with some dude I had just met two minutes before. We walked all the way back across the bridge to Ottawa together, thick as thieves, and I invited my new friend to crash at a girl's house that I had met the night before. Nobody was around when I woke up, and I never saw either of them again. Not that I would remember what they looked like if I did. I barely knew who they were. I have dozens of these bizarre drinking stories but it always amazes me that, as in dreams, each of them seemed like perfectly reasonable sequences of events at the time.

Anyway, after a bunch of carrying on at this bar I decided it might be a good idea to try and find the others. The alleged dealer disappeared and Lee, Nikki, and I started the walk back to wherever Geoff lived. I had to rely on them to get us there since I didn't know where that was. Lee stumbled all over the place and talked all kinds of bullshit. Nikki seemed straight as a judge. Until all of a sudden he picked up this huge stick and started swinging it at people's mailboxes and anything else in his path. He was like Christian Bale's character in fucking *American Psycho*, straight-faced but just completely scaring the crap out of everyone. I told him to get sorted, and he just laughed and heaved the stick at someone's house. We kept walking.

When we finally got back to Geoff's, we found him still awake watching TV. Lita and Marc are also there, sleeping in other rooms. Geoff told me that he brought both of them back home, and that he just hung out by himself for the remainder of the night. He was bitter, and I didn't blame him at all. I felt awful about the whole thing. It was about 5am. Geoff told me to tell Nikki to leave, as the coke thing put him off. I don't remember what happened to Lee. Later that morning on the six-hour drive back to Toronto no one spoke more than five words each.

I don't talk to any of these people anymore. It's funny to look back on those times and try to make sense of the dynamics that drove them and made them possible. I used to have a lot of friendships with different types of people based on different types of shared interests or characteristics, and I suppose I still do lately. But I did learn my lesson that night. Mixing associations is better left to guys like Jerry Seinfeld.

I don't know how long Tony had been in that snug little box of a building beside Hakim Optical, but right around the time I left home for university in the late 80s Tony relocated his business to a space at least three times the size right across the street. Business had really improved for him, and he became super successful. When I did go into Tony's new and seemingly improved store in 1990, I found that while it probably was more aesthetically pleasing to the common customer, it had lost that sense of organic identity that made it so great. It wasn't necessarily that vibey place where I wanted to hang out anymore. It was a lot more like other stores instead. Derek was still there, but I was uncertain if his capacity was that of employee or hanger-on. It was awkward, because we didn't speak anymore. I wasn't even sure if he knew who I was, or if he ever really did. It was so unnecessarily weird. The weirdness was largely my fault and I did nothing to step up and relieve it, and I regret it to this day. I sometimes wonder about Derek and his unusual application in my younger life, and it disappoints me that I didn't have the foresight to recognize him as more than just an application that wasn't useful anymore during my social shape-shifting. It makes me focus more on not being such a superficial prick these days.

Business was booming at the new Records on Wheels, and the focus seemed to be on hard rock and heavy metal. If you were into that, Tony was still your guy. At this point, I was starting to pay much more attention to the fact that Tony was equally capable of setting you up with something you would immediately cherish based on your request, be it metal, jazz, country, or otherwise. He knew his stuff across the board and he really had an inherently genuine charm that allowed him to bring people back into his store, even if it was approaching the borders of commercialization. I was happy for him. I liked his immense character and I liked what he stood for. He was a good man and he was good at what he did, and he deserved his success.

Years later, after I had graduated from school and moved away from the North, I happened upon Tony on a Queen Street crosswalk in Toronto. While we continued to walk in separate directions, we had a very brief exchange that inspired me to visit his store when I returned to Sudbury over the Christmas holidays in 1998. I was heartbroken when I did.

Tony's huge store on the west side of Elm Street that had been thriving through the early 90s had been closed up and the space was available for rent. The entire downtown area was eerily dismal and hushed, like a sad epilogue to a story that had already been told. The City Centre mall was rife with empty stores. A single Music World record store existed on the lower level that had not been there when I was last in the mall. The entire upper level of the mall, which used to house the A&A Records store where I bought Dangerous Toys' debut record, had been converted into a call centre. The food court where we nervously ate pizza before the Iron Maiden concert was diminished to a handful of restaurants, deserted and on its last lifeless legs. Sparse handfuls of elderly people quietly sat grim and vacant-faced. The entire scene took on a dark brown hue in my eyes and it made me a bit sick thinking that such an important part of my childhood was awaiting its death knell. Tony had retreated to a new location, back across the street to the space that Hakim Optical had previously occupied but had now vacated, directly beside the building that originally housed that first magical Records on Wheels location that time had now left behind. Now it was a Pizza Pizza outlet.

The sign on the storefront said Records on Wheels, but the design was completely different. It was crudely manufactured in an airbrushed homemade facsimile of the original, obviously by an amateur. The inside of the store was difficult for me to experience. It was barren. It looked like a room in a house that attempted to masquerade itself as a business. Vinyl records sat at the back of the store conveying the allure of a flea market. A choppy amalgam of compact discs occupied smallish bins that forced me to consider the tragic incongruity of what I was seeing before me against what I had seen seemingly not so long ago. The entire operation was a bleak, wistful shadow of its former self. Tony himself looked the same, notwithstanding an increased number of understandably grey hairs.

We shook hands and exchanged pleasantries. I didn't quite know how to approach the subject of the sea change that had occurred since I had last visited him, or even if I should. I asked him how he was doing, and it all came out.

The advent of the 'big box' shopping plazas had come to the east end of the city, introducing Sudbury to the world of Wal-Mart. With it came the very unfortunate squeeze that every little businessman in the community felt. Customers had been buying their records at these big box stores, and Tony was feeling the pinch in a huge way. As awkward and difficult as it was to see what had unfolded over the years, I was glad to see that Tony was sticking it out and still making a decent go of it. He mentioned during that time that there were people from all over Canada and the U.S. like myself that still returned to his Records on Wheels shop to buy product, and that these people played a significant role in keeping the business alive. It was nice to hear.

Recently, after having heard my endless blathering about how great Tony's record shop was, my wife suggested that I create a Records on Wheels Facebook group. This isn't the sort of thing I would typically ever do, but in this case I thought it would be a meaningful and fitting gesture. Because Tony was so old school that he eschewed the use of computers in his business, I didn't think to search for a pre-existing ROW group. But it turns out that there already was one, with more than 300 members – a good number of those being from somewhere other than Sudbury, and whose comments on the page nostalgically reflect back to their days as younger regular customers.

In my mind, returning to Records on Wheels today represents a quasi-tangible portal back to teenage times. But more importantly it's also one of the last bastions of musical and social purity in the area that's been unrefined by inevitable economic and technological advancement. And as much as I love my gadgets and the increased ease of living in modern times, the principle that places like Records on Wheels were built upon becomes more progressively distant each time the New Economy becomes the New New Economy.

Having recently entered my forties and thus not quite at the *tight-slacks-in-a-Corvette-convertible* stage of middle age life yet, I'm reluctant to go into the geriatric routine decrying innovation and efficiency. Every adult looks back on their youth with a personal bias, and the bias tends to take on renewed vehemence as one continues to age. But even beyond the pleasure and security of nostalgia, I'm contemplative of the increasing absence of that yesteryear *purity* - that base, simplistic, direct approach that applied to making and enjoying music, doing business, and dealing with people. Maybe the fact that Tony's record store is still standing during these times means that I'm not alone in my position.

Eight
Kerrang!

Somewhere along the course of my many visits to Tony's record store, I discovered *Kerrang!* magazine in his shop. I estimate the timing of this event to be late 1985 or so because I distinctly remember buying issue number 117 as it came out, which was around April 1986 and featured Wolf Hoffmann and one of the other Accept guys on the cover. I had already been pretty familiar with the magazine at that point - familiar enough to develop a manageable obsession with it. I remember reading about Accept's newest record *Russian Roulette,* along with all of the other great content that *Kerrang!* offered within its pages, on a Greyhound bus trip to see my then-girlfriend. She lived in a neighbouring town west of Espanola, a sleepy little place called Massey.

Massey had a population of maybe a thousand people, smaller than Espy but bigger than McKerrow. It was also bigger than Webbwood, which was more or less the Greyhound stop along the highway just before Massey. As everything is relative, these places made Espanola seem like a metropolis. A number of the roads in Massey were of the gravel or dirt variety. Wearing a jean jacket ensured the comfort of placid commonality. Interest in the pursuit of higher knowledge earned you the social scarlet letter, and maybe even one or two punches in the face depending on what day of the week it was.

Massey was primarily agricultural, and the farm boys who lived there were known for being some of the toughest in the entire region. There was one particular clan from Massey who had a well-established reputation for being good with their fists, but I don't remember their family name at this moment. Just that one of them may or may not have been called Marvin. You did *not* fuck around with these guys, especially when booze was involved. And it usually was. There was plenty of time for the Massey boys to practice pugilism – there wasn't much else to do up there other than drink and fight. And maybe that other thing, which I may or may not have been too young to do at the time.

Speaking of which, my main interests during this time were girls, music, food, sleeping, and maybe one or two other minor intermittent interests that could be categorized as 'Other' in the pie chart to balance out the number at an even one hundred percent. Playing on my high school's sports teams was one of these interests, but my primary interest in the fairer sex dramatically superceded the sports interest. Really, I was more interested in meeting girls during sports trips to other high schools than I was in actually winning games, a proclivity that positioned me on the bench for more time than I would have normally served there for just being a mediocre athlete.

I can't dispute the fact that my extra bench time was well deserved, however. Without realizing it, I once held up a team bus trip back to Espanola from Blind River because I was sequestered in a private area behind the school, deep in conversation with a brand new bright yellow-sweatered and tartan-skirted friend while the bus containing our high school's three basketball teams waited and waited. The coach really tuned me in for that afterwards. But, it didn't deter my friend Johnny and I from accepting an invitation to a little impromptu party a few months later. This get-together was at the house of a girl whose parents were leaving for their cottage at midnight that Friday night, immediately after her dad's shift at the paper mill ended. Johnny and I had a volleyball tournament in North Bay the next day, and the bus was leaving from Espanola High at six in the morning for the two-hour trip. After some careful deliberation we decided it would be okay to take the *carpe diem* approach, and we showed up at the house just after midnight sharp with party favour contraband in hand. The next day started with me waking up very confused, to the combined sound of female shrieking and blaring bus horn. It was six-thirty and the team bus was waiting for us outside the house. I gathered my belongings and stumbled out the door, snickering upon learning that Johnny had thrown up in the fish tank at some point during the previous evening. There would be no snickering once we got on the bus though. At least not for the first fifteen minutes or so anyway.

The kids from Massey all bussed in to the imaginatively named Espanola High School, and integrated with the Espy kids thusly. My Massey girlfriend had been the object of my giggly grade ten affections from afar the year before we dated. Of course, I passive-aggressively contributed to all of that *professions-of-love-under-her-picture-in-other-people's-yearbooks* nonsense in my pursuit of her. Christ, I *lived* for her during that courting period. Just as I did for the next girl and the next one after her while I was a naïve, impetuous teenager. I didn't know any better. No one did.

It's no secret that supercharged hormones have made girls the prime focus of most any red-blooded male sixteen-year-old since the dawn of history. But it just seemed so elementary for me back then because idle hands weren't the devil's workshop - an idle *mind* was. At that age, there were no responsibilities, and what felt like eons of time to burn. Teenage emotionality is so overblown and dramatically dramatic because there was really not much else of any significant purpose in life at that point. Even less in a small town. What else was there? University and adulthood were a lifetime away when I was sixteen. There's an obvious suggestion of beauty in innocence and purity in this premise, and I guess that's the desired translation I should arrive at when I think about the bullshit melodrama I went through as a teenager with intense weekly crushes. I miss the carefree days of high school only as far as the *carefree* part goes, though. The emotional maelstrom that came along with being an unwise, infatuated, hormonally overdriven teenager was the devil's bargain.

Anyway, Massey Love Interest would become Girlfriend, and the floodgates would give way to tidal waves of much adolescent gooey mushiness. I didn't know much about Girlfriend during my wooing stage. I only knew what she represented. She was one year older than I was and unfortunately, hindsight would have me think that this was most likely a prime factor of my infatuation. I did notice at a later stage in the courting period that she had uncommonly large breasts for a girl of her age. This was not a concern of mine either way at the time. Even if it were, I most likely wouldn't admit it here anyway.

While she didn't have that textbook prettiness that went mostly unrepresented in either of our small towns other than in the Health & Beauty section of the Rexall drugstore magazine rack, she did have a certain look that allowed her to stand out in a crowd in my mind. And if we're being honest, this actually made her *more* attractive in my eyes. Personally I've never been a big fan of that cookie-cutter, plastic flower beauty. It doesn't seem legitimate to me somehow. I liked a certain contrariety. The subtle kind. The kind that doesn't necessarily make an individual unusual looking, just unique. The kind that can only be exclusively governed within the eye of the beholder. This is what made her compelling to me at that point of my wonderfully insipid teenage life[3]. Sometimes you know what you're looking for, and sometimes it's better when you don't.

This was my very first exclusive Boyfriend-Girlfriend relationship, as defined by the variable of the oft-dreaded Parental Meeting. Yes, I'd had fair-weather girlfriends before, but the relationship only really becomes exclusive when you're invited to the girl's home to meet her parents, have dinner, and be an overnight guest (sleeping in separate quarters of course). And this was my very first one. I was on my best behaviour during these visits, and as nerve wracking as the first couple of dinners were for your longhaired humble narrator, I actually developed quite a nice relationship with the parents.

Girlfriend's mother was a very kind, friendly, soft-spoken woman. Smiled a lot. Her father was a big, gentle giant of a man whom I was

---

[3] *Please note duly that uniqueness is* not *a euphemism for ugliness.*

convinced was that matinee idol-looking kid when he was a teenager. The one who drove around in his Thunderbird convertible looking to score poodle-skirted chicks and bust greaser heads. More Jeff Conaway's Kenickie than John Travolta's Danny Zuko. I would look into his face as we sat around the dinner table and be reminded of the lyrics to the John Cougar Mellencamp song "Pink Houses", particularly the part when the man says to the woman doing the dishes, *"Hey darling, I remember when you could stop a clock"*. I always thought this was a peculiar thing to say to a woman, especially one's wife. But he was that guy in my mind (even though the man referenced in Mellencamp's song was black), the kind that could say these words with an earnest adroitness that would somehow make it charming. He seemed like a young man unfortunately exiled to an older man's body, and his melancholy eyes suggested that he was more than just a bit considerate of it.

Sometimes he would pull out his acoustic guitar after dinner and regale us with a couple of country songs or whatever. This was something I remember being mildly uncomfortable with at first, but I don't remember why. It just made me feel weird. I did eventually grow to enjoy it, and long afterwards there were times when I thought very fleetingly and hypothetically about whether or not it would have been cool to go back and jam with him after I learned how to play guitar in university five or six years later.

I also thought about what it must have been like for him and Girlfriend's mother, or for any set of parents for that matter, to have their daughter's boyfriends over to the house. I considered what a bizarre and awkwardly amusing exercise in appearances it all must be, knowing what the prime directives of most teenage boys are in diametric contrast to the image they typically try to convey in the company of parents, who are not at all fooled. Especially Girlfriend's father, Kenickie. He knew what the score was.

Girlfriend visited my family's house as well, traveling from Massey to Espanola in Kenickie's big black and grey Ford Bronco. She was a licensed driver, a luxury that I did not enjoy at that time. I was happy to take the Greyhound bus to Massey though, because it meant I could read *Kerrang!* on the way. In fact it actually turned into a little ritual, and got to the point where I didn't go unless I had a fresh copy of *Kerrang!* with me. I suppose that it was during these little trips that I really got into the magazine. And, both unfortunately and fortunately I suppose, gradually less and less into Girlfriend.

The time eventually came during the following summer when Girlfriend would no longer be. We moved through our denouement with the requisite recklessness that immature teens do, holding those inevitable public shouting matches loaded with wicked hurtfulness that is fully intended. The last time I ever saw her was on Mead Street in Espy, in the road. I was walking with Johnny to his house across from the baseball field and she drove by in her mom's Dodge. I had been trying to avoid her up until that point. Wasn't returning her calls. When she saw us, she hit the brakes and jumped out of the car screaming like a fucking crazy person. And it all came out right there in the road, in less than savoury language for everyone to see and hear. And then it was all over forever.

My mom told me years later that she eventually went on to marry one of the Massey boys from that pugilistic family with the surname I can't remember. I was genuinely happy for her, still am.

Kerrang! was a riot to read, and the more I read the more hooked I got. I tried to keep up with the weekly distribution and buy up the back issues I had missed at the same time. This wasn't easy, on top of having to travel to Sudbury to buy the damn thing, which was more than five dollars an issue in 1986 given that it was imported from the United Kingdom. But this is mainly why I liked *Kerrang!* as much as I did.

Kerrang!'s most important point of difference was that it was much more genuine than any other rock magazine. I sometimes struggled to understand what some of the writers were saying in their Cockney deliberations, but that just added to my level of interest. From my perspective, the general thrust of *Kerrang!* was that it was produced by a gang of loutish drunks that genuinely loved hard rock and heavy metal, who had a damn good time being part of the movement. The title of the magazine was derived from the sound of a power chord played on an electric guitar, and it was originally intended to be a one-off supplement of the *Sounds* publication in 1981. But it thrived in a big way throughout the 80s on the strength of an anti-establishment type of feel. There was no artifice, no bullshit. The writing was informed enough, but it was conversant and loose. It conveyed a more informal association, making it more credible and authentic when compared to the other metal magazines.

Before I discovered *Kerrang!*, I bought *Hit Parader* and *Circus* for the full-page posters that conveniently fit on the door of my locker. But that was really their only allure. *Hit Parader* and *Circus* were essentially record company corporate gladhanders. The glossy layouts and overall presentation of these magazines always made me feel like I was reading a hard rock Sears catalogue. The articles were kife that had goofy by-lines like *"Ratt: Metal Titans Back On Top with New Magnum Opus"* or something stupid like that. *Hit Parader* in particular was notorious for those constant Top Greatest of All Time lists, which were always bullshit. The articles themselves were fabricated and banal, like reading a children's story version of Sodom and Gomorrah. I remember reading a Motley Crue article wherein the writer, most likely Andy Secher because it seemed like he wrote every fucking article in every issue of that magazine, was apparently in a limousine with the band when Mick Mars stuck his head out of the window and shouted, *"Show me your tits!"* (unusually racy for *Hit Parader*) at a female passerby. Come *on.* Anybody who knows anything about Motley Crue knows that Mars was the last guy in the Crue who would have done that. Tommy Lee? Bet on it. Vince Neil? Duh. Nikki Sixx? Quite likely. But Mick Mars? Nah. He probably just wanted to get out of the car and go and get wrecked somewhere by himself.

Axl Rose referred to Secher's journalistic integrity in Guns N' Roses' tune "Get in the Ring", actually name checking Secher in the song and saying that he was "printing lies" and "ripping off the kids paying with their hard earned money". But then again, Rose calls out pretty much everyone in the magazine business in that same rant, including his former friend and *Kerrang!* writer Mick Wall.

I recently procured the *Kerrang!* issue (number 159, October 1987) wherein Wall reviews a Guns N' Roses / Faster Pussycat show at the Manchester Apollo. This was a nice surprise, as I wasn't aware the review was even in there when I bid on the magazine on eBay. The review seems to be his first encounter with Guns N' Roses based on the article's content (he makes a bemused comment about the uniqueness of "the singer's" name, referring to him as W. Axl Rose). This interested me because this concert review was likely the starting point of the personal friendship that would develop between Rose and Wall, as documented both in subsequent *Kerrang!* issues and also in Wall's 2007 unauthorized William Axl Rose tell-all book[4]. It was also mildly interesting to me that Wall didn't necessarily seem to favour one band over the other in the concert review (Faster Pussycat opened up for Guns, but the article content was more or less evenly split between both bands), indicating at the end of the article that he was "hooked" on both. I distinctly remember playing the debut cassettes of both bands interchangeably in 1987, and aside from the differences in production and the musicianship edge Guns had, I didn't really notice a huge difference between these bands until much later either, despite the fact that *Appetite For Destruction* went on to become a highly vaunted classic rock cornerstone and Faster Pussycat's record sadly being more or less relegated to the bargain bin. When I first heard *Appetite* I immediately loved it, but I didn't recognize any particular brilliance at that time. It just sounded like a really savvy, straight-ahead hard rock record. But then again I really only listened to side one of the cassette. I rewound it continually because I liked those songs so much that I paid no attention to side two until many years later.

Kerrang! magazine had substance. It had guts. It was real. The *Kerrang!* scribes in many cases discovered, befriended, and hung out

---

[4] *Fun fact: according to Wall, before the book came out Rose cornered him in a club flanked by an entourage of large gentlemen, and advised Wall it would be in his best interests not to go ahead with its release.*

regularly with the who's-who of the genre, and it was clear that they were a genuine extension of the massive party that was hard rock and metal in the 80s. The writers had character. They hacked on each other, they hacked on themselves, and they hacked on the rock stars they wrote about. Their album reviews were unbiased. The writing was heartfelt, even dumb sometimes, but it made the magazine legitimate. In fact, the writers were actually able to establish themselves as personalities in the movement, no small feat in a genre where image and visual representation accounts for a considerable piece of the pie.

The content was not overly informative award-winning journalism. In fact, it was the sarcastic opposite. The magazine was perfectly aligned with its subject area and it was much more entertaining than it was factual. The facts just happened to come along secondarily with the stories the writers recounted about being a part of the hard rock and metal inner sanctum. As with heavy metal itself, a substantial part of the allure for me was the connective aspect, and feeling like I was there. Like I was involved. And *Kerrang!* was able to help me feel as though I was much more involved than I ever was. I pored over the commentary about what it was like in the *Kerrang!* offices, seemingly a big heavy metal frat party. Drinking, 'ligging' (though I'm not certain, I suspect 'ligging' is slang for hanging around backstage and sucking up free drinks), and blasting advance copies of countless hard rock and metal records at full volume in the office 'death deck'. What a wonderful *métier*, thought I as I read this magazine. It wasn't uncommon for someone like Lars Ulrich to drop by the *Kerrang!* offices unannounced for a few laughs with a bottle of Absolut in hand. Issue after issue I almost felt like I got to know Mick Wall, Xavier Russell, Malcolm Dome, Geoff Barton, Steve 'Krusher' Joule, Dave Ling, and the rest of the contributing staff. There was even a splash of Canadian patriotism in the mix, as Paul Suter had a special fondness for Canuck bands (really mostly Lee Aaron) and actually came to Canada often to check out the groups that were playing Toronto's version of Hollywood's Sunset Strip clubs – venues like Larry's Hideaway, The Gasworks, Rock n' Roll Heaven and the El Mocambo.

Of course now, in my vast adult wisdom, I'm more considerate of the stark likelihood that these poor bastards most likely worked long hours under harsh timelines for shit money, and that they probably butted heads regularly as a result of having to meet deadlines in getting the magazine out every week (it was available every two weeks up until late 1987). Either way, *Kerrang!* provided me with an additional cerebral channel, a corresponding visual component to the aural element that heavy metal music represented, and they did a damn good job doing it.

As I mentioned earlier, thanks to the World Wide Web I've enjoyed the luxury of being able to obtain the missing copies of my pre-existing *Kerrang!* collection with the help of eBay. My collection stops around issue 400, coinciding with the fade-to-black of real metal sometime during 1992, that point some people refer to as being the time when grunge wiped out metal. By *real* metal I mean the original old school stuff, not the also-ran foolishness that was foisted upon us post-grunge: emo-metal, nu-metal, and all the other piffle that followed.

While I'm on the topic, actually...some people charge Nirvana, Pearl Jam, Soundgarden, and the rest of grunge movement with the demise of heavy metal. But really, these new bands were just playing out their namesake, serving as a more cerebral and less flashy 'alternative' to a longstanding movement that had achieved mainstream success mostly as hair and pop metal. Most of these new grunge bands were actually hard rock and metal based. They were just dressed in different clothes and had a more sombre message. Alice in Chains singer Layne Staley was a metalhead whose early bands played Armored Saint covers, and Alice in Chains started out under the name Diamond Lie. A lot of people, Kurt Cobain included, criticized Pearl Jam for having too much lead guitar in their songs. "Alive" featured a long solo outro that Pearl Jam guitarist Mike McCready admitted was completely lifted from Ace Frehley's solo on "She". The changing of the musical guard, while lamentable, shouldn't have been a shock to anyone knowing what we do about popular culture and more specifically musical history. Punk rose up with the same countercultural intentions to overcorrect the commercial gluttony of 70s stadium rock. Grunge didn't kill metal. Metal killed itself by collapsing under its own corpulent bloat. The end was inevitable. Metal's (kind of) death was pre-ordained by its own tragic hubris.

Ahem.

Anyway. As *Kerrang!* moved on to cover Nirvana *et al*, magazine founder and editor Geoff Barton and some of the other key scribes from the good ol' days jumped ship. They started their own magazine in the late 90s called *Classic Rock*, an alternative for vintage metalheads who would rather focus on the glory days. I'm an avid reader of the magazine, but that cult of gonzo rock journalist personality aspect that made *Kerrang!*'s approach so interesting to me isn't quite there anymore. It doesn't exist in the age of electronic media. For all of its advantages, technology has a terribly pious way of sterilizing these things.

Reading *Classic Rock* is a similarly double-edged sword. On one hand, it's a solid rock magazine with great content, provided by mostly the same chaps that were responsible for *Kerrang!*. On the other hand, reading it always forces me to consider the following: 1) that *Classic Rock* is a substitute of something that I was once so dialed into as a kid, 2) how much of an afterthought the whole nostalgic exercise can be, as my interests in the magazine's content are largely rooted in nostalgia at this point in my life, 3) this is more or less microcosmic of my entire nostalgic fascination with heavy metal at this point, and 4) the unpleasantness of plotting nostalgia against reality is a by-product of the blessed curse of being equipped with temporal lobes and a new mammalian brain able to conceive of the concept of time, segment it into quantal moments, and lament its passing.

I love those back issues of the mighty *Kerrang!*. Who am I kidding? If I'm going to live in the past I may as well go all the way with it. Just like Kenickie did.

Nine
Gunter Glieben Glauchen Globen

One of my shortcomings as a human being and contributing member of society is my initial tendency to categorize everything in an attempt to actualize a greater organization. It's a compulsion, actually. It's also hypocritical, because I typically oppose the concept of artistic labeling. But sometimes I can't help myself.

Where German heavy metal is concerned, I still tend to go back and forth in thinking that it has this certain something about it as a metal sub-genre that makes it special. When I was younger, it made me want to go out and find more and more German metal bands after I heard one or two good ones.

When I thought about what that certain something was now, the first thing that comes to mind is the crunch and the sustain of the guitar riffs. But, while it may seem that some Teutonic bands take an almost textbook approach to the composition of the metal riff, I don't know that I could provide an example that couldn't be matched by other bands from England or anywhere else.

That certain something was not the production, because while German producer Michael Wagener was partially responsible for two literally perfect heavy metal albums, Accept's *Restless & Wild* and *Balls to the Wall*, he also produced Poison's *Look What the Cat Dragged In* and White Lion's *Pride*. So it wasn't that.

The vocal delivery in German metal is unique, which is an almost stupid statement to make because it's so obvious. But as obvious and stupid as it may seem, this was the characteristic mainly responsible for my tendency to compartmentalize German metal into a separate segment. Germanic linguistic imperatives, including the lip and mouth configurations required to speak German with proper effect, just lend themselves so well to the heavy metal lexicon. Sharp, aggressive, and even weirdly erotic at the same time. This whole dynamic of consideration is unfortunately governed by stereotype. It can make certain languages representative of certain characteristics. Like for example, that French and Italian are typically recognized for being overly amorous languages. No self-respecting metal band wants to be received in that light. Other Indo-European dialects (with the polarized exception of that classic British rock inflection) don't seem to marry well with hard rock and metal either. And yet German, on the other hand, almost seems made for it. It has a sharp, steely, militant coolness about it that could make even crap songs like Nena's "99 Luftballons" sound interesting. Falco's "Rock Me Amadeus" actually *was* cool, mostly because of Falco's combination of German inflection mixed with a rap-style delivery. I always secretly thought Falco (actually an Austrian) was kinda badass.

While some German metal riffs were powerful enough in their own right to contribute to some of the genre's best songs, it was the vocal performance that persuaded my mind to conclude that German heavy metal was more isolated and singular than it really was. In actual fact what was really happening was that I had come across one German band that I loved called Accept, and three others that released albums that I really got into. These were Helloween's initial four-song EP and follow-up debut LP *Walls of Jericho*, Warrant's (no, not that one) *The Enforcer,* and Underdog's *Rabies in Town*. The problem was that I wasn't giving them enough credit for being special in their own right. I lumped them together as being representative of what I thought German metal was or should be. The whole thing was wishful thinking. To sum it up, I wanted every German metal band to sound like Accept, because musically they seemed like the perfect heavy metal band to me. Some of the greatest heavy metal purity exists within the grooves of the aforementioned *Restless & Wild* and *Balls to the Wall*. However, this is unique to Accept and not at all to 'German Metal'. Let's face it. For every Accept in Germany, there's probably at least eight or nine Rages or Living Deaths.

And then there are German bands like Scorpions. Scorpions exists on another plane because the band has a broader, richer, pre-*Blackout* and *Love at First Sting* musical history dating back beyond its 80s heyday. It's hard to conceive of the fact that Scorps was actually formed in 1965 (!) by rhythm guitarist Rudolf Schenker. Singer Klaus Meine pronounced words like blackout as *bleinkount* in his speaking voice and the band was plenty German, but they evaded my German metal compartmentalization as a teenage metalhead because I never considered Scorpions to be a real heavy metal band. They were too crossover. As it did for Aerosmith, the 80s hard rock and metal explosion afforded Scorpions a second career in addition to their first as more of a Deep Purplish / UFO hard rock outfit, back when Uli Jon Roth and Michael Schenker had been in the band.

Back then I didn't know a lot about Scorps other than the fact that the band's record covers invited curious speculation, particularly 1976's *Virgin Killers* (with a very young naked girl whose genital area is cleverly obscured), 1980's *Animal Magnetism* (featuring a kneeling woman beside a Doberman, both looking up submissively at a man wearing tight slacks and standing in front of them with a beer in his hand), and the original 1979 cover of *Lovedrive* (set in the backseat of a limo, a man wearing a suit is pulling his hand away from an also formally-dressed woman's exposed breast, the man's hand being attached to it by a thick elongation of bubble gum). As misogynistic as TKO's *In Your Face*, maybe just more abstractly thought provoking.

The difference between Scorpions and most of their 70s brethren was that they a) were able to adapt because of their metal tendencies as heard on the 1981 release *Blackout*, and b) recognized the perceived value in hard rock ballads. Mind you, Scorps only started to get really popular in 1978 after *Lovedrive*. In a way their *Love at First Sting* record was similar to Deep Purple's reunion record *Perfect Strangers* and UFO's *Making Contact*, in that they were all shots at entrenchment in the burgeoning 80s metal sweepstakes. Alice Cooper attempted the same move three years later in 1986 starting with the awful *Constrictor*, and then again with the equally awful *Raise Your Fist and Yell*, finally getting some traction with *Trash* in 1988 on the back of the hit single "Poison". Not at all to disrespect Alice, but beside records like *Killer* and *Billion Dollar Babies* these albums were fucking terrible. He'd probably agree with me on this point, actually.

Anyway, Scorpions were a 70s band able to really capitalize in this new early 80s market, spinning some of their previous 70s material like "Make it Real" and "The Zoo" into commercial gold on their 1985 live record *World Wide Live*, and even managing some new hit single ballads later on like "Send Me an Angel" and "Wind of Change".

Scorpions walked the line deftly because while you might be able to argue the fact that *Blackout* was a metal record, Scorps were never actually a heavy metal *band*. Nor do I think they ever considered themselves to be. Sure, they may have borrowed some basic rudiments from the heavy metal genre, in essentially the same way Motley Crue did with *Shout at the Devil*. But this was only to disguise themselves as blend-ins. They had the good sense not to reinvent themselves too radically with the glam image of the day to fit into the movement. And yet their distinctive band logo was right there, sewn into the denim jackets of the headbanging faithful, right alongside the patches of Maiden and Priest, the biggest metal juggernauts out there at the time. Scorpions had a successful formula, spelled out clearly in the title of their 1989 greatest hits compilation *Best of Rockers n' Ballads*. And it only worked as well as it did because they were never really a heavy metal band.

Accept was polarized to Scorpions in this way. I discovered Accept right around the time of their *Restless & Wild* release, and I probably bought it because of the cover. Background: a stage lined with a wall of amps. Foreground: a live action shot of the band, the singer choking the guitar player, who was facing him and bent over backward while playing his guitar. What's not to like?

Restless & Wild starts with the crackly sounds of a needle being placed on a record, and into an old 1800s German song called "Ein Heller und ein Batzen" ("A Farthing and a Penny"). What sounds like a woman singing *"hi dee, hi doe, hi dum"* (folks have said it's actually producer Dieter Dierks, but I'm not sure about that) is interrupted after a couple of bars by someone grabbing the stylus arm and dragging it across the record. A loud high-pitched shriek is then heard compliments of Accept singer Udo Dirkschneider, and metal pandemonium ensues in the form of album opener "Fast as a Shark". The story goes that the old German tune was a popular marching song during the Nazi era, and it rubbed some people the wrong way as a result. Accept claimed to have not known this fact until after they released the record. Ironic, since these days bands are intentionally looking for this kind of stuff to put on their records for the media attention it commands.

That unusual intro was literally the only musical ground my older sister and I would ever have in common. *Restless & Wild* was the only cassette that ever had the distinction of playing regularly on both our tape players during the years we lived under the same roof back in Espanola. She was three years older than me and heavily into Michael Jackson, Prince, and all of that stuff. We were at each other's throats daily; we really stuck it to each other all the time. It was *war*, man.

She had this great big boom box and I had this much smaller ghetto blaster (hard to believe the term 'ghetto blaster' was actually popularly used at any point. But then again, I suppose Archie Bunker was also popular around this same time). My player was so small that it was much more ghetto than blaster. We both had completely separate music collections, and the only time one of my tapes other than *Restless & Wild* ever played on her machine was when she wasn't around. It was like a periodic truce because she was, for reasons unknown, fascinated with that "Fast as a Shark" intro. I only obliged her because I delighted in hearing my music blast out of that monstrous deck. But she only ever played the intro, and after it played a few times it was right back to wartime.

We used to have these inane arguments about music, during which I used to try to convince her that my player was louder than hers because of what was playing in it. For example, I would say that when my blaster was playing Scorpions' *Blackout*, it was louder than hers playing whatever lame Prince song she was listening to at the time. Heavily flawed logic of course, but I did stuff like that all the time just to wind her up.

It's been said that "Fast as a Shark" has the distinction of being among the first thrash metal songs ever recorded. It almost doesn't seem right though, given the fact that *Restless & Wild* came out in 1982 (1983 on these shores) and Metallica, Venom, Slayer *et al* were definitely lurking about during this period, playing much faster and with much more intention of doing so than Accept did. If "Fast as a Shark" is a thrash metal song, it's surely unintentional because the rest of the record would lead me to believe that Accept seemed happy enough cranking out mid-tempo metal riffs. Much to the delight of young aspiring rockers like your humble narrator.

The songs on *Restless & Wild,* even "Fast as a Shark", can hardly be considered thrash knowing what we know now. If anything, these songs are superb examples of pure, standard heavy metal. In fact, *Restless & Wild* is one of those records that stand out among its peers because of the fact that Accept did innovative things with the songs to set them apart. Nothing radical that would earn them a Nobel or anything, just very minor but interesting subtleties. The pick scrape intro in "Ahead of the Pack" is an example of those little nuances that I liked about *Restless & Wild*. I remember thinking as a kid that these minor details really gave this record a unique character. And that subtlety has always been the margin that differentiates great bands from mediocre ones.

An example of how Accept struck a perfect balance between the use of these variations while still delivering the rudiments that make pure metal what it is, was the whammy bar intro to "Shake Your Head". It's simple and just a bit unorthodox, and may not be something you'd necessarily expect as a main riff construct. But from a linear standpoint it's so perfect, especially because after four bars the first guitar is joined by a second for an additional four bars. This device in particular, the twin guitar attack, has to be my favourite in all of heavy metal. Hearing the riff played on one guitar for a measure through the left monitor, and then hearing the second guitar player come in through the right monitor playing the same riff, followed by the drums and bass come in on both sides paving the way for the vocal...man, it comes across like a fucking jet taking off if it's done the right way. It's the reason why, for as many iPod-driven Bose systems I might position throughout my house, I still have a traditional left channel-right channel stereo system in the music room with two powerful speakers positioned on opposite sides of the room. No compact sound system will ever be able to fully deliver the majesty of the twin guitar attack. Convenience is one thing and I certainly embrace technology, but these are things that I just can't do without as a traditionalist. People laugh when I tell them this, but it's not like we're talking about a bloody eight-track cartridge or something. I remember listening to Triumph's *Progressions of Power* on one of those. Even if the big selling point of the eight-track tape was like listening to your stereo in the car, the logic of the four-program operation still escapes me. Cassettes must have been received as a technological marvel in comparison.

The overall consistency of *Restless & Wild* is impressive. It's one of those records that you can play front to back without having to skip any tracks. Yeah, there might be a couple of borderline ones, like maybe "Flash Rockin' Man" and "Get Ready", but even those are held together with crisp, strong guitar riffs. Even if the record was just loaded up with grinders it would be fine, but the closing track "Princess of the Dawn" shows some depth and maturity in an impressive capacity. It's a very special thing when a band can harness heavy metal power and deliver it with the sophisticated style that Accept does on *Restless & Wild*. It's one of those records that proves to be an essential listen not only in Accept's career but also within the genre, because it's that quintessential record that straddles the divide between the naïve rookie material and the ever-impending commercial offerings that every band has. It's Accept's *Rubber Soul*. Even if you didn't know any better where it fell in the succession of Accept's recording history, you could probably guess based on the quality of the material. The point where naiveté has been shed and the band hints at being capable of great things. And of course Accept would confirm that with *Balls to the Wall*, the zenith of their recording career.

The absolute best thing about *Balls to the Wall* is those thick, crunchy, pulverizing guitar riffs. I honestly think that the way the guitar sounds on this record could be offered as a textbook example as to how metal guitar should always sound. The record kicks off with the title track, and the fat slabs of guitar are so voluminous that they envelop you. The song itself is perfectly representative of heavy metal proper, and is as good as any metal song I've ever heard, really. One of the greatest moments in all of heavy metal may actually occur in this song, beginning at 2:56. The buildup to the guitar solo begins at this time, and you know something cool is going to happen as the drum fill takes you up to the end of the measure. At precisely 3:11 singer Udo Dirkschnieder screams *"Here we go!"* and guitarist Wolf Hoffmann's lead begins with two heavily bent notes and a series of eight ascending notes, and he hangs on the highest one briefly before backing off with a very quick muted descending slide. The harmonic note Hoffmann hits twice at 3:20 squints your eyes, and a perfect solo culminates in that ominous minor key lead riff that starts at 3:28 and continues through to the song's breakdown at 3:45. This thirty-two second piece of music has compelled me since age fifteen and still gives me chills every time I hear it. I'm probably around upwards of having heard it two thousand times at this point, seven of those happening as I was writing this.

The massive guitar sound continues throughout the record. The sustained crunch of the power chords ring out so intensely that they may actually make you wince, in a good way. Because it's one of metal's most perfectly produced albums, *Balls to the Wall* actually does sound much better when it's louder. Ever since I started listening to music, when I found something that really appealed to me I would turn it up loud enough to feel as close as I could to it. Like I was almost inside it. After I got my first high-quality stereo system I cranked all of my favourite songs up loud enough to create a density, a massive thickness that almost felt like an all-enveloping sonic liquid. So many artists invite the listener to do this with that *"to be played at maximum volume"* claim on their record liner notes. In the case of *Balls to the Wall* though, the listening experience really is in fact enhanced with volume. The production allows the listener to aurally receive the guitar in what feels like multiple dimensions. It's goddamn brilliant.

Balls to the Wall blazes on through the controversial "London Leatherboys", and as I listen I think for a minute about how one of the benefits of growing up sequestered in a small town was that I wasn't privy to the controversy that songs like "London Leatherboys" generated. A very considerable part of the magic in experiencing these records as a teen was that they were received with a blankness that was absolute. Little media influence, and no socio-political counterpoint to temper my impression. Despite the peculiar album cover art and supposed 'gay metal' overtones of songs like "London Leatherboys", I hadn't the faintest idea about homosexual S&M subcultures growing up in a small northern Ontario town. I was oblivious to all of that. Ignorance was bliss, an immeasurable luxury of the young (and geographically secluded). The other morning I was at the gym listening to *Balls to the Wall* on my iPod while I was doing pushups when I realized that it was a bit peculiar to be repeatedly lowering my face towards my iPod, positioned on the floor screen up and displaying that album cover shot of a man in bikini briefs and a leather jacket squeezing a ball in his hand. Crikey.

As a kid one of my favourite tracks on *Balls to the Wall* was "Fight It Back", a paean for the teenage metalhead if there ever was one. The gut-wrenching shriek that Dirkschneider unleashes at 1:55 (that lasts until 2:08) is like a sonic nuclear firestorm. Today that scream is stylistically reminiscent of Axl's 'siren' wail that opens "Welcome to the Jungle", and back in 1984, it may have been obliquely similar of Bruce Dickinson's introductory vocal salutation at 1:17 of "Number of the

Beast" as Iron Maiden's brand new singer in 1982. I will boldly say here that I think Dirkschneider may have an edge on both of them in this example in terms of flat-out fury.

The common thread here is that Accept isn't one of your typical headbanger bands, and *Balls to the Wall* closer "Winterdreams" affirms this. Its sing-songy acoustics may only fit on this record because this fact this clear, and because it takes nuts to finish an album like *Balls to the Wall* with such a jangly (ahem) *ballad*. The album's atmosphere darkens the song accordingly and makes it work.

The period I spent around early 1985 waiting for Accept's next record, *Metal Heart,* to come out reminds me of how indescribably thrilling it was to anticipate a new album from one of your favourite artists. A new *album*. I'm loath to describe the ritual at the suggestion of it making me sound old, but I have to because it was such a big deal. It was practically compulsory to what it meant to truly experience music.

Music is such a disposable commodity today, those glorious days of *album rock* long gone. The days when the concept of a complete group of songs formed an *album*. And I'm not talking about a concept album, just cohesive bodies of work that gave you a sense of theme without you even realizing it. A new album was an event. The release always included artwork, photos, liner notes, and a visual component complimentary to the aural one the music provided. And I spent hours and hours in my bedroom poring over that stuff.

Whenever one of my favourite bands released their newest album, I would wait for that record to arrive at the local music shop. I would walk over to the New Releases display and pick it up, smiling as I acknowledged the band's logo and briefly scanning the new product's artwork front and back before bringing it to the cash register to make it my own. It was a special feeling. There was crazy anticipation before I loaded the album into the deck or onto the turntable. The perusal of the materials that accompanied the record while I listened to the new songs was always done simultaneously. The complement of photos, notes, and all those other materials that came with the package added that additional dimension to the listening experience, growing my conceptual understanding of what the band was really about and shaping the band's own unique specificity. A block of time was always set aside for new release acquisitions. I would go to my room and close the door behind me, expecting not to be interrupted. My complete attention was focused on this event. I listened to these albums very intently and each one carved out its own identity in my mind, unique from the last and the next.

By 1985 there was a new record store in Espanola called The Disc Depot, and a guy who had just recently graduated from Espanola High established it. This guy was an outcast in town, but completely by his own design. He flouted all of the typical small town rules of dress and decorum in a very loud and obnoxious way, and he relished it. He also may or may not have been involved with my sister in a romantic capacity around that time, though I have to lean heavily towards the former. He was that guy every small town resident loves to hate. The non-conformist. He was kinda like a much chubbier version of Kevin Bacon's character Ren in *Footloose*.

Of course, he was subjected to the usual stuff that Espy non-conformists were dealt. Hurtful slander. General vitriol. Being goaded into no-reason fights by the conformists. But he just took it. And he was still taking it when I left town. The funny thing is that these types of guys usually have the last laugh in the end, which is the only time that life actually imitates art and lines up with the ending of the movie. These guys seem to know something everyone else doesn't, much in the same way that every nerd in your high school went on to be successful in life while the coolest high school kids typically went on to be underachieving fuckups. I can't definitively say that I didn't like this guy because he was a blatant non-conformist or because he was an asshole, because I had a difficult time determining where the line was that differentiated those two back then. Looking back now on the position I took with him, it was probably because I secretly resented him for having the massive balls that it took to be completely oppositional. And a bit because he actually was an asshole.

Regardless, his store was cool insofar as it at least made an effort to bridge that gap between Wally's House of Rip-Offs and a real record store. It was small, but the right records were in there. The Disc Depot carried W.A.S.P.'s *Animal (Fuck Like A Beast)*, proudly displayed for all conformists and non-conformists alike to see. After I bought it, another copy promptly went on display. And this place wasn't just a metal shop, because Ren wasn't even into metal, at all. He liked Joe Jackson and Wang Chung and Platinum Blonde's *Alien Shores* record, and played stuff like World Party's "Ship of Fools" over the store system.

And then, one day, there it was prominently displayed in the New Releases section. Accept's newest record, *Metal Heart*.

Metal Heart didn't carry the same ferocity that *Balls to the Wall* did, but this was to be expected. As previously noted, ferocity is fleeting and finite in an artist's career arc, and Accept had just moved through their solstitial apex period. The precious blend of intensity and naïveté was no longer usurping self-awareness. The unfortunate bane of popularity set in. This isn't to say *Metal Heart* is a bad album, because it's definitely not. The languid darkness of *Balls to the Wall* was gone, but the power was still there. "Up to the Limit", "Dogs on Leads" and "Wrong is Right" were fierce. The guitars were still crushing in the production, now accompanied by drum tracks that seemed a bit more crisp and up front in the mix. On *Metal Heart*, Accept even took the listener down a jazzy path in the very interesting "Teach Us To Survive". You can almost hear the gasps and see the screwed-up faces of diehard Accept fans as that bass line bounces down the fretboard. Because it's Accept it works though, and it really should have come as no surprise. It stands to reason that a band as musically intuitive as Accept would continue to break new ground creatively. The hints were there on previous records. The tragedy here is that Accept's real *raison d'etre*, the riff-mad headbanging fan, will sometimes tend to frown upon these artistic indulgences. And per the solstices theory things will begin to unravel, as they sadly would in Accept's case after this record.

I bought *Metal Heart* on both vinyl and cassette. I did this because as I mentioned earlier, I loved the completist experience of having all of the accoutrements of the vinyl record, most importantly the lyrics. But I still needed the option of Walkman mobility. I did it when I had to, but I hated taping albums onto blank cassettes because a) the sound quality suffered, and b) I didn't like the way the Maxell cassettes looked in my cassette collection, with band and album names printed in compromised cursive to accommodate that smallish space afforded by the spine of the cassette liner and written using different pens that usually had different colours of ink. I know, I know. Not quite control *freak*, though. That's an aggressive term. Maybe just a bit control *freaky*.

Yes, of course I made mix tapes. Lots of them. And yes, there was a certain artistry involved in making an outstanding mix tape to be sure. I was very mindful of this fact, right down to the titling of the mix tape. Instead of calling the tapes passive-aggressively stupid names like *Mixed Shit* as so many folks did, I tried to be more imaginative. I gave the tapes funny and cryptic names like *The Lordosis Reflex*. I know this is still stupid, but at least I was a bit more cerebral in my stupidity.

As a faithful fan I happily bought Accept's next record, *Russian Roulette,* though I admit that I didn't listen to it much. Whether it was intended or not, I didn't pick up on the irony of the cover photo at that time - Udo Dirkschneider dressed as a high-ranking officer and being handed a revolver by a defiant-looking Stefan Kaufmann, with the rest of the band looking on sheepishly. Dirkschneider would soon leave the band, the group probably beleaguered by the prospect of trying to perpetuate their fame.

You can hear it at various points in the record. The first sign is album opener "T.V. War". It just doesn't have the same dramatic heft that the previous album openers did, something Accept had almost come to be known for. The next two tracks salvage the proceedings slightly, but the next song, "It's Hard To Find a Way", has a chorus that borrows slightly from Dokken. Side one closer "Aiming High" sounds more like Accept, as does side two opener "Heaven is Hell", complete with a full "Balls to the Wall"- like breakdown before the last chorus. "Man Enough To

Cry" reminds me of Rainbow's "Man on the Silver Mountain", "Stand Tight" is just peculiar, but "Walking in the Shadow" was the most telling example of Accept's state of affairs. Wolf Hoffmann's solo in "Walking in the Shadow" is very reminiscent of that fantastic harmonic accompaniment style he previously used in the "Balls to the Wall" track (the gang chanting also appears in both tracks), but it just doesn't have that same...*gravitas*. As a result, the song's title provides a grim irony – the material gives the impression that it's destined to exist in the shadow of Accept's earlier material. *Russian Roulette* would be my last Accept record, but that doesn't take away from the fact that Accept was a ridiculously gifted band, and that *Restless & Wild* and *Balls to the Wall* were two of the greatest heavy metal records of all time in my opinion. I still listen to them all the time.

 I used to wonder if Deaffy, the name credited with writing the lyrics in the liner notes, was some kind of acronym, anagram, or nickname of someone in the band, as in the way that Jagger and Richards are credited as The Glimmer Twins in their liners. But before long, as it would in so many other areas, the Internet would also enlighten me on this topic. It turns out that Deaffy was a pseudonym for band manager Gaby Hauke, who took it upon herself to write all of the band's lyrics, much of them controversial. Bizarrely interesting. Wolf Hoffmann eventually married Hauke and moved to Nashville.

 Wolf Hoffmann has been one of my favourite guitar players since I first heard him play. I couldn't resist reaching out to him when the Internet (more specifically, his photography website) afforded the opportunity for me to gush a bit as a fanboy. Poor Wolf. He very graciously responded to my first couple of emails, but when I descended into a mild stalking spiral given my fascination that he actually answered, he stopped. I took that as a sign that I should refrain from sending him drunken idiotic notes like, "*Wolf, where would the best place be for me to pick up a copy of Breaker?*".

 I can sometimes see why celebrities get frustrated with the rigours of being famous, but I was happy to find out that (before I tested his patience) Wolf actually seems like a genuinely engaging guy. Jokes aside, I'd still like to shake his hand one day. I see that Accept has recently reformed *sans* Dirkschneider and is currently touring a new record at the moment, and I wish Wolf and the band all the very best. I might even catch them live if they play Toronto. Unless I'm somehow banned from attending because of any security concerns Wolf may have.

✸ **Ten** ✸
Achtung Rabies

My second favourite German band is one that not many people have heard of. Hell, I don't even know an awful lot about them.

Before I started working at The Met in my late teens, I used to hang out at the dubiously named Espanola Youth Centre during the summers. Time was mine to kill, and the Youth Centre was a hangout along a very small circuit of very few hangouts I strung together throughout Espy to mitigate the melancholy of my small town boredom. I completed that circuit several times daily as a kid during those summers. Staying in one place for more than an hour seemed like madness. Keep in mind the Xbox was an Atari 2600 then, and I could only play so much hyper-pixelated Pitfall before it made me want to go out on an adventure of my own. I was a vagabond anyway, and it was my thing to move around. I didn't stay in one place for too long.

The Youth Centre was actually just the gym of Espanola High School. You could either play basketball on one court or badminton on the other, or floor hockey along the side of the courts with these weak-ass plastic hockey sticks and a plastic hollow puck. The rest of the school was closed off, but sometimes as the centre was closing for the night we would hide in the bathroom and then roam the darkened halls of Espanola High after the centre's employees unwittingly locked the place up with us inside.

There was something about walking around the school, and around town for that matter, in the dead of night that I really liked as a kid. I used to stay out all night wandering all over town, undisturbed and unafraid, accessing Espy's placidity and mining her secrets. The nighttime was my silent friend. It was paradoxically vulnerable and yet not without a solemn power, and it offered something more for me to discover during its hours despite the obvious reality that there was even less stimulus at night than there was during the day. This was because nighttime presents an opportunity to deviate from reality just a little bit. I exploited the dark of night as an adolescent thrill seeker and I was engaged by every mystery it provided back then, much more than at any point of the day.

Funny how things change. If I happen to be out walking after dark these days and I see a group of kids coming in my direction I'll cross the street, even after I've had a few. The magic of the nighttime is definitely a young man's game.

There were only two employees at the Espanola Youth Centre. One of them was a girl named Jane, whom I estimated to be maybe five or six years older than me. Jane was a very pure, natural-looking girl who didn't wear makeup or attention-getting clothing. This worked to her advantage in the same way that WKRP's Bailey Quarters' plainness trumped Jennifer Marlowe's* overdone sex siren-ness. While my teenage crush on Jane was predicated on her good looks, it was equally rooted in the fact that she carried herself as if to seem unaware of them.

I only saw Jane for one or two summers at the centre. I remembered her when we crossed paths again several years later, in a most unlikely environment. I happened across her in my second year at university in Sudbury, as she sat on the bed in the room of a guy who lived down the hall from me in dorm.

A gruesome perversion of circumstance had befallen me at that moment. Here was goody-goody Jane, the unblemished angel, juxtaposed against the dirty, drunken, debauched misgivings of our dorm

---

* *Don't ask me how I remember these TV character names thirty-plus years after watching WKRP in Cincinnati. I need a calculator to do simple math and yet I somehow retain this knowledge.*

environment. And I can tell you that this guy she was with indeed had his Keith Richards merit badge, rightfully earned. When I first saw her there, I recalled the disdain I felt the first time I saw my teachers smoking in the staff room back in grade school. Shattering images both. To think that Jane may have engaged in the devil's embrace with one of my dirty dorm mates was strangely repulsive to me, as much as it didn't have to be. I found it to be a shame in a Holden Caulfield sort of way.

The other Espanola Youth Centre employee's name was Van. Van was an athletic, alpha-male BMOC type that used to beat me up with regularity back when I was grade seven and he was in grade eight in Sacred Heart School. He went on to attend high school at St. Charles College in Sudbury, and the first time I saw him after my last grade school beating was behind the counter at the youth centre. He seemed to have forgotten all about it. Even though I didn't, I looked past it as we played out our roles in one of those peculiar situational and transitory 'friendships' that summer in 1985. He was a funny guy and we had some decent laughs. Mostly at each other's expense.

One day Van approached me with a Maxell cassette that he said I would be interested in. He got the tape from one of his Sudbury school friends, and it featured two albums by bands I had never heard of before. On one side was a band called Chateaux, and on the other side was Underdog, a band from Germany that Van told me he really liked. The Underdog album was called *Rabies in Town*. I furled my brow in skeptical curiousity as I read the handwritten liner. I still didn't fully trust ol' Vandal at this point.

I don't remember the details surrounding how I would get my own copy of *Rabies in Town*, and why Chateaux was not included in this transaction. I think Van must have taped it for me on a cassette I gave him. Just now, I went and dug the actual tape out of my old collection that I've kept since those days. Sure enough, Underdog appears on Side B of the Maxell XLII 90 I must have given him. Side A had already been taken up by a suite of Iron Maiden favourites – "Aces High", "Invaders", "Gangland", "Two Minutes to Midnight", "The Trooper", "The Number of the Beast", "The Number of the Beast" live version that appeared on the "Aces High" vinyl single (I liked Adrian Smith's guitar solo), unreleased b-side "King of Twilight" also from the vinyl single, "Run to the Hills", and "Back in the Village". This little collection was assembled on August 4, 1985 according to my all-caps penmanship on the liner. As such, *Rabies in Town* shows as having been recorded two days later on August 6. My younger self also checked off Dolby noise reduction on the liner, in case that's in any way relevant.

Rabies in Town got tons of play on my crappy little boom box, and it just got better and better with every listen. I may as well have just had *Rabies* taped on both sides of the cassette, since I just rewound it every time it reached the end of the side (with no disrespect to Maiden, of course). Riff after crunchy guitar riff and soaring vocals interwoven with all of the other key essentials to comprise an outstanding record. This was the heavy metal that I heard in my head, especially the intro and colossal main guitar riff in "I Do It". Ridiculously good.

A curious aspect of this record was the lyrical content. Getting back to what I was saying earlier about vocal delivery relative to ethnic origin, I loved that the Underdog singer's Teutonic inflection rendered words like 'wheels' into *whilce* – it added a jagged edge to the songs. The funny thing about *Rabies in Town* (other than the title) is that, while all of the songs have English titles and the lyrics are in English, it almost seems like the words are just a collection of various English language clichés like *'eye of the hurricane'* and *'set my soul on fire'* assembled to form verses and choruses. Maybe the lyrics were written in German and translated to English to appeal to a more global market, I don't know. The lyrics of the Alice Cooper "Under My Wheels" cover that appears on the record are all sung in English per usual, except the one line in the second verse after *"And then I say honey I just can't go"*. I think the line in English is *"Old lady's sick and I can't leave her home"*, but that's not what comes out of the speakers. It appears to be sung in German instead. Or something other than English. It's kinda funny to try to decipher any meaning from the lyrics on *Rabies in Town*, because the more you listen the more confusing it gets, if not because some of the lyrics are unintelligible. Except the lyrics in title track "Rabies in

Town", which describe the trials and tribulations of an enthusiast who delights in biting a *"lovely lady with a big fat ass"*. Weird.

Yes, *Rabies in Town* had terrifically cheesy moments but it was that beautifully stupid, glorious kind of cheese that makes good heavy metal so fun to listen to. It's requisite, and it's not limited to just heavy metal. Every genre had and has its idiosyncrasies that were considered tantamount to the style, and definitive to the genre's constitution. Music, regardless of (and specific to) genre and era, should always be considered in terms of its perceived application. I don't let any obvious gaps in chronological relevance hinder my appreciation of the music itself. It wouldn't be fair. Listening to the Beatles' 1962 B-side of "Please Please Me", named "Ask Me Why", can be the same as listening to most heavy metal. They both need to be heard contextually for what they are in terms of period, intent, and for the application they best serve. With this in mind, I listen to *Rabies in Town* these days with the same mindset my mom should be employing if she's still listening to her old Boney M records.

As time passed after I first got that *Rabies in Town* cassette, something that had come to be equally compelling as the music was the fact that I didn't know a thing about this band. Like, at all. I had the recorded music itself, the band and album name, the song titles, and the fact that they were from Germany. That was it. No musician's names, no year of release, no band history, no pictures, nothing. Van had gone back to Sudbury less than a month after he gave me the tape, and I never saw him again. Google wouldn't be available for another thirteen or so years. Any time I asked someone at a record store about a German metal band called Underdog, they would screw up their faces like George Costanza and shake their heads from side to side. The positive that I took from this was that Underdog, like their lyrics, could thus be imagined and interpreted in any way I chose. And if we're being honest, I kinda liked it that way. Based on the pictures the music painted in my mind, I had free license to imagine what the band looked like. For some reason, I imagined the singer to look like TKO's Brad Sinsel from the cover shot of *In Your Face*. For a while, I didn't want to know what their names were, or anything else about them, for fear of ruining the image of Underdog I had already established in my head. I risked disappointment, like when I saw a picture of Malice's singer James Neal a couple of years after wearing out Malice's *License to Kill* cassette. It's not like he looked like The Elephant Man or anything, but it just snuffed out an image I had already construed in my mind. And this rationale lends itself considerably to heavy metal. The genre relies almost as much on implied fantastical perception as it does on the music.

Fourteen years later, in 1999, I met a guy from England named Paul Rose. Paul was participating in some kind of work exchange program here in Canada and he received a placement in the company I was working at in Toronto. We worked together in the same department. Through some chat we had discovered that we had very similar musical tastes, and we became personal friends after spending a lot of time blathering about hard rock and metal bands we loved. Paul was probably ten years younger than I was but mature far beyond his years. We had some laughs cracking on each other about the obligatory stereotypes of our countries. He still calls me a lumberjack to this day.

One day at work I asked Paul about Underdog, and I wasn't surprised to hear that he hadn't heard of them. As we had been in the Internet Age for a few years by this point, I figured I might as well go ahead and type it in to the Copernic search engine Paul had recommended and see what happened (Google wasn't yet the omnipotent juggernaut that it is now). For all I knew about this band, *Rabies in Town* could have been a singular offering recorded in someone's basement. I wouldn't have been surprised, as the recorded copy I had sounded like it had been recorded inside a toaster.

Lo and behold, the *Rabies in Town* search yielded one hit, on a Japanese website. The site looked like it was put together to reference someone's personal music collection. It boasted thousands of LPs, CDs and cassettes, and *Rabies in Town* was listed as being a part of this person's vinyl portion of the collection. Paul and I thought it might be worthwhile to email the Webmaster to explain my situation and ask some questions about the ultra-mysterious Underdog from the other side of the world. I would use my work email so as to retain a measure of anonymity. What harm could come of it?

The day after I sent the email, a response came back. It was from someone named Koichi Matsunaga, the owner of the website. I jumped out of my chair and waved Paul over to my desk. The email was written in broken English, but the message was that this person was extremely familiar with Underdog. Turns out the band had recorded three albums, *Rabies in Town* being the second and best album. The *Rabies in Town* album was actually referred to in the email as 'Raby Town', which made Paul and I laugh hysterically until we couldn't breathe. The email itself was written in an extremely engaging and congenial way. And Koichi ended it with an offer to make cassette copies of all three albums and send them to me through the mail, free of charge.

I'm ashamed to say that my small town skepticism made me reluctant to send out my home address via email, even if this guy seemed nice enough to do this for me. Not knowing what would or could come of this, I provided the company's mailing address instead of my own.

Sure enough, not two weeks later, a package arrived for me at my place of business. Inside the package were two recorded cassettes. One was a TDK 45-minute tape containing the *Rabies in Town* album, and the other was a 90-minute Maxell cassette featuring two albums, one called *Underdog* and the other called *Out in the Night*.

I couldn't believe my good fortune in receiving these tapes. Purely out of the kindness of his heart, this person had taken the time and expense to do this for a complete stranger. I sent him a long email thanking him profusely, and asked him if I could return the favour by sending him something from Canada he may not have access to in Japan. His response was that there was no need, and that having a friend in Canada was enough. Heartwarming stuff.

The other albums, debut *Underdog* and the band's last album *Out in the Night*, were... *okay*. There was a good song here and an okay song there, but they sounded nothing like *Rabies in Town*. There was little cohesion, lots of keyboards and even some goofy space-age robot voice sound effect stuff. I dismissed these records and focused on this new *Rabies* recording, which even featured an intro to the first song on the album, "Nightmares", that I hadn't previously heard because it wasn't on my original Van version - whoever had made that original recording erroneously pushed the record button after the intro and missed it.

Koichi and I corresponded about bands via email for a while, and I finally coaxed a request for Canuck band Helix out of him. We sent a few CDs back and forth, exchanging the Japanese version of Raven's *All For One* for a Zappacosta CD I can't remember the name of that wasn't available in Japan. His emails were always extremely kind and enthusiastic, and full of statements that made me smile. He would say that he was *"so proud having excellent Canadian friend like you!"*. Our last exchange was about two years ago, when he informed me that a friend of his was traveling through Toronto, and he asked me if I would mind to take an afternoon to show her around the city. I was happy to do it.

Paul went back to England one or two years after we had first reached out to Koichi, but he was a houseguest here a few years back. We still correspond regularly through Facebook, and we've arranged a mutually exclusive agreement wherein accommodation would always be available if one of us is traveling in the other's country. I haven't taken him up on it yet, but I will one day. He advised me recently that he picked up a vinyl copy of *Raby Town* for me from one of the English shops.

As for Underdog, an official website still in its formative stages popped up a few years back seemingly via members of the band. I emailed to ask some questions about the possibility of the release of their records in CD format, and someone responded from the site that the plan was in fact to release everything on CD, which would be made available through the website when it was completely built up. When I tried to return to the site a few weeks later, it had vanished without a trace.

I was finally able to pick up a CD version of *Rabies in Town* on eBay after having checked every six months or so for the last five or six years.

Knowing that original label Mausoleum Records never did release this record in CD format, I figured it was going to be a passable vinyl-to-CD conversion at best and a crappy hiss-laden gong show at worst. When it arrived, I was actually pleasantly surprised. I can hear that it's a vinyl conversion, but only barely. If one didn't know any better, one might not notice that this is anything other than a standard CD release. The liners and CD itself are pro quality featuring a close-up image of a foamy-mouthed canine on the cover (duh), and the names of the band members, nicknames and all. When I looked at the band photo on the back cover, I was chagrined to find that the singer, whose name is Mike 'Spider' Linster, does not resemble Brad Sinsel in any way. Dang. In fact, none of these guys look anything as I imagined they would. With the exception of Linster and a Uli Roth-looking guy, they kinda look more like a Dr. Hook tribute band than the blokes who were responsible for such badass music.

Anyway, the great mystery of Underdog is more or less solved, and it's great to crank this record for the first time through a proper system and really connect with it. As I listen to *Rabies in Town* now, I consider a couple of things.

The first is how two completely opposite people like Van and I could have been connected by Underdog. Van was raised in an affluent nuclear family by parents who bought him a new hockey stick every time he scored a hat trick during one of his hockey games. Which he did often. His social status was that of an influencer, and he was socially powerful in Espytown. This would turn out to mean zilch later on in life of course, but the point is that Underdog wasn't for kids in Van's position. Music like Wham! or Depeche Mode was more properly suited for Van and his social circle.

I remember being on a high school basketball trip once and watching a warm up for the Lo-Ellen Park Knights girls team, during which they were playing "Wake Me Up Before You Go-Go" by Wham!.[*] Lo-Ellen Park was a Sudbury high school known for its good-looking

---

[*] *Between Wham! and Kerrang!, I must say that it's a punctuational pain in the ass to deal with these exclamation-marked titles.*

preppies and in-crowd kids. As I watched the girls gleefully bounce through their lay-up drills in time to the music, mouthing the lyrics to each other through dramatic and sassy expressions with perfect smiles, I remember considering the role music played in social class distinction. Happy shiny people listened to happy shiny songs, and angry malevolent people listened to angry malevolent songs in an almost territorial construct. It was almost a self-advertisement of their life situations. Anything else was musical mockery, because irony wasn't *en vogue* yet and because image was everything. But Van, who was attending a private school in Sudbury that may have been even swishier than Lo-Ellen Park, did not subscribe to my crude socio-musical suppositions. Of course, Van couldn't have known as a teen that post-adolescent angst would allow us to enjoy a *you-don't-pick-your-favourite-music-it-picks-you* existence any better than the rest of us. More likely is the fact that he was actually masquerading as a preppy while secretly manifesting his suppressed rage by listening to *Rabies in Town*. That would at least explain the regular beatdowns Vandal meted out back at Sacred Heart School. I did my share of role-playing as a preppy as well, just to a lesser degree. My mullet always gave me away, however.

In terms of direct musical connectivity, I also consider how cool it is that this album actually did become a connective force between three individuals from remotely different parts of the planet. Paul Rose and I had already been friends, but the *Rabies in Town* mystery contributed to a stronger bond. And I would have never had the pleasure of interacting with Koichi Matsunaga from Japan had it not been for Underdog. Little did the band know when they released a heavy metal album about biting fat chicks' asses that they would have been responsible for initiating goodwill and forging lasting friendships on this type of multicultural and international scale.

✡ Eleven ✡
Former Things Passed Away

After looking up that old Underdog cassette, I went back into my big old fake mahogany multi-drawer cassette organizer that contains my still-intact 80s collection to look around a little bit. Everything was exactly as I left it all those years ago. Alphabetized by band and then sorted in order of release date. Things get started with Accept's *Midnight Highway*, the version with a woman dressed in a frock holding a chainsaw on the cover.

This collection of tapes is a musical summation of my adolescence. As I look over these little rectangular totems, I'm mindful of the significant application these tapes had in my life during my teen years. An aggregate memento of former things passed away. I look through the drawers and I'm transported back into my rock poster-emblazoned teenage bedroom on Tudhope Street in Espy, where this cassette organizer sat beneath the credenza my tape player occupied. That crummy deck conjured up the music from these cassettes as best it could, given its quality and my mother's consistent aversion to the devil's noise. Since my bedroom was on the other side of the wall from the family TV room, I would be asked multiple times per evening to turn my music down. Eventually I would just load Loudness' *Thunder in the East* cassette into my Walkman, cued up to "We Could Be Together", and leave the house to patrol the unremarkable streets of Espy looking for something remarkable.

Here's a tape that I'm surprised I didn't wear out – Cinderella's *Night Songs*. Cinderella entered my life in 1986 with the subtlety of a cruise missile. The launching of Cinderella and this pink-n-purple debut cassette was no doubt a marketing coup, but I wonder if the branding was almost *too* good.

Most people who *got* Cinderella most likely came for the bombast and stayed for the music. Ideally, this is the way the man behind the curtain at the record company would best have it. The music video medium served as the perfect vehicle by which to foist a band like Cinderella upon the public. The video for "Shake Me" had an intro featuring the requisite flashy-trashy big hair and makeup girls strutting their way through a campy tongue-in-cheek storyline. The single itself cranked out staccato power chords that recalled KISS' "Calling Dr Love" and Motley's "Ten Seconds To Love". Did the lyrics narrate the pubescent Holy Grail glory of anonymous, random sex at command? Of course they did. The opening lyric of "Shake Me" sums it up perfectly – "I met this girl around quarter to ten / I made her once she said make me again". I still smile when I think about how much that opening line, rendered in Brian Johnson-sings-Bruce Springsteen salvo, was the tip of the spear that so perfectly manifested the whole red-blooded rock and roll experience as I saw it through wide seventeen-year-old eyes.

The live concert theme in the video showcased the band's Philadelphia-cum-Sunset Strip image, and it raised the ante of that guitar-over-the-shoulder trick that I had only seen Yngwie Malmsteen and that dude from Lita Ford's band do previously. The trick involved throwing the guitar over the shoulder and catching it again as the strap naturally orbited it around the body, behind the torso and then back up into the hands. In the "Shake Me" vid all three guitar players do it, including the bass player. And they do it forwards *and* backwards for crissakes. I couldn't believe what I was seeing. My teenage mind was Cinderella's for the taking at this point.

Incidentally, years later when I was at university one of my dorm mates appeared in my doorway one night after a couple of drinks. He was holding the expensive guitar of his roommate who had gone home for the weekend. He decided that it would be a good idea to try this guitar throwing trick, though he a) had never done it before, b) didn't even play guitar and c) wasn't privy to the fact that strap locks are an important part of this feat. He put his drink down, lifted the strap over his shoulder, and stepped out into the hallway so that he could have some additional room to perform his trick. He looked at the rest of us with a stupid-ass Peewee Herman grin and threw the guitar up. It didn't even begin the revolution it should have taken around his back. The strap came off immediately after the guitar left his hands. The guitar sailed up to the ceiling, smashing against it hard enough to crack the guitar's headstock and repel it back to the floor faster than gravity would have normally delivered it. It was effectively broken into two pieces that were connected only by the strings. Peewee Herman scrambled to reassemble it in shock, shrieking *"Fuck! Oh fuck!"* at the top of his lungs. Like he was surprised that this was the outcome. I think he may have even been crying. I was too, having fallen to my knees convulsing with gut wrenching, eye-watering laughter. To this day, witnessing that exercise was the closest I've ever come to laughing hard enough to piss my pants.

Night Songs was only successful because of Cinderella multi-instrumentalist and frontman Tommy Keifer's (and ergo Cinderella's) greatest advantage – the fact that his musical abilities and mystique as a performer reached beyond the cartoony corniness of Sunset Strip hair rock. Keifer was legitimate, and he was believable. This couldn't be said of many of his frontman peers. Keifer may have been at the vanguard of a movement that colourfully reconfigured the hard rock heroes of the previous decade for screaming girlies the world over, but his downfall was that he was labeled as the same - a parochial figure in a genre that is taken seriously by very few and ridiculed by a great many. In the same way that Michael Richards couldn't escape his Kramer typecasting post-*Seinfeld*, Keifer and his band still suffer the fate of a simplified hair band labeling. Tommy Keifer could hold his own alongside hard rock's elite, but because of that *Night Songs* album cover alone, he was doomed to die by the same sword by which he lived in Cinderella and in the minds of his fans.

Keifer's androgyny channelled the smooth fluidity of a late 60s Jagger-Richards composite, mysteriously asexual and as offensive as he was intriguing. Keifer had a Steven Tyler-esque carriage about him that allowed him to pull off the routine where so many others failed. Even if the music is, as Martin Popoff once said, *"fake blues"*. On *Night Songs,* Keifer uses a falsetto singing style that while not quite as shrill as say, Mark Slaughter's, is just bluesy enough without nodding *too* deliberately in Tyler's direction. I've always thought that Keifer was a victim of circumstance born a decade too late. He used the pop metal environment as a launch pad in the same way Guns N' Roses did, because every Cinderella record that followed *Night Songs* moved further away from hair rock and closer to the blues. Unfortunately, Keifer and Cinderella made too much of a pink-n-purple impression in their early years and they would never be able to get up from underneath the hair band mantle the way that Guns did.

Cinderella's sophomore record *Long Cold Winter* tried to do away with the *Night Songs* fake metal formula, the only visual reminder being the band's dubious pinky purply colour scheme of the band's lousy logo on an otherwise blasé album cover. With the exception of the logo, the back cover of the album is exactly identical to the Stones' *Beggars Banquet*. Coincidence? I doubt it.

The band attempted to send a very clear message when they kicked off *Long Cold Winter* with an unaccompanied slide guitar number called "Bad Seamstress Blues", played by none other than Tommy Keifer

No Sleep 'til Sudbury

himself. As much as I really dig Keifer, I have to admit that moments like these validate Popoff's *"fake blues"* condemnation of Cinderella. Despite the blues declaration, "Bad Seamstress Blues" launches this album into a familiar pattern – the track sequencing is pretty much identical to *Night Songs*. "Fallin' Apart at the Seams" is "Night Songs". First single "Gypsy Road" is a less salacious and more rootsy "Shake Me". It's followed immediately by the ballad "Don't Know What You Got (Till It's Gone)", the second single from the record. Just like "Nobody's Fool" was as the third track on *Night Songs*. The leadoff tune on side two of *Long Cold Winter*, "Second Wind", is basically a reworking of *Night Songs* side two opener "Hell on Wheels".

Any intended likeness to Aerosmith or the Stones is eliminated by Cinderella's formulaic approach to track sequencing. With *Long Cold Winter*, they basically released another version of *Night Songs*. Most likely it was at the behest of the record company, maybe in a bid to stretch out their newfound fame away from the Philly bar scene. It's not surprising that a formula was followed given the time. Or that each of the newer songs showed slight signs of maturation against their predecessors. But this may have been a problem for hair band fans, Cinderella's main draw. Hair band fans don't want signs of maturation. The same thing happened to Ratt when guitar whiz Warren DeMartini tried to pass off "Way Cool Jr." as a Ratt song. Ratt isn't a blues band in the eyes of their core fan base. They're a Sunset Strip hair band, and they always will be. Nobody cares who a hair band's influences are.

Poor Tommy Keifer. There are some moments on *Long Cold Winter* that give a glimpse of Cinderella's potential to move beyond the poseur pale, mainly in Kiefer's lead playing on the otherwise generic title track. There's some creativity in the arrangements. The breakdown of "Second Wind" recalls early Aerosmith, but it flames out before taking the song somewhere worthwhile. And really, this is the unfortunate paper tiger that is *Long Cold Winter*. It flashes some brief elements of greatness, but it falls short of the bands it emulates. The songwriting and musicianship are more than capable, but formula and an 80s sheen prevents Cinderella from stepping out of the long shadow cast by the "real" blues of their rock and roll forefathers.

"Heartbreak Station" from Cinderella's 1990 album of the same name is probably their best song from a songwriting point of view. It must be so frustrating for Keifer that it's overlooked in favour of the likes of Poison's "Every Rose Has Its Thorn". This is a great example of how Cinderella played the game by the same rules as their peers during their time, but couldn't escape from a hard rock purgatory that must have been more like hell for Tom Keifer. He knew the blues. But because he came in through the front door with Cinderella, he was and still is trapped in a closed system above Sunset Strip vapidity but beneath Aerosmith and the Stones.

If we're being honest, Cinderella is essentially The Tommy Keifer Band. With no disrespect to the other members, Keifer represents the band much in the same way that Jim Morrison did The Doors. In both cases, their respective bands would virtually be non-entities without the charisma of their respective frontmen. Look no further than Ray Manzarek's pitiful attempts to cash in on The Doors brand by trotting out The Cult's Ian Astbury in Morrison's place on tour in the 90s for proof. Blaspheme! I like Astbury, but shit like that just shouldn't be allowed.

I contemplate Tom Keifer's position in the genre, and I think I understand why I consider him in the way that I do. His swagger and musical ability are compelling beyond the manufactured image of *Night Songs*. When Martin Popoff calls Cinderella *"fake blues"*, I do have to admit that he's actually right. But, Keifer is the closest thing to the prime eras of The Rolling Stones and Aerosmith that 80s hair rock was capable of producing. Sometimes a part of me wants to believe that Tom Keifer has the same gravitas as Steven Tyler because I'm faced with the dim prospect that while Aerosmith wasn't my generation's music per se, Cinderella and 80s hair metal to a large degree was. I do resign myself more comfortably and justifiably to the fact that my generation's Rolling Stones was actually Guns N' Roses (never a hair metal band),

and maybe The Black Crowes. I could just leave well enough alone and respect the veracity of the rock and roll hierarchy as it exists. Wherever he does fit in however, I'll still always dig Tommy Keifer.

                                                                     ∽

A couple of sleeves over in the big tape box is Fastway's *All Fired Up* cassette. I liked the "All Fired Up" riff I heard on MuchMusic, Canada's answer to MTV, and I bought the tape on a lark in 1984 with fingers crossed. Turns out I ended up really liking it. Keeping in mind that I learned the hard rock hierarchy backwards by not getting to the Aerosmiths and Rolling Stoneses and Led Zeppelins until having first heard all of their hirsute musical spawn, and even as a lover of Anthrax and Metallica, I still listened to the heavy blues on *All Fired Up* quite often. I had a definite soft spot for this record. Particularly for "Telephone". This being the case, I wonder sometimes why I wasn't more into Zeppelin, even despite the fact that I flatly dismissed them as being 'older people's music'. The first time I heard "Kashmir" was on the radio in a car when I was in St John's, Newfoundland in 1983. Even though I instantly loved it, I never did follow up on it because I didn't know who or what it was, and I just kinda forgot about it until I heard it again in university. The funniest thing about learning rock backwards is that any affinity for the 80s stuff is intensely bolstered by the nostalgic element that comes with pairing the music with memories of being a kid. I really feel that ardour as I pore over these tapes. For other peeps that listened to Springsteen, The Clash, and Elvis Costello in the 80s this music is drivel, and I completely get that. One of my best friends Garvin is one of those peeps.

    I 'met' Garv three times. The first time we crossed paths was at summer basketball camp when I was sixteen and he was fifteen. At that age, you wear your musical tastes on your sleeve as part of your identity. Not many other things are as important. I was a Metallica fan and Garvin was a Springsteen guy, so we were opposed from the get go. He actually left Sudbury to see The Boss on the Toronto stop of the *Born in the USA* tour right in the middle of camp, that fucker. The second time I met Garv was three or four years later in university. He shared a dorm room with some guys I used to drink with, and he answered the door when I showed up one night. We just kind of looked each other up and down, and went about our business.

Four years after that, in September 1993 I walked into my first psychology thesis class very much a stranger in a strange land. There was one last vacant seat remaining, right beside none other than Garvin. Ironically, this time we were both happy to see a familiar face given the circumstances. It was really only through the disdain we harboured for the nerds that made up the rest of the class that we found out we actually liked each other. The class was difficult enough that we were obliged to look out for each other that year, and as a result we went on to become very close friends to this day. Garvin introduced me to the majesty of The Rolling Stones via *Sticky Fingers*. I heard "Bitch" for the first time in his little Ford truck and I rewound it and rewound it. Recently I've heard Garv play Metallica's "Seek and Destroy" on the guitar. It's astonishing how much of your destiny is absolutely imperceptible to you as a young person.

'Garvey' is not his real name. It's a nickname, after that old Saturday Night Live *Fred Garvin: Male Prostitute* sketch. It featured Dan Akroyd looking at the camera in a close-up and introducing himself as such a couple times during the bit. The nickname came about the summer after we graduated from thesis and scored ourselves jobs at the same resort. We were still in our early twenties, so the setting would get pretty Roman more or less every night. One night in particular, we were playing pool against each other in the bar. There were some girls hanging around, maybe three or four. Garv and I came down to the eight ball. It was his turn. It was one of those shots that was easy for the average pool player, but it carried that same uncertainty as the three-foot putt with a one-stroke lead on the 18th at Augusta. Neither of us were particularly good pool players. Even if we had been, being faced with trying to sink the eight ball for the win with a group of birds watching is a formidable fucking task. Garvin and I both knew he was going to blow the shot. We also both knew that I was going to laugh when he missed it in front of the girlies.

The cue connected with the ball with that abrupt clunking sound that compels the listener to make a face. You know the one. The cue ball did not make contact with the eight ball. The cue ball may not have even reached the eight ball. Two long seconds of ugly, frozen silence hung in the air. Before I could complete the inhalation required to let out the mammoth laugh that was requisite in such a situation, I looked over at Garv. He was still leaned over the unfortunate shot, and he slowly turned his head to look at me with that same dry, pursed-lips Fred Garvin male prostitute face. Except his face didn't say, *"Fred Garvin, male prostitute"*. His face instead said, *"And now I'm going to wrap this pool cue right around your fucking head, you fucking motherfucker"*.

I'll never forget that. I've been calling him Garvin ever since. And right behind the guitar over the shoulder caper, it ranks as the second best laugh I've ever had in my life. I love ol' Garv, he's one of my best friends in the world.

So one day in the late 90s Garvey and I were out on a booze-up the night before a long drive from Toronto to Sudbury. He and I used to really rip it up back then, and we always paid for it the next day. However, Garv is one of those guys who really suffers through his hangovers. Like *really* badly. Super grumpy while he's doing it, too. He was having a terrible go of it during this particular ride. I don't remember who else was in the car, but he was in the back seat and I was driving. A couple of days before this trip I had been flipping through CDs at Sam the Record Man's flagship store on Yonge and I saw Fastway's *All Fired Up* combined with their first release on one of those imported double CDs, and I picked it up. I just let it play in the car during this drive with Garvey, figuring it wasn't a bad way to split the difference between our musical tastes. I thought I was doing him a bit of a favour. After all, I could have been cranking the Metal Church.

Poor Garvin didn't say a word during the entire drive. When it was time to drop him off at the end of the trip, he slowly opened the car door and said in a monotone voice, *"Who were we listening to?"*. I perked up, enthusiastically letting him know that it was Fastway, a band I used to listen to in high school. *"Pretty good, eh?"* I said.

"It's fucking terrible and I hate it" Garvey grumbled, and slammed the car door before hobbling away.

On through the cassettes. Just before Quiet Riot's *Metal Health* is Queensryche. Queensryche has always been interesting to me because they blatantly exploit my hypocrisy.

I really like Queensryche's music. In the 80s, Queensryche was to heavy metal what Pink Floyd was to "classic rock". Both bands worked within the parameters of their respective genres, but each added nuances that expanded their boundaries and took the music to new places beyond expected convention.

That's where the hypocrisy part comes in. I couldn't get my head around the fact that these boundaries could or should be compromised. As an 80s heavy metal fan I took things at face value because with definition came understanding. Meaning. And to a degree, security. Colouring outside the lines was not appreciated. Metal bands that hung their hats too intently on their intellect weren't necessarily metal anymore, because too much intellect distilled the fundamental paradigms heavy metal represented. In a way, experiencing Queensryche visually and aurally as a metal fan in 1986 would be like going to McDonald's and ordering a salad. That's not what you go there for.

I was wrong about Queensryche, of course. And I knew it. I didn't *want* to know it. As much as I was a shill for Metallica's use of historical and biblical references in their lyrics being proof of the fact that heavy metal wasn't for stupid people, it was just a silly social trapping for me. Back then I did wonder if heavy metal that was too intellectually involved could actually be considered heavy metal. In Queensryche's case, the music itself in addition to the lyrical content was highbrow for the average metal fan. I mildly bristled at the fact that I liked it within the same context that I liked guttural, primitive heavy metal.

As such, the reasons for my Queensryche intrigue allowed the band to elude any categorization I might have normally imposed upon them. One of those reasons was the immense skill and emotionality in Geoff Tate's vocal delivery, which represented probably ninety percent of the band's intrigue in my mind. The guy *sang his ass off* on these records! Queensryche may have been elementarily labeled a progressive metal band, but that would have been unfair because a) prog metal was and still is douchey and b), the progressive metal band sub-genre was only ever created to account for metal bands that 'overachieved' beyond the parameters of what heavy metal is believed to be anyway. Prog elements finessed the pleasure out of metal. Prog was counter-intuitive, and Queensryche didn't seem to belong to that grouping somehow in my mind. I perceived the band as something altogether different, which was perplexing in a way that would eventually repel me because I was too myopic to give it much thought.

The album cover of their debut EP was pretty weak for a band of their creative ilk. I suppose that this was because it had been released on their own independent label 206 Records. Back in 1983 my curiosity was piqued by this album sleeve, displayed on the wall in the New Releases section of Wally's Music. Over a black background, the jagged purple and pallid yellow lettering of a single word I had never heard before – *Queensryche* – was etched front and centre in an amateurish font. There was an umlaut over the 'y', most likely to emphasize darkness and crazy Nordic power or something. Motley Crue may have beaten them to this punch, but I don't remember if I saw the umlaut used here first or in the *Shout at the Devil* ad in *Hit Parader* magazine. And this would have impacted my decision to buy this record, because I frowned on bands that may have lifted other bands' ideas. My youthful naïveté also prevented me from realizing that, despite the name of opening track "Queen of the Reich", the band altered the spelling of their name to avoid neo-Nazi connotation. I just figured it was spelled that way for the same reason Motley Crue, Led Zeppelin, Def Leppard, and other bands fooled with the spelling of their names. Because as young, snotty, defiant rock and rollers, they could.

Because there were no band photos or anything else to look at on the sleeve, I bought Queensryche's EP partially on the suggestion of this sinister European-ness they conveyed. But really it was mostly by default. In 1983, the immediate laws of supply and demand worked against me in my situation. I was coming off of records like KISS' *Creatures of the Night* and Maiden's *The Number of the Beast*, and I had to have *more*. But in secluded Espanola, there wasn't much more to be had. Wally had me right where he wanted me, in a small Northern Ontario town pre-driver's license, with the buying power of the glorious World Wide Web still more than ten years away. Wally actually told me that Queensryche was this exciting new young group who made a demo tape that was picked up by a record store owner, who in turn offered to manage the band after hearing it. I probably asked him about it first though, because I always played right into his hands like that. Twenty-two dollars and ninety-nine cents later, this four song EP cassette was now my property.

Overpriced or not, the record was well worth it. The intro for "Queen of the Reich" is textbook, perfect heavy metal, and Tate showed off a set of pipes that would eventually put him up there with the Halfords and Dickinsons. The EP was rookie rough and raw considering the potential they would prove to have, and it was ideal for me at the time. It was heavy metal as I expected. How it was supposed to be.

Queensryche's next record, *The Warning*, was not what I expected. I liked it, but its sophistication distracted me, just slightly more than guitarist Chris de Garmo's passing resemblance to Jamie Lee Curtis. The only thing metal about 1986's *Rage for Order* was the overt domination theme, exemplified in Lisa Dalbello (a Canadian) cover "Gonna Get Close To You". Otherwise the record was something that defied categorization and occupied a unique space between metal and some other thing that could have only existed in the 80s. I did have a special fondness for *Rage for Order*'s lyrics back then however.

At the height of my hypocrisy, I snubbed Queensryche's next record *Operation: Mindcrime* completely. Its success made me even less interested than I already was. I was always much more compelled by the underdog. I was too cognitively lazy to contemplate Queensryche in the light they deserved to be cast in, based on the immense talent I may or may not have cared that they had. When the poignancy of "Silent Lucidity" caught my ear a few years later in university, I had reinvented myself away from metalheadism in favour of artists like The Beatles, Neil Young, and Led Zeppelin. Because I couldn't reconcile Queensryche's application in my life at that point I only superficially enjoyed "Silent Lucidity". And I pretty much ignored every other Queensryche recording that followed it.

I started over from scratch with Queensryche recently by rediscovering the first three records and moving on to realize the greatness of most of their later releases. All of a sudden Queensryche is kinda like the ex-girlfriend that was never really that good looking but had a really great personality. I sidestepped concept albums like *Operation: Mindcrime* as a kid because I thought that concept records were too rigid, and that they polarized what heavy metal was supposed to be about. Translation - *Operation: Mindcrime* intimidated me intellectually as a teenage listener.

The next cassette I pull out of the box features a pre-domestic violence Tawny Kitaen on the cover - *Out of the Cellar* from Ratt. With the exception of maybe Poison, Ratt might be *the* band that unequivocally personified the entire 80s hair band movement. I'm talking about the Sunset Strip, New York, and anywhere else the hair band scene was even marginally popular as a result of Aerosmith and newish Strip progenitor Van Halen. I know Ratt didn't have a ballad during the pinnacle of their success, but they were the first real hair band to launch the scene. I don't count Motley Crue as a hair band participant during that period. Ditto the equally successful Twisted Sister and Quiet Riot. Motley was faux-satanic in 1983, Sister was S&M freaky, and Quiet Riot was metalhead-ish and not androgynous enough. And I could never completely stomach Poison. So Ratt it is.

Ratt had smash single "Round and Round" and fake-metal super record *Out of the Cellar*. They puckered pretty in their makeup. They copped Joe Perry swagger, and used cowboy Wild-West imagery to their full advantage. They had industry juice, inserting friends like Ozzy and Nikki Sixx and Tommy Lee in their videos. They even had one of the best guitarists on the Strip scene in their ranks at the time in Warren DeMartini. Really, Ratt was the only hair band to have all the bases covered (except that ever-important ballad), where most hair bands had one strength they tended to capitalize on. Dokken had guitar phenom George Lynch. Winger had the looks of pretty boy frontman Kip Winger. Motley had the image. Alcatrazz had Malmsteen. Keel had singer Ron Keel's pipes, if that could be counted as a strength. But Ratt had everything. What they didn't have, they had you believe they did. Frontman Stephen Pearcy was a poor singer, but his vocals were triple tracked in the studio and his puckery persona distracted us in the exact same way Vince Neil's did.

Ratt was even perfectly representative of the hair band movement throughout the arc of their career. Ratt is the Lindsay Lohan of hair bands, even to this day. I was a big Ratt fan in 1984. I had these *Ratt EP* and *Out of the Cellar* cassettes and I played them constantly. I had all the videos and interviews taped on VHS, which was no easy feat in cable television-challenged Espanola. I followed the band in the press as best I could. I even had one of those little Ratt buttons of the *Ratt EP* album cover that you could pin on your jacket, which I proudly did.

Ratt were huge around this time and when *Invasion Of Your Privacy* came out in 1985, I politely overlooked the fact that it was a sub-par record, mostly in denial. I was rooting for this group of cool-looking, pose-striking musical Svengalis who gave me "Wanted Man" and "Round and Round" to dig a bit deeper and deliver another *Out of the Cellar* album. Never did happen though.

The next record would be 1986's *Dancing Undercover*. I didn't even buy it. *Invasion* at least had "Round and Round" redux "You're in Love". *Dancing Undercover* had nothing that compared. Ratt had seemingly played all their cards, and their undoing would soon start to unfold a la Dana Plato. The typical band-killing culprits all took their places - ego clashes, addictions, women, et cetera. The band experimented with new musical directions on subsequent records, always a career killer in specified sub-genres. Guitarist Robbin 'King' Crosby would wrestle with addictions, contract AIDS, and suffer a heartbreakingly sad demise by heroin overdose. Other band members dropped off, and peculiar addition Michael Schenker replaced Crosby for a while on guitar. And at one point, there were two Ratts out on tour, each talking shit about the other very nastily and very publicly. Three of the five original members reunited to cash in on their 80s popularity with guys like Quiet Riot's Carlos Cavazo filling in for Crosby and Robbie Crane for bassist Juan Croucier. After milking the teat of a nostalgia-starved generation of hair metal fortysomething fans who had money, they talked more shit about each other in the press. The most cringe-worthy comments came from drummer Bobby Blotzer, who said that Ratt was a business that he needed to continue because he wasn't a 'trust fund kid' like Warren DeMartini. Ouch. Blotz also got a book out this year for everyone to enjoy which contains several fun facts, one of those being that Bobby is a better driver when he's drunk.

The unfortunate circumstance for bands like Ratt, who essentially embody the 80s hair band movement past and mostly pitiful present, is the reversal of fortune they experienced as a result of their own hubris. Their story is motion picture fodder – meteoric rise to fame, worldwide recognition as rock superstars, with a long, unsightly drop to the bottom as victims of their own success. The bad news for Ratt is that their story is missing that happy ending piece present in other VH1 *Behind the Music* segments. Blotzer and Pearcy's feuding and the noted absence of original bass player Juan Croucier marred their latest 'triumphant' reunion tour. We all know the reunion tour is a blatant cash grab. But in Ratt's case, the ugly little man behind the curtain is exposed for all to see by the band's public comments. The Greek tragedy is real, but not romanticized and without any kind of valour or dignity. That may be because there wasn't any valour in the first place, but I was okay with the fact that the media and the record industry just wanted us to believe that it was there back in Ratt's glory days. I kinda wish Ratt had been okay with that too.

When MuchMusic debuted in Canada in 1984, the first video played on the Power Hour was W.A.S.P.'s "I Wanna Be Somebody". After I figured out that the segments repeated every four hours, I watched it again and again even though there wasn't much to it. I remarked that guitarist Chris Holmes and then-drummer Tony Richards looked like bizarre skull-faced ghouls when they made their crazy anarchy faces. I only noticed after the third or fourth viewing that frontman Blackie Lawless is actually drinking blood from the skull at the end of the vid. I did notice on the first viewing that the big W.A.S.P. sign behind the band that Blackie lights on fire initially fails to ignite on the top left side the first time though.

I was able to capture this video on VHS the following week on Wednesday afternoon, when the Power Hour was regularly scheduled. It was right in between Rail's "Fantasy" and a segment wherein Thor blows up a hot water bottle by blowing into it during an interview with J.D. Roberts. I also got Armored Saint's "Can U Deliver", Heaven's "Rock School", and Aerosmith's "Lightning Strikes". I didn't care for the Aerosmith vid and I tried to record over it with something else, finally succeeding with none other than Autograph's "Turn Up the Radio" from *Friday Night Videos*. Christ. What was I thinking? Life is funny. I had that VHS tape loaded and ready every time any of those video shows was on, hoping to pick up pretty much any metal vid I could, recording and re-recording, taping over stuff because I could never time it properly. And now, YouTube is just a couple of lazy keystrokes away.

Before I saw the W.A.S.P. video I was already very familiar with the band. The debut cassette got a lot of airtime in my player, and I used to have side one of *The Last Command* rewound and ready for insertion into my Walkman before setting out into the cold, dark winter mornings to walk to 7 a.m. basketball practice before school. Even though they were essentially facsimiles of each other with the blood and fire routine, I always kept W.A.S.P. and Motley Crue completely separate as a fan. Motley had that slight edge over W.A.S.P. based on the sexual angle that Nikki Sixx built into the band by inserting Vince Neil into the frontman slot. This strategy probably irked Lawless more than a little bit. I'm sure that actually pissed a lot of people off, particularly the members of L.A. bands like Stormer and Odin. It may have even pissed off W.A.S.P. wastecase Chris Holmes, based on that horrifying clip from Penelope Spheeris' documentary *The Decline of Western Civilization Part II: the Metal Years* that shows Holmes floating in a swimming pool downing bottles of vodka and describing himself as worthless while his mom sits and watches poolside. The fact that his mom is there witnessing this makes it that much more unnerving and horrific. Chris Holmes should have been a member of Ratt. It's probably not too late.

We used to play a drinking game with Whitesnake's *Slide It In* cassette. The contest involved playing it from the first song on side one and taking a shot every time we heard David Coverdale sing the word 'love'. After side one was over it would be a challenge to get up and turn the tape over to try and do the other side. The game improved somewhat in later years when the CD became available.

Aside from its social applications and endless proclamations of love, I always thought *Slide It In* was a really great hard rock record. The first time I heard Whitesnake was when I saw the "Slow and Easy" video. I instantly loved it. The band members all looked cool, the singer and the song sounded great, and whether or not the consummate hot chick getting strangled by her own pearl necklace was intentionally allegorical, that was cool too. It was all there. The marketing magic of music video had woven its delicious spell yet another time. Off to Wally's Music I went.

With *1987*, I realized that Coverdale had steered the good ship Whitesnake away from its bluesy hard rock roots and into the more glamourous waters of *hair band-slash-easy listening* to keep up with the Bon Jovis and the Poisons du jour. Guitarist John Sykes had been disposed of, as were bassist Neil Murray and drummer Cozy Powell. A new flashier ensemble was put in place to play all of the riffs that poor Sykes had already written for the new record before getting sacked, "Still of the Night" included, glammed up with 80s-affected harmonics and overproduction. But this was the order of the day. Coverdale knew what he had to do in order to sustain his newfound foothold in the U.S. market.

I sometimes wonder what would have happened had Coverdale simply kept the old band and released another *Slide It In*. I know that under the governance of the music business, and maybe even of band evolution, this may have been impossible. I just think it's a bit sad that Whitesnake is probably remembered more for its hair band output, considering that after a few years after Coverdale left Deep Purple he put out some decent hard rock records between 1979 and 1982 under the Whitesnake banner even prior to *Slide It In*. The underlying reason *Slide It In* was so great was because it was simple and organic. There was no makeup on it, and there was no need for any.

In essence, there were two Whitesnakes. One bluesy Brit-rock Deep Purple direct descendant, and one that was eyelinered and puckery, borne of record company capitalism to win over hair band, party rock-mad America.

It was only my interest in the former that compelled me to go along with the latter for a while, in exactly the same way I went along with Judas Priest's *Turbo* and maybe Ozzy's *The Ultimate Sin*. I did it for as long as I could, despite their blatant slickness and attempted mainstream appeal. I did it because I knew what was really in there, behind all of the packaging necessary to have any sustainability within the MTV Generation at that time.

Because somewhere in there, in that second Whitesnake, was the guy who once sang "Burn".

✵ Twelve ✵
The Pit

Among the Ratts, Cinderellas, Queensryches, W.A.S.P.s and Whitesnakes, and of course the Motleys, Maidens, Metallicas, and Metal Churches of my humble little cassette collection, are some additional tapes that I've also enjoyed in varying degrees. Every cassette I bought in the 80s is still in here, and each of these drawers speaks to my hit-and-miss odyssey as a hard rock and metal fan that bought albums based on what my gut told me.

As I mentioned earlier, sometimes I hit the bullseye and other times I missed the shooting range altogether. Icon was a great little unknown band out of Phoenix, and their self-titled debut record got plenty of airtime on my tape player. It was a bullseye. Their second record, *Night of the Crime*, which I bought excitedly at some truck stop in North Bay, was a shameless sellout and a major disappointment to me.

The first Badlands album was purchased out of sheer interest in former Ozzy guitarist Jake E. Lee. While I didn't know it would be more of a bluesy record, it was actually a welcome surprise as was Ray Gillen's superior voice. Great record. Another bullseye.

I see the first Bon Jovi cassette in here and wonder if I bought it on the strength of "Runaway". Nah. There had to be another reason. Not a bad record all in all, if you're enjoying it for what it is. Sometimes when

I listen to Springsteen I can't help but be reminded of Bon Jovi, and there's something mildly perverse about that.

Britny Fox's debut, a copy of Faster Pussycat's *Wake Me When It's Over* still in the shrink-wrapping for some reason, and a 1982 MCA copy of Diamond Head's *Borrowed Time* containing only seven songs are all in here. Metallica's original *Kill 'Em All* and *Ride the Lightning* pre-Elektra Banzai cassette releases, in addition to Slayer's *Show No Mercy* also on Banzai are also here. I once saw both of these Metallica Banzai cassettes on eBay for $2,500 each and I wonder if the seller got that for them. I wrestle with the notion of having two cassette tapes possibly worth five thousand dollars in my collection.

Helix's *No Rest for the Wicked* was one of the first cassettes I ever bought, because it had a song called "Heavy Metal Love" on it. Of course this song had little to do with heavy metal, because Helix was never a heavy metal band. I was also intrigued by the fact that the band was from Kitchener, and that in their travels across Ontario they actually had played in Espanola at some point in the late 70s at a place called The Pit. The Pit was a bar in the basement of an old rundown establishment called The Espanola Hotel. It was directly across from the paper mill, which pretty much guaranteed the establishment a daily revenue stream. This guarantee was further secured by the fact that The Pit was also a strip joint, one that did not card its patrons at the door no matter their known or presumed ages.

I used to go to The Pit when I was sixteen with some guys who were considered the in-crowd at our school. The funny thing about going there with these guys was that the tacit coolness I always faked when I was out with them was really amped up in a place like The Pit. I guess because we were in the company of older guys who drank there. There were a few peculiar anthropological rules that always applied in The Pit. Most of these were rooted in insecurity and passive aggression, and some others I haven't completely figured out to this day.

In The Pit, it wasn't cool to look at the strippers for longer than a couple of seconds. If you did, it was like it was some sign of weakness or something. Nobody who was cool ever did that. It was also very uncool to demonstrate in any way that you looked excited, surprised, shocked, panicked, or happy that you were drinking Molson Golden in a strip club at age sixteen. It was supposed to look like it was no big deal. Normal, run-of-the-mill stuff. Maybe even boring. It certainly was not boring for me, man. The assumption that any of this was normal was the biggest joke ever. Almost funnier than the fact that every member in this in-crowd group made it clear, in one way or another, that they had never masturbated. Ever. Because if you had, you were gay. And thus by default very uncool.

I have to admit that I had a difficult time navigating all of these rules. As a sixteen-year-old it was hard for me to be nonchalant when I was in the same room as a girl who was taking off her clothes and writhing around on the floor a couple of feet away. These girls would all dance to three songs, and they would all follow the exact same routine each time. The first song was dancing, and the top came off at the end of the song. The second song was also dancing, and the bottoms came off towards the end of that song. The third song was called 'the floor show'. During this song, which was always a ballad, the young lady dragged a blanket to the front of the stage and there was no dancing.

It was okay to have a look at what was on offer at this juncture, but only for a second. And only in a disinterested way, like it was a mechanical course of procedure. Making the same kinds of faces Mike Damone did in *Fast Times at Ridgemont High* would have been considered cool. Like you were doing the girl a favour by acknowledging her while she bent over backwards (and forwards) to entertain you. So ridiculous.

Alright, back to these cassettes.

In looking at Dokken's first album, the cassette that I bought along with *Kill 'Em All*, *All For One*, and *Show No Mercy* because of the band logo, I see that the liner notes list Ratt's Juan Croucier as the bass player, not Jeff Pilson. Hmmm. Didn't notice that before, or know that was even the case until now.

There's all kinds of stuff in this collection that I had long forgotten about. Flotsam and Jetsam's *No Place For Disgrace*, Riot's *Restless Breed*, a copy of Frehley's Comet *Live + 1* with a hole punched through the spine of the cassette case like a used deck of Vegas cards. Jetboy's *Feel the Shake*, a tape I bought hoping every song would sound like the title track. Not so. Helloween's 1985 five song EP released on Banzai with the 'this side' and 'that side' labeling in the place of side one and side two. Most definitely a bullseye. Kingdom Come's debut record, Keel's *The Final Frontier*, Kix's *Blow My Fuse*, Kreator's *Terrible Certainty*, Laaz Rockit's *City's Gonna Burn*, Michael Schenker Group's *Built to Destroy*, Tokyo Blade's *Midnight Rendezvous*, and Y&T's *Mean Streak*. I might be tempted to play a couple of these if I had a tape player.

Here's the rare 1983 Ratt EP, whose liner notes contain this message, devoid of syntax: *'to all our families and all heavy metalists and dangerous women everywhere'*. Heavy metalists? Blotzer must have been responsible for that. In among the special thanks list of the Ratt EP, rife with family members and unfamiliar names, is Scorpions drummer Herman Rarebell. Makes me wonder what the relevance is.

As I continue to pull open these drawers and investigate their content, I'm reminded that there are some really lousy and obscure albums in this collection that I don't remember buying at all. Ruthless' completely unremarkable *Metal Without Mercy*, Samain's *Vibrations of Doom*, Sanctuary's *Refuge Denied*, Heathen's *Breaking the Silence*, and USA Warrior's *Fighting For the Earth*. Vinnie Vincent's two solo records are also here. And as clowny as they are, I actually wouldn't mind listening to them. Probably only once though.

I move on to some of the more obscure cassettes that spent a lot of time in the player back in my high school days. If you're like me and you like the *chu-chu-chug* muted note guitar riffing, Malice is your band. I was always disappointed that this band wasn't bigger than they were, but I wasn't surprised. I think that people didn't necessarily know what to do with Malice, because the band couldn't be compartmentalized. They sounded like a slightly less heavy version of Judas Priest, but a heavier version of Ratt. They weren't as good looking as most hair bands, but dressed better than most of them. It's funny, because the individually posed pictures of the band on the sleeve of their *License to Kill* record actually look nothing like the band. The shots of guitarist Jay Reynolds and singer James Neal may as well be of someone else entirely. Tricky bastards.

Malice didn't have any videos that I ever saw, and I have no idea why I bought *License to Kill*, nor any recollection of buying it. I'm assuming it had something to do with the calm and collected chap on the front cover who appears to be wearing panty hose over his head and swinging a hatchet. Spillover from my Lizzy Borden fascination maybe. I loved the *License to Kill* record and I still listen to it regularly, despite the demo inclusions of "Murder" and "Vigilante" that appear on the CD I bought a few years back on eBay.

I'm ambivalent when it comes to bands adding demo version material to re-releases. On one hand, hearing demo tracks of songs that you've already heard is kinda like gaining access to a behind-the-scenes vantage point. It allows for a greater insight and perspective into the work, which can be really cool. The problem is that you may not care to have witnessed the laid bare performance because sometimes, it ain't pretty. It can conflict so drastically with the finished product that it may actually take away from your interest in the band. In Malice's case, I almost wish I hadn't heard the demos. Neal's singing is so out of key he sounds like a drunken karaoke enthusiast. Vastly different from the slick finished version that appeared on the original record.

This is detrimental because it opens up the possibility that the quality of his vocal on the mixed and mastered record may have been purely attributable to studio trickery. Every musician benefits from the studio perks, but some much more than others. It's the exact same scenario that Motley Crue proposed when they released the demos for the "Shout at the Devil" and "Looks That Kill" tracks on a *Shout at the Devil* re-release. It wasn't terribly surprising that Vince Neil would sound like shite on the demos, but Jesus. I generally appreciate bands sharing that stuff but when I heard those demos, I developed a newfound respect for the musical wherewithal of record producers like Tom

Werman. It took big balls for Motley Crue to let those demos see the light of day, even if it was financially motivated. But it took even bigger cojones for Malice to do it, because Motley had already made their money and nothing to lose. Poor Malice had nothing to gain.

Of the more lesser-known cassettes in this collection, Dangerous Toys' debut is one of the better ones. I liked that Dangerous Toys didn't just sound like the standard twelve bar boogie hair metal band. They came from Texas and they sounded like it. It's a shame that bands like this who didn't necessarily sound like anyone else but who have obvious talent, didn't do well for themselves in the rock and roll sweepstakes. But Dangerous Toys had a vague pre-Kalodner Aerosmith vibe combined with a heavier sound that didn't really fall into line with musical trends of the day. Around the time Dangerous Toys came on to the scene Aqua Net and Revlon were mainstays in hard rock, but judging by the picture of Toys' frontman Jason McMaster in the liner notes, he'd likely blacken your eyes at the suggestion of applying mascara to his. And yet, the band exudes a self-deprecating disposition throughout their debut record, not taking themselves nearly as seriously as the aforementioned picture might suggest. In fact, on songs like the goofy "Sportin' a Woody", Dangerous Toys comes closest to sounding like just another Sunset Strip throwaway act. The album is full of disparities, enough to perplex the listener into wondering what DT was really about. But this worked to the advantage of the band, whether it was intentional or not. Like Malice, they couldn't quite be compartmentalized despite their being lumped in with the hair metal movement at large and marketed alongside the likes of Warrant.

Guns N' Roses were another band that bristled in the company of their hair band peers, and while Dangerous Toys had something of a Guns look and released their debut around the same time, they had little else in common. The first Dangerous Toys record didn't light the world on fire but there were some great songs on it – "Queen of the Nile", "Scared", "Ten Boots" and "Take Me Drunk" make it a really interesting listen. Hell, pretty much every song was good, except album closer "That Dog" and filler "Feels like a Hammer". The lyrics aren't your typical garden-variety *fire / desire* rhyming couplet fare, even though most of the songs rely on the drink-fuck-fight construct most hard rock and metal fans have in their DNA. What made this record unique and listenable through multiple spins was that blend of disarming, self-effacing charm with believable, colourful, shitkicking hard rock, which provided the suggestion that the band was capable of transcending a genre dominated by Poison clones.

Inversely, some bands don't care about being clones if that's what it takes to make it. And as is always the case in the wake of a new(ish) musical movement, there are millions of these secondary and tertiary unsigned bands teeming through the system. There was a group out of Detroit in the 80s called Halloween (not at all resembling German speed metal outfit Helloween) that could have represented every one of these bands that, but for any of a multitude of unfortunate reasons, didn't make it. The interesting thing about Halloween is that when you experience them, it occurs to you that they're basically the 'before' version of a Motley Crue or a W.A.S.P..

Halloween brings most every pre-requisite to the table that Motley did. They had a competent guitar player with plenty of great metal riffs. They had a weak singer that made up for his chops visually. An evil and mysterious bass player. A flashy drummer that probably could have faked being on par with Tommy Lee. And it was all united by the consummate dark, ambiguous, evil leather-n-spikes image and a huge reliance on a carnival-like stage show. In fact Halloween almost out-Motleys Motley Crue on this 1985 cassette, *Don't Metal with Evil*. The only real difference between *Shout at the Devil*-era Motley Crue and Halloween is that the latter didn't have a guiding force behind them like Motley did in the team of the aforementioned producer Tom Werman, Doc McGhee, Doug Thaler, Geoff Workman, Tom Zutaut, and whoever else was involved in a corporate capacity.

I only came across Halloween while watching an obscure late night video program that was broadcast out of Detroit called *The Beat*, hosted by some WKRP-looking dude with a fivehead* and big glasses so thick he could probably see germs with them. Ironically, Motley Crue was co-hosting the show. It must have been around late 1985 since they were wearing their *Theatre of Pain* getups and were past the black leather and pentagrams stage at that point. Halloween's video for "What a Nice Place" played, and it instantly captured my attention visually but also aurally. I only happened to see this vid by chance, since *The Beat* played mostly local unsigned talent, and I only happened to catch the show while toggling through the three or four channels we had in Espy at the time. The video was amateur, but there was something special about this band that made me wonder why they never got picked up by a major because even I could contemplate them in their 'after' version. I don't think the songs Motley Crue brought into the studio for the *Shout at the Devil* sessions were that far beyond the Halloween songs featured on *Don't Metal with Evil* in terms of quality. In fact, I think that *Don't Metal with Evil* is basically *Shout at the Devil* without the refinement and makeover abilities of Team McGhee. Yeah, *Don't Metal with Evil* has an ample amount of awkwardly cheesy moments. And yeah, the band goes to the well one or two times more than they should have with elements like the use of feedback and vocal delay. But rookie hindrances like these were most likely abundant on the *Shout* demos too. Brian Thomas' vocals on *Don't Metal with Evil* might be slightly slipshod, but we all know that Vince Neil's vocals before any magical mixing was performed were no better than the average loutish drunk at your local after-hours booze can. *Don't Metal with Evil* wasn't given the opportunity to become, with all of that record company-backed professional songwriting mentorship and skillful studio refinement and production, the polished final product that *Shout at the Devil* was. I often wonder what it would sound like if it had.

I also wonder why no one else saw that spark in the band that I saw. Was it because Halloween was located in Detroit and not L.A.?

---

* *Bigger than a forehead*

After all, had Philly's Cinderella not been seen live by Jon Bon Jovi in a chance encounter, they may not have had the career they did. Was Halloween just slightly behind the times with the spooky faux-goth theme in 1985, already beaten to the punch by Motley Crue and W.A.S.P. a couple of years earlier? It's hard to believe that nobody was willing to sign this band.

Maybe Halloween should have picked up and moved to Hollywood. There was plenty of appetite for theatre there, even that of which not implied. Lizzy Borden's stage show was full of malevolent theatrics, implied and otherwise, and their *Love You to Pieces* cassette was the perfect record for budding young sociopaths everywhere.

I listened to this cassette a helluva lot. While the music was great, it was only ever an enabler for Lizzy Borden's image. Which, really, was my main fixation. What I may not have realized as a Borden fan in 1985 is that the lyrics and imagery that comprised Lizzy Borden's overall dictum to me as an observer, may have actually made the songs themselves seem to be of a higher quality. Bands like Lizzy Borden, as KISS and Motley Crue had before them, offered an additional channel of opportunity for involvement through connection with fantastical imagery. The offer is based purely on escapism, catering specifically to an audience most likely lacking something in their everyday lives. The elements are completely unrealistic, but they suffice as an alternative in navigating the conflicts posed by everyday society. At its core, heavy metal as a genre acknowledges and provides unrealistic resolutions to an audience with very real social needs. And this was Lizzy Borden's *raison d'etre*.

Also gracing my cassette collection is TKO's *In Your Face*. In an email I sent to Martin Popoff responding to his review of this record, I commented that lead singer Brad Sinsel was the Rodney Dangerfield of 80s hair rock. I initially said this in a sarcastic way, but I actually might have been on to something the more I think about it.

In Your Face's cover features a shot of a glammed-up Sinsel (that again, looks nothing like him) standing over a vanquished requisite big-haired hottie lying at his feet presumably unconscious, and wearing only Everlast trunks and a pair of boxing gloves that just so happen to be covering her otherwise nekkid boobies. It would appear that the boxing gloves didn't do her any good against Sinsel. I'm wondering if Sinsel and his band are just overt misogynists, or if maybe this damsel is perhaps the engineer or some other person responsible for the mastering of this record, because it's bloody terrible. I actually like the *In Your Face* material and I bought the CD later anticipating an improved sound quality, but it was equally poor. And, there's a picture of poor Brad in the CD liner that makes him look like a late-period Liz Taylor. So not quite a bullseye.

✵ Thirteen ✵
Everybody Wants To Go To Heaven, But Nobody Wants To Die

Apart from all of these hard rock and heavy metal bands from my cassette collection and beyond, there are hundreds of bands from the genre that I didn't listen to for any multitude of reasons. The most popular reasons most likely had to do with a band's songs, singer, or style. Or, there were bands like Junkyard that I may not have known about until much later that I actually *did* like when I eventually heard them. I decided to make a list of these bands and provide some speculation as to why they were excluded from my teenage hard rock and metal adventures. There are a million of them, but here are the ones that instantly come to mind:

Motorhead
Venom
Krokus
Saxon
Megadeth
Keel
Tesla
Van Hagar

T.T. Quick
Overkill
Black 'n Blue
Trixter
Firehouse
Danger Danger
Tuff
Pretty Boy Floyd
Bang Tango
L.A. Guns
Junkyard
D'Molls
Love Hate
Kik Tracee
Enuff Z'Nuff
Pretty Maids
Giuffria
Tigertailz
Vain
Sleeze Beez

Find a comfy chair, because I have something to say about every one of these acts. And Poison too.

One of the main determinants in whether or not I could get into a band, and still is, is whether or not I like the singer. The lead vocalist is the representative focal point of the band and if I don't like the singer vocally or otherwise, I tend to take a pass on the band as a whole. I look at it this way - the relationship between a band and its singer is directly parallel to the relationship between a woman's face and her body as they relate to her overall level of attractiveness. A woman with a beautiful face and a lumpy body gets a lot more latitude than an ugly woman with a smashing body. That's just the way that it is. A rock band's level of positive reception works within the same context. The band could be comprised of crack virtuoso musicians that write and perform great songs, but if the singer isn't cutting it in some way for the audience, the group ain't happening.

When I was first exposed to Motorhead in the mid-80s, it was like, *"Who the fuck are these geezers?"*. It was obvious that bandleader Lemmy was a card-carrying rock and roll cretin, but I completely missed his point back then thanks to my childhood KISS programming.

I think the first time I had ever heard Motorhead was at the same basketball camp where I first met Garvey. There were a lot of fifteen and sixteen-year-olds from all over the place at this camp that spent the week in the same residence, and there was a lot of fraternizing going on at night. There were these two French guys from somewhere north of Sudbury who shared the last room at the end of the hall, and one of them was named Gilles. Gilles smoked, was kinda paunchy, wore wife-beaters, and had a moustache and enough back hair to make him look like a man amongst a bunch of teenage boys. He spoke in that heavy French accent, the one you could only have from growing up in the farther reaches of northern Ontario. Gilles also carried himself with a certain Jeff Spicoli flavour.

He blasted Motorhead's "Ace of Spades" when I was in his room one day and I thought it was a riot. It was perfectly representative of Gilles and his fuck-it attitude, but for me the music was more jokey than anything else. I didn't *get* Motorhead back then, partly because I dismissed the band as bordering on hard rock and metal parody (dubious observation considering some of the bands in my cassette collection at the time), but also because Lemmy's voice wasn't at all to my tastes back then. I still don't own a Motorhead record, but now I respect and understand why they're as celebrated as they are. And I love Lemmy. Motorhead is a great example of why it's important to take the time to stick your head inside and take a really good look around to make a properly informed assessment rather than sitting back and dismissing the book on the merits of its cover. That being the case, I still snicker like Beavis whenever I hear "Ace of Spades".

With Venom, I took the same look around but there wasn't anything in there. I will say though, that after seeing the "Witching Hour" video a few times on the MuchMusic *Power Hour*, I was captivated by the concept of how a band could be so good at being truly horrible in the way that Venom was. It's a rare trait that few bands have pulled off over the years.

Krokus ran afoul of my vocalist rule on every front. Singer Marc Storace pushed all my buttons with his voice, his grey tights with knee-highs, and his attitude. The 70s afro didn't score any points either. With Storace as their frontman, Krokus struck me as the favourite band of that guy who makes a point of cracking his neck with or without the use of his hands in a public place, usually a crowded elevator. I gave *The Blitz* a few spins back in the day, but I borrowed it based solely on the strength of that femme fatale in their "Midnite Maniac" video. I watched the video again just now on YouTube, and then I read some of the comments. Turns out I was right about Krokus' fan base.

I bought Saxon's *Power & the Glory* on cassette in 1983, but I never really developed an interest in the band beyond a few interesting riffs here and there. Not sure why, but it was probably because they didn't have an image to compete with Priest, Maiden, or Motley. Fickle teenage me.

There was a glut of crappy thrash metal bands, and a handful of good ones who actually *got* it. And even though Dave Mustaine and Megadeth certainly did get it, as I mentioned earlier, I just couldn't get past Mustaine's vocals. I bought Megadeth's debut cassette when it came out. It featured "Mechanix", which was the reworking of "The Four Horsemen", one of four songs he was involved in writing with Metallica before his firing. The cassette didn't do anything for me. It just sounded so bloody laboured, and the production was lousy. As much as I hate to say so, I think my disdain for the record could be partly attributed to Mustaine's sacking from Metallica.

I reached my own conclusion that the album was a foreign, amateurish version of *Kill 'Em All*, and that Dave Mustaine was just an embittered cast-off that didn't deserve my attention. I did keep an eye on Megadeth as they progressed however, and did some occasional sampling over the years, like buying *Youthanasia* for "Reckoning Day" and "Train of Consequences". I liked the band much more later on, but that cursed vocal still prevented me from really getting into the band. That coupled with the fact that Mustaine always seemed so overwrought by this intense *hatred*. It made him seem petty and small. Metal bands generally have a tone of aggression that comes across in their image without it tempering their likeability. Yet Mustaine always seemed to always have this ultra-nihilistic nastiness about him that went beyond the standard, even for thrash. He just seemed like he was too affected by the Metallica thing, and it seemed like everything Megadeth did was done reactively to something that Metallica had done.

The other day I saw Mustaine's autobiography in the bookstore and picked it up. I shouldn't have, because at the moment I have five books going that I really need to finish up (Ian Christe's *The Van Halen Saga*, Richard Dawkins' *The God Delusion*, Keith Richards' *Life* biography, Carl Goldberg's *Speaking With the Devil*, and some financial investment book I don't remember the name of but don't feel like going upstairs to check). But, I had read a snippet of Mustaine's book in the store and while I knew that it would be interesting based on his retelling of the Metallica dismissal, I kinda wanted to see if the book could turn me around on Mustaine. Not by reading his account of the events that shaped Megadeth's career (because I thought I more or less knew how that would go), but more so to hear his account and draw my own conclusions based on whether I thought he was full of shit or not. And, I had an upcoming flight from Toronto to Munich to kill, so I figured I might be able to read the whole Mustaine autobiography while on board. I can't sleep on planes.

I finished reading the last page of the book just as the flight was touching down in Deutschland, and Mustaine's memoirs were compelling enough to distract me from thinking too much about the fact that I was one human error away from getting more closely acquainted with the Atlantic Ocean at 800 miles an hour. Jensen 1, giant squid and other mysteries of the deep 0. But the book was more than just a distraction. I enjoyed reading it for the most part.

It was a bit sad that Mustaine had to live most of his life in the long, dark shadow of his former band Metallica, based on the kind of guy he was – already seething with hatred before joining Metallica as the result of all manner of emotional trauma and weirdness endured in his childhood. The unfortunate aspect of Mustaine's ouster from Metallica is that complicity was initially a wash. Mustaine was consistently acting like a drunken asshole and couldn't be tolerated any longer, and Lars Ulrich and the rest of Metallica sorted things out by kicking him out of the band and sending him home on a bus from New York to California with no money. Score settled. Until, of course, Metallica went on to rip up the metal world in the 80s and then popular music at large in the 90s, leaving Mustaine in their wake and never looking back.

It sucked to be Mustaine before, but it really sucked after that – a point Mustaine makes light of in Metallica's documentary *Some Kind of Monster*. In the documentary, Mustaine makes references to his dismissal resulting from his 'disease', meaning his excessive drinking. Alcoholism isn't a disease. It's a coping mechanism. Mustaine had deeper-seated issues that gave rise to his alcoholism and these issues were the real impetus behind his dismissal, but he didn't acknowledge these facts or take responsibility for them in his emotional reunion with Ulrich.

Mustaine's book spells the issues out clearly. There is much evidence of the severe self-esteem damage he'd suffered in his younger travails at so many points throughout. He mentions how badass a fighter he is on way too many occasions. He reminds the reader countless times that he is a superior guitar player. He notes more than once that his *'fingers dance across the fretboard'*. Ech. But it's easy to see where that insecurity and overcompensation comes from.

Towards the end of his book Mustaine describes his seventeenth meltdown, this one different from the first sixteen because it actually puts his marriage in jeopardy along with the prospect of losing his kids. In response, Mustaine gets sorted. At last, he finally beats drugs and alcohol after seventeen rehab visits. At the same time, he finds the lord and becomes a Christian. And by his account, he was only able to get clean because he 'gave' himself to Jesus Christ.

Mustaine's diatribe about finding god is superficially disappointing because of the relationship between religion and life cycle. No one is interested in god when they're young and virile, out drinking and screwing and tearing the world up. Mustaine certainly wasn't. Religious faith tends to come into the picture later, at a point of weakness. It comes along when people get older. Not necessarily after they've lost their sense of invincibility in their later twenties or early thirties, but not too long after they start to contemplate the inevitability of their own mortality and begin to be more cognizant of the remainder of the road ahead. They need a magic crutch, and the ambiguity and convenience of the Jesus concept suits this purpose sufficiently. And now, The Original Cynic, Dave Mustaine was leaning on that crutch.

By Mustaine's own account, he seemed to have kicked substances on his own. And yet for some reason, he gave credit to religion for this achievement. This is the source of the real disappointment. Mustaine was faced with a grave dilemma – get sorted or lose your wife and kids, and maybe your life while you're at it – and he did it. The real reason he was successful was because his maturity finally took hold. Mustaine made mention in the book that everyone deals with addictions and substances differently. What that really means is, everyone has varying levels of emotional maturity. Sooner or later it kicks in and allows you to take stock and suck it up. Which is what Mustaine did.

Dave Mustaine's story isn't the first, and it won't be the last. Horrible home life growing up, mind-warping religious dogma drilled into the head. Defence mechanisms created against it out of fear and anger. Some of us notice that the fear and anger lends itself to great purity in artistic output. But the pain can't last. The intensity subsides and the pain is quelled. Wisdom and maturity present themselves eventually if suicide or recklessness resulting in death was avoided in youth.

From this perspective, Mustaine is finally a winner. A hero, maybe. But his heroism is heartbreakingly tragic because for all of his overcompensation bravura, he can't bring himself to accept credit for his greatest achievement of all. Mustaine likely can't comfortably acknowledge the fact that he accomplished such a feat himself, and feels the need to defer to a placebo rather than fully embrace the feeling of true pride and genuine self-worth. If anyone feels bad for Dave Mustaine, including Mustaine himself, it should be for this reason. Not for being kicked out of Metallica.

Jesus sells, but Dave Mustaine sold his soul to the wrong devil.

Though they have absolutely nothing at all in common with Megadeth, Keel is another band whose singer soured me in the 80s, and that consideration is even more pronounced when I listen now. It's clear that on *The Right to Rock* frontman Ron Keel sang like Christina Aguilera did on her records - with one big continuous self-aggrandizing vocal throughout the entire song. It's not that Keel's voice is bad, but it's not exceptional either. His vocals are done in such an overambitious way that he could never possibly deliver on the level that he's leading the listener to believe he performs at. It's unnecessary overkill. It's the same overkill, in fact, as when Keel's old Steeler band mate, Yngwie Malmsteen, noodled through endless million-note solos on his guitar. Poor Yngwie. So ridiculously talented but so misguided. Yngwie was like that exceptionally hot chick that was pathetically vain, dramatically posing and making a seductive pucker face whenever there was a camera in the vicinity. It just ruins it for everyone. In Keel's case, and Yngwie's too for that matter, more was unfortunately less.

Speaking of seductive pucker faces, I wish I could say Poison was on my list of bands that I didn't listen to, but in all honestly I can't. I did have a Poison album, though I don't remember which one it was. I remember thinking that Poison was like that little pre-packaged sushi number you see in the deli section of your supermarket. It doesn't carry a lot of substance or quality, it's not at all good for you, but it's there to satisfy a spontaneous jones. And if you recognize it for what it is in and of itself without comparing it to anything else, you can secretly enjoy it and derive a certain pleasure from it. I will say that these days I enjoy sushi in Japanese restaurants without exception, however.

No Sleep 'til Sudbury

I never understood how a hard rock band could be so fascinated with an obscure scientist. I think the main thrust behind Tesla's devotion to inventor Nikola Tesla stemmed from the fact that they were trying to shed some light on the fact that Tesla was the actual inventor of the radio, and not Guglielmo Marconi, as popular legend would have us think. Regardless, still not sure why a gang of dirty rock degenerates, the leader of which being a former cement truck driver, would take such an activistic and noble stance on this topic to the point of actually naming their band after him and carrying on about his trials and tribulations in the liner notes of their records. Little bit weird.

Before they changed their name at the suggestion of their manager, they called themselves City Kidd, which I suppose is a weaker name. Or is it? Back in the day, I passed on Tesla and the name was one of the reasons I did. I vaguely knew who Nikola Tesla was from Grade 11 physics class, and school and rock and roll had no business intermingling in my mind back then. Unless it was in the context of Australian hard rock outfit Heaven's "Rock School". For all I knew Tesla was some kind of douchey prog band.

Then I heard "Signs". Strike two.

I thoroughly disliked the song and still do. I got the wrong message from the band. The fact that Geffen didn't seem to put a lot of effort into marketing Tesla didn't help their cause much either. I had never seen any of their videos, and they didn't really seem to be out there as much as the other hard rock and hair band b-listers like BulletBoys and Britny Fox. Had I seen the video for "Modern Day Cowboy" things would have been much different. I would have most likely bought the record on the strength of that one song alone. It almost seems like Tesla were disadvantaged by being lumped in with the Poisons and the Warrants of the time, when in actual fact they were more akin to a no-frills AC/DC style. There were loads of bands like that on the scene, like Johnny Crash and Dirty Looks, that opted for the Guns N' Roses sans-pouting lipsticked approach, but the "Signs" cover misfired as a single. Tesla was like a man without a hard rock country.

But y'know, I kick myself now. Just a couple of years ago, after hearing "Modern Day Cowboy", I decided that Tesla must have a couple more songs in their catalogue that sounded more like this and less like "Signs". So I previewed their four studio records on iTunes, and I found out they did indeed. I went on a big Tesla kick after that. Bought all four CDs and listened to them in order of release. I started in on the second one, 1989's *The Great Radio Controversy* after hearing their first record, 1986's *Mechanical Resonance*, about 10 times or so end to end. It's fantastic, and I think it's so funny that I somehow completely missed this record. I likely overlooked the peculiar cover and crappy song titles at the record store. Despite the titles, most of the songs stood up. Particularly "Modern Day Cowboy". My favourite aspect of the record, and maybe the band, is that singer Jeff Keith sounds like the hybrid product of a Gregor Mendelian cross-pollination of Steven Tyler and the Black Crowes' Chris Robinson. After having heard the remainder of Tesla's essential catalogue, 1991's *Psychotic Supper* and 1994's *Bust a Nut*, I realized that I had made the mistake of overlooking one of the most underrated hard rock bands of their ill-fated time.

While I was listening to these 'new' records, as I do any time I listen to music outside a social setting, I set aside time and focus completely on the recording. I usually do this on Friday nights, upstairs in the music room of my house. This is where my main stereo system is located, along with a couple of sofas and all of my guitars and other musical gear. I have to be alone during these sessions, which means no talking. Interruption is frowned upon. As such, Alison can be nonplussed by the Gestapo-like conditions imposed during listening time. But you won't find me chatting her up during an airing of *The Young & the Restless*, so things even themselves out.

I'm actually pretty lucky. Alison's fine with *The Boneyard, Hair Nation,* and Eddie Trunk's show being on the radio during our hour-plus work commute during the week. We joke about the importance of these Friday night listening sessions, because even though I'm afforded these satellite radio liberties during our commute, I cite examples like the one that happened just the other day. Ace Frehley's "Rocket Ride"* was playing on *The Boneyard*. Just as the best part was about to come on, the crescendo of the song, that part at 2:22 just before the solo where Frehley ad-libs the *"Grab a hold of my rocket!"* vocal, I reach for the volume control to crank it and open my mouth to sing along, when Alison says, *"We should stop and pick up some cheese bread"*.

Dang.

Now, it's important to clarify that the suggestion of cheese bread consumption or anything else Alison says is never ignored or discounted. Never has been. We both understand why there is a need for solitude during the Friday night listening sessions. She's really awesome about all this stuff, and this is one of the reasons I married her. We coalesce in the same logic.

For example, Alison shares my theory that men (and women) should be given a period of three seconds to visually familiarize themselves with a woman's breasts at the beginning of any social interaction if they're being advertised by the woman in even a mildly suggestive manner. If you count it out, even in Mississippies, three seconds is just enough time without compromising the borders of lechery. The reasoning here is that this three-second timeframe would eliminate uncomfortable leering and any shifty-eyed weirdness during the interaction. The point is that guys are going to look either way at some point anyway. That's just a scientific fact that can't be refuted. If they're out there, they're going to be observed. We all know that. And if the boobs are being put out there, it's not by accident. So why not just cut through that bullshit social tango that everyone pretends isn't going on and just take the three seconds, familiarize, and be done with it? No need for any further looking after that, no comments, no disrespectfulness, no weirdness, and on to the next piece of business. It's obvious that respect is the catalyst of this theory and that the only downfall involved is the absence of respect, but that's up to the individual. I've always been of the opinion that this approach just makes more sense for everyone

---

* Yes, "Rocket Ride" is technically a KISS song, but we all know that this was exclusively a Frehley song, that he worked up in his home studio in Connecticut and mailed to the rest of the band because he hated being in KISS at that point.

involved. Plain and simple. Alison supports the theory, for no other reason but because it's logical.

Van Halen with Sammy Hagar was like Axl Rose and his newest collection of musical ringers – both bands should have been called something other than their original name. I know that Edward Van was the real bandleader in VH throughout each of its permutations, and *yada yada yada*, but I consider Van Hagar a completely separate entity from Roth-era Van Halen. In fact, they actually could have called the band Van Hagar (I think it was actually suggested to them at some point). And I'm not knocking Van Hagar, because Sammy really does seem like one of the nicest, most humble guys in the business. And I like that. He's the kind of guy you'd want to go on a massive bender with. As much as I like David Lee Roth, I sense that he may *not* be that guy. Regardless, Van Hagar and Van Halen don't mix. I don't even compare them to each other. They exist on two completely separate planes. My attitude towards Van Hagar is more agnostic than atheist. I don't oppose, I just politely look the other way.

Bands like Firehouse, Danger Danger, and Trixter were at the forefront of a movement in the late 80s and early 90s that homogenized hard rock and metal to make them more digestible in the mainstream, in the same way that country music was diluted and 'popified' to make it more marketable to a larger audience a few years later. I knew nothing about these bands other than what they represented, and I wasn't interested. Danger Danger's tacky flamboyance and overly juvenile sexual wordplay made me want to vomit. There were so many more of these bands, the also-rans that emerged to clog up the landscape in the wake of a genre explosion - Southgang, McQueen Street, Sweet FA, Pretty Boy Floyd, Tuff, and on and on and on. I don't profess to know a lot about these bands, but there wasn't really any need. I do know that Tuff singer Stevie Rachelle founded the Metal Sludge website, which was a brilliant idea and has been a source of a lot of laughs and great information for me since the late 90s. Rachelle definitely gets it.

In the hair rock genre, there was no artistic or musical integrity. The movement was more about the pursuit of debauchery than it was about music, especially for the second and third tier bands that sprouted up post-Warrant and Poison. Fame, the endgame in this pursuit, was just an enabler to raise the debauchery level to stratospheric proportions. Unlimited access to record company money was converted into more and better drugs, more and better girls, and newfound controls over those who had previously controlled. It was about getting fucked up, getting laid, being in absolute and complete control of how often you were able to do both, and raising a middle finger to anybody who stood in the way of these objectives.

In this sense it was a dirtier, sleazier version of rock and roll. Hair rock was obviously not at all about musical depth or sophistication. The over-the-top glitter-glammy posturing that was the order of the day in this period was initially ironic, because the use of supposed beautification elements like Revlon and Aqua Net were spat back into the face of the establishment and mocked by otherwise unhygienic men-urchins who wore it to the degree where you might have difficulty being able to tell if they were actually in fact men. The real irony lies in the question of whether or not these guys understood this, or if this behaviour was just cribbing from the 70s glam movement to get some attention that might translate into stardom. And maybe some exploration into their own homoerotic identities too.

For whatever reason, the last group of bands on my list - Bang Tango, Junkyard, D'Molls, Enuff Z'Nuff, Kik Tracee, and Love Hate - just weren't accessible to me despite the fact that I shelled out for the cassettes of most of their contemporaries. As lengthy as they may have been, I suppose their marketing tentacles couldn't reach me all the way up there in Espy. I hadn't even heard of some of these bands until much later. In Bang Tango's case, I was exposed to singer Joe Leste's band Beautiful Creatures first. I initially liked the Beautiful Creatures debut record but eventually soured on it after I realized how desperate it sounded in trying to straddle the old and 'new' hard rock eras. And while I thought that Bang Tango was a band that did well to operate a bit left of the Sunset Strip centre with some unique approaches to hair band songwriting, something about Leste prevented me from being interested in making room for him and his band. Can't put my finger on it.

I heard Junkyard for the first time by accident in 1998, on a Rhino Records compilation CD that I bought for TNT's rifftastic "10,000 Lovers in One". I was delighted to discover that the CD contained some surprise gems in D'Molls' "D'Stroll", Enuff Z'Nuff's "New Thing", and Junkyard's "Hollywood", all songs I would have loved to have heard ten years earlier. It also contained a Pretty Maids song "Future World" that was my first and last sampling of Pretty Maids (see singer as band focal point and beautiful woman with unattractive body analogy). I loved "Hollywood" and checked out a few other Junkyard songs, like "Blooze", but didn't really follow up on it at all. As far as Enuff Z'Nuff went, I wrote them off immediately for their poor choice in band names. However, I can't dispute the fact that their biggest single, "Fly High Michelle" is an incredible composition loaded with hooky melodies that deserved much more attention than it got. It kinda reminds me of The Beatles' "Something", in that "Something" is an outstanding song but because George Harrison wrote it, it was doomed to languish in the shadow of the Lennon and McCartney compositions. "Fly High Michelle" may well have been one of the best hair rock songs ever written, but because of the command bands like Poison have over the hair rock faithful, "Every Rose Has Its Thorn" will always obscure its real value.

Giuffria did not have representation in my cassette collection, but their song "Call To The Heart" has one of those strangely compelling melodies that immediately took me by surprise when I heard it for the first time. As I listened, it challenged me to consider why I liked it so much. My only explanation is that sometimes notes can line up a certain way to form a melody that just takes hold of you beyond explanation.

Giuffria hasn't given me any reason to like them otherwise, but I will admit that I love this chorus. It's like that piano intro arrangement in Coldplay's "Trouble" – an insanely compelling melody is derived from a sparse piano line.

And a good song is a good song, no matter who writes it.

Welsh hair band Tigertailz got my attention in the same way. Their obligatory hair ballad, "Heaven", stands out among others because of that additional chord in the chorus that changes the entire harmony. The performance of the song is standard hair band fromage, but the chorus arrangement makes it attractive.

Another band from across the pond, Netherlands' Sleeze Beez, eluded my attentions in the 80s despite my regular perusal of *Kerrang!*. Of course, with a name like that I would have overlooked them anyway unless they had a video in rotation in Canadian markets as fellow Norsemen Shotgun Messiah did (though they relocated to Hollywood). I heard Sleeze Beez last year for the first time, and I liked them enough to dig through their catalogue a bit. I definitely would have dug them in the 80s. Despite the obvious glam overtones, the Beez were a bit more edgy and more palatable than that cluster of Warrant-lite hair bands that would swell the genre to its inevitable and bloated critical mass point. The hair band schema became too inflated and trendy. Like those ridiculous gargantuan Central Perk-issued cappuccino mugs on *Friends*. And like women's sunglasses in the last couple of years. How much bigger are they going to get before they qualify as welding shields?

Vain was another band that I came across maybe four or five years ago after hearing their tune "On the Line". It occurred to me after listening to Vain that their point of difference from other hair bands of their ilk was that they didn't have a 'shredder' in their guitar player. And *every* hair band has one of these. Right down to the most obscure ones, like Spread Eagle and Princess Pang. Maybe this was a good thing, I don't know. You could make an argument for the fact that the showy guitar acrobatics were soulless and that they trivialized the culture, but that was the whole point. Hair rock was never about soul. No matter what Bret Michaels would have you believe.

Hearing these songs at this point in my life was interesting to me because it allowed for the opportunity to assess them in a different way, separate from any emotional investment I would have made in them as a teenager. Back then, I experienced these songs immediately from the inside, without taking the time to look around from the perimeter first and then go in.

With age, of course, come deeper consideration, broadened perspective, and more involved scrutiny. I liked Junkyard and D'Molls in 1998, but I knew down deep that I only liked them back then on false merit, in a twice-removed sense because of the nostalgic bias of my teenage affinity for the hair rock genre. I wasn't kidding anybody. It's obvious now, more than ten years after that, that there was bias. I just didn't want to accept it then, because I was twenty-nine and still hanging on to the past in ways that I had intended to be indiscriminate but really were probably more passive-aggressive. And that's the thing. I still listen to these songs today, but the way that I enjoy them has become far more delineated as time passes because I'm not as far inside them as I used to be. In fact, the scale has inverted itself. The songs are inside me now, and contextually they represent something altogether removed from what they previously had.

✷ Fourteen ✷
Heavy Metal or Hard Rock?

It irks me when people call Van Halen and Def Leppard heavy metal bands.

Van Halen and Def Leppard were never heavy metal bands, and Guns N' Roses was never a hair band even though it may have vaguely resembled one in the group's earliest days. The line that separates 80s hard rock from heavy metal may be a blurry one in some cases, but that's only because people fall back on the term *heavy metal* reflexively to conveniently categorize most music from that period that featured repugnant guitars played by repugnant looking individuals. I realize that sometimes even that category of people who know a thing or two about music, and maybe even heavier music in particular, will tend to deploy subjectivity over objectivity in their considerations of musical genre. Music can be a very personal thing, understandably so. There is a discernable difference between hard rock and heavy metal however. And despite tunes like "Fire Your Guns" and "Touch Too Much", AC/DC is not and never was a heavy metal band.

Differentiating the two genres is not an exact science. As with anything, there are exceptions to every rule. And there are a lot of things to consider beyond simple checkpoint characteristics. Punk is similar to heavy metal in a couple of ways, one notable similarity being that their aural and visual characteristics are both so sharply defined that they can be rendered Halloween costume cliché. This is a problem, because definitions are established but misappropriated because of stereotyping.

The Clash is an example. They're considered to be a 'punk' band first and foremost, but songs like "Train in Vain" and "Rock the Casbah" would imply anything but. I don't profess to be an expert on The Clash. But, if you consider their beginnings from the same mid-70s punk-pioneering circle that included The Sex Pistols, and what the band was really about from a socio-political perspective, it's easy to conclude that even though they were considered sellouts for signing a record deal and turning out to be gifted songwriters, they were actually a punk band at their core.

Another problem is that heavy metal is often made a malleable concept beyond its specific musical constitutions. Sammy Hagar proved this in 1979 by naming a song "Heavy Metal" that was really no heavier than anything in Foreigner's catalogue. This is exactly the kind of loose ideology that obscures what's really heavy metal and what's really hard rock.

Quickly as a side note - it also pisses me off when non-metal artists use metal imagery as an attention-getting prop in songs and videos. Seeing a studded-leather-wearing-jet-black-big-haired Sammi Curr-looking character playing a tapping solo on a Flying V in an R&B number at the American Music Awards boils my blood. It's callous, exploitative, lazy, and demonstrative of music industry sliminess. Stick to using your own fucking genre imagery.

Now then. Specifically defining the heavy metal genre from a cut-and-dry technical standpoint *is* possible. But it gets messy. The immediate visual and aural cues bands provide can be misleading, because beneath the surface there is convolution brought about by the fact that heavy metal and hard rock were both borne of the blues. Metal is a blues relative farther removed, but a relative nonetheless.

Before getting into technical intricacies just for fun, the point needs to be made that the key difference between heavy metal and hard rock is *attitude*, plain and simple. Any band you can name can be defined as either heavy metal or hard rock by this variable. Attitude is the lone precursor that predicates every other factor in shaping metal bands and hard rock bands.

Both are equally unrepentant but heavy metal attitude is militant and aggressive, often with a focus on dark imagery and adventure, overt domination, and power themes. Hard rock attitude is aggressive too, but in a more sexual, romanticized way, with less focus on violence and sword 'n' sorcery content and more on the double-entendre swords lurking within the trousers of the hard rock musician.

Heavy metal is fierce and mighty and larger than life, and hard rock is too-cool-for-school swagger, groove-laden and sleazy. Metal is cold and steely, hard rock is warm and wet. Hard rock's measure is *one-two, one-two* (think Aerosmith), while heavy metal is *one-one-one-one-one*. Metal wants to bash your head apart and gargle with your blood just for the sake of it, and hard rock wants to bang you and drag deep on a cigarette afterwards, just for the sake of it - and look really cool doing it.

Of the aforementioned examples Van Halen, Def Leppard, and Guns N' Roses, it's clear by this rationale that none of these bands are heavy metal bands at all. Hard rock? Absolutely.

There's no denying that a small handful of pure heavy metal bands existed in the 80s. But, a band's complete body of work has to be considered. Accept's first couple of albums weren't metal by their own admission. They really didn't settle into being a real heavy metal band until they released *Breaker* in 1981. But they stayed metal after the movement was over, and because they started to take real shape in the late 70s (Udo started forming the band in 1968...!), they could be considered metal pioneers.

And what about Judas Priest, the band Accept opened for on their first big tour in 1981? Priest was one of those groups that could easily be recognized as heavy metal right off the bat, if not for the simple reason that they *told* you in no uncertain terms that they were heavy metal and damn proud to be. Genuine heavy metal bands in the 80s always used the term *heavy metal* in their lyrics and in their song and album titles, and referred to themselves as heavy metal bands. Because heavy metal is more of a discernable 'lifestyle' genre than is hard rock, there are a number of criteria that could be relied upon to define metal. Like wardrobe. The consummate heavy metal outfit probably best represented in Rob Halford's stage clothing for the past thirty plus years – head-to-toe black leather, studs, massive armbands with spikes, and handcuffs with maybe a couple of bullet belts to accessorize.

I remember as a kid seeing Halford in his metal uniform in the pages of *Circus* with those huge wrist-to-elbow leather armbands featuring actual *spikes*, not just those square little pyramid studs. The studs were okay, but they were lame in comparison. I wanted the spikes. Sloss and I would wear all that stuff when we really rocked out. The bandanas, the Japanese rising sun or Union Jack t-shirts, black Levis, and the studded wristbands, right up to the elbow on both arms. All of it. My parents thought I was a goddamn lunatic. I scoured Sudbury looking for the spikes back in the day. While the studded versions were sometimes available (among a bunch of homemade crap versions that I bought by default because I couldn't possibly go home empty-handed), the spikes were never available. I concluded that they were banned from milquetoast Canada back then just like all of the other fun things I wanted, like Yummy Mummy (snicker) cereal, Chinese throwing stars, and Hostess Twinkies. These days, I see the damn spikes in every headshop I walk past in Toronto. Not much good to me at this point however.

Halford had the spikes, en masse - on his armbands, on his jacket, on his boots, and who knows where else. He was probably the textbook example of how a prototypical metalhead would be dressed, just as Judas Priest serves as the most obvious example of the prototypical heavy metal band. With the exception of commercial gaffe *Turbo*, Judas Priest was essentially the monarch of the heavy metal court in the 80s. So much so that the complete Judas Priest music-plus-image package could possibly be used as a reference point against which other metal bands are measured, or even to define the heavy metal genre itself.

But again, something is amiss. In all of his years as Priest's lead vocalist, Halford never really grew his hair that long. Most card-carrying headbangers would tell you that long hair is mandatory to be considered a metalhead. Halford is also gay. Though he hadn't made this fact public knowledge until the 80s were long over, the fact that "The Metal God", as Halford was widely known, was a homosexual likely and quite unfortunately failed to line up with what heavy metal represented in the opinions of some headbangers.

An interesting thing happens when Judas Priest is used as a measuring stick for all things heavy metal - purported metal originator Black Sabbath is seen in a new light.

It's actually a light that Ozzy Osbourne had always argued that he and the rest of Sabbath should be seen in - that of a heavy blues-rock band. Ozzy has always been adamant about the fact that Sabbath were never a heavy metal band, a somewhat alarming assertion given that Black Sabbath are considered by many to be *the* originators of the heavy metal genre. But, it makes sense when you consider that Sabbath started out doing blues and jazz stuff and only decided to get 'heavier' by doing two things – taking on a darker image in name and lyrical content, and writing heavy, distorted, chugging guitar riffs to match those lyrics. Aside from those albeit very important aspects, Black Sabbath dressed more like hippies than anything and you could hear the blues foundations in most of their music, particularly on their debut record. Considering that they took the scary approach for their first few records because Sabbath bassist Geezer Butler happened to notice that people enjoyed watching horror films (one of those films in particular being called *Black Sabbath*), it's interesting that the band inadvertently created a musical genre they didn't even believe they should be a part of. To make the assertion that Black Sabbath was not a heavy metal band seems almost perverse, and yet the argument can be made. I would say that in Sabbath's case, because of the fact that they created archetypal heavy metal riffs like the one in "Children of the Grave" first, and actually initiated the entire heavy metal movement (though without really intending to do so) makes them a heavy metal band by default at the very least.

Later on when Ozzy left Black Sabbath, he recruited one of the finest heavy metal guitarists of all time in Randy Rhoads, and somehow still didn't consider himself to be heavy metal. Ozzy's solo material is an example of the *reverse* of the situation, where bands are inappropriately labelled as heavy metal when they're not. Ozzy says his music is not heavy metal, and yet it employs most if not all of the devices that would define metal; particularly the heavy, chugging minor key guitar riffs and lead breaks played using Dorian and Mixolydian scales amid all of the dark imagery. Hell, there's even an inverted cross on the cover of *Diary of a Madman*.

For me, Ozzy's scene was really just a slightly more commercially streamlined version of earlier Black Sabbath. You can't tell me that "Mr. Crowley", "Bark at the Moon" and "Miracle Man" aren't heavy metal songs. Ozzy knew that he was playing metal songs during his solo period, but for some unknown reason he just didn't want to acknowledge it. Maybe this is because Ozzy was a rock and roll guy at heart, having been influenced most heavily by Sir Paul McCartney. Maybe he just went along with the flow of what he did with Sabbath and the metal movement that he and Sharon saw coming in the 80s. I'm not sure that Ozzy ever even made a reference to heavy metal, at any point. During shows he would shout out *"Rock and Roll!"* to the crowd instead. Ozzy, like Sabbath replacement Ronnie James Dio (RIP) in his witches-and-warlocks imagery approach, played bona fide metal music without completely being a real heavy metal outfit per se. Ozzy and Dio had a lot in common, actually. Both were 80s post-Sabbath singers, and both were managed by their wives. Dio was a much better singer, but Ozzy (and Sharon) somehow managed to grab the better guitar players.

Welsh guitarist Jake E. Lee actually played for both Ozzy and Dio, in fact. Lee's playing provides some perspective in noting the differences between heavy metal and hard rock. If you listen to his playing on Ozzy's *Bark at the Moon* record, in particular on the "Bark at the Moon" track itself, it's definitely heavy metal in tone and style. But if you listen to Lee's playing on the Badlands records post-Ozzy, it's heavy blues-rock, no question. Big difference. Same goes for Zakk Wylde on *No Rest for the Wicked* versus his non-Ozzy Pride and Glory stuff.

This is why the body of an artist's work has to come into consideration if we want to see them for what they truly were. Dio's work with Elf and Rainbow position him as a hard rock singer. When he joined Sabbath and then formed his own band afterwards, that didn't change in his mind. His roots were in hard rock, just like Ozzy's. Motley Crue is the inverse example. Motley may be considered metal by some on the merits of their *Shout at the Devil* material, but their previous release *Too Fast For Love*, subsequent record *Theatre of Pain*, and everything else after that was anything but heavy metal. Motley Crue is a hard rock band, pure and simple. A band can write metal-style music and be a metal band perhaps without intention (or admission, in Ozzy's case). On the other side of the coin, a band can also convey the image and use all of the clichéd devices to pass themselves off as metal, and still not be a metal band. This was essentially what Motley did circa *Shout at the Devil*.

Most of the time, before the evaluation of a band's body of work, you can tell a metal band from a hard rock band just by listening to them. The trickier ones like Ozzy, Scorps, and maybe a handful of other artists, are rarities. Ninety-five percent of the bands you hear on Sirius XM's *The Boneyard* are easily distinguished. There are certain discriminating elements that represent what it was understood to be. If there were a technical argument to be made in this medium, the following would be it.

The music comes first. The heavy, crunchy, galloping guitar riffs have to be there for a song to be considered heavy metal. Metal riffs contain certain features that differentiate them from hard rock riffs. One essential element is the palm-muted chugging notes between chords. Some examples include Accept's "Love Child", Dio's "Holy Diver", and Raven's "Seek and Destroy", but the best ones come from heavier bands like Megadeth and Anthrax, who use this picking style in pretty much every one of their songs. Also, metal riffs are typically played using the staccato (unconnected notes) as opposed to legato (flowing notes) technique, adding a crunchier, more aggressive vibe to the riff.

Another distinction is note selection in the riffs. Depending on what scale is used, the riff will sound bluesy (pentatonic blues scale) or 'scary' (Dorian, Locrian, Phrygian). The reason is because blues scales mostly use what are called 'whole step' intervals, with less sharp and flat notes and sound 'fuller', and the other scales use 'half-step' intervals and as a result sound slightly dissonant and more 'evil'. The best example of this motif is the theme from *Jaws*. It only uses two repetitive bass notes, but the half-step interval naturally creates tension with that 'evil' sound.

Next is playing style. There's a limit to how eerie a song can sound based on scale choice. But when players do things like holding on to certain notes, or bending them out of the expected key somewhat, it contributes to that sinister sound. Playing style and delivery are critical to whether songs are interpreted as metal songs, especially in light of the rule exceptions encountered. For example, it's difficult to be more metal than Dave Mustaine. He relies on the pentatonic scale in his lead playing, because this scale was the one he learned when he first picked up the guitar, and you can hear it in his leads. However, how he incorporates this scale into his overall playing style is significant to how Megadeth's music sounds.

As such, the sound or *tone* that the riff is played in is another factor. Metal riffs simply wouldn't be metal riffs without distortion. The way a riff sounds in the overall mix and how it's produced on an album makes all the difference, although production along with things like tempo and groove are considerations that involve the overall musical product itself. Not just the riff.

If the riffs and leads were played using all of the aforementioned devices, it would stand to reason that the band playing them would be a metal band. But again, non-metal examples like Motley's "Looks That Kill", and "Wasted" by Def Leppard contradict the argument. At this point, you should almost use an algorithmic approach - *if* the riffs seem to qualify as metal, *then* you move on to the overall instrumentation of the band, and so on. You could continue this formula across all of the metal 'signifiers' to determine of a band is really metal or not[5], because there are some dead giveaways that will allow us to come to a speedy conclusion. The most obvious one is the presence of synthesizers. Synths are added to band's recordings to 'fill out the sound', but really they're in place to improve a band's commercial viability and get them on the radio. This is not heavy metal. Hammond organs might be an exception, but just barely.

Guitar melodies are also game changers. When you press play to hear Def Leppard's "Another Hit & Run", the first six seconds of the track lead you to believe that you're about to hear a heavy metal song. The guitar melody line that comes in at 0:07 assures you that you are not. These melodic implements, subtle as they seem, are the most telling of a band's musical position and inclination. Albeit seemingly one-dimensional, old school heavy metal is very straightforward. It doesn't contain overly melodic guitar lines (Maiden came close, but they were always sure to remind you in other areas, at least on their earlier records anyway, that they were a bludgeoning headbanger's band). Even though they were hailed as being at the vanguard of the New Wave of British Heavy Metal movement, Def Leppard was never a metal band. They were at their 'heaviest' on their first two records and maybe on some parts of *Pyromania*, but during this period they were essentially an AC/DC that was okay for girls to listen to. And I don't mean that detrimentally. I'm a big Leppard fan.

The song lyrics can be about lopping off the heads of evil and big-breasted Valkyries with a broadsword but if they're sung unintelligibly, as most metal and hard rock lyrics are, it's a wash.

So, if that's all in place, you have a metal *song*. But not necessarily a metal *band*.

As far as image goes, there were few heavy metal bands that didn't specifically dress the leather-and-studs part. Particularly at the beginning of their careers. Manowar did before they adopted the *YMCA-meets-Conan-the-Barbarian* thing, and Accept also did before Udo

---

[5] *I can't believe I'm using scientific reasoning in trying to make a point about heavy metal. My poor high school teachers might be proud of me after all.*

buzzed his mullet and donned army fatigues. James Hetfield wore black leather and spandex and a bullet belt back in the *Kill 'Em All* days, and Slayer wore the full leather and spikes outfits in their early period. But there's where the algorithm approach comes in. Loads of Sunset Strip bands used to dress in leather and spikes, but the metal music wasn't there to justify calling them metal bands.

Labels can be misleading. The 'hair metal' tag was created to define the 80s Sunset Strip movement as a matter of catch-all convenience. This movement was only called 'hair metal' because there's no other convenient name for it. Like 'classic rock'. You can't say 'hair hard rock'. It's the same as 'glam metal'. It's a misnomer. Technically there's no such thing as 'hair metal' or 'glam metal', because bands like Poison were more pop bands than metal bands, even if the riff from "Look What the Cat Dragged In" was curiously similar to Armored Saint's "Can U Deliver". Again, that's where attitude constituted the difference between hard rock and metal. Ratt exploited this motif with "Round and Round" by disguising a pop song inside a Judas Priest staccato guitar picking style riff, thus setting the tone for the 'glam metal' explosion. But really, the only thing that was vaguely 'metal' about this movement was the riff masquerade. Armored Saint was one of those pick-and-shovel metal bands that epitomized the genre with tons of great metal riffs. Even though they were based in Los Angeles, they stood out among their Sunset Strip brethren because of how they expressed themselves. And therein lies the real difference between heavy metal and hard rock. Attitude.

Sometimes the little nuances contribute to the telling of the story. Things like backing vocals can generally be pretty good barometers of whether bands were heavy metal, hard rock, or otherwise. If heavy metal bands did employ backing vocals, they were barked or spit out in militaristic fashion, and rarely exceeded two syllables for the most part. If not simply jumping in on the chorus and backing up the lead vocalist whenever they sang the song's title, the most popular metal backing vocal was the *"Hey!"* gang vocal. You know the one.

And yet even this device can be hard to lock down as an exclusively metal element. Bands of every stripe tended to use it, including Bon Jovi and KISS. Marilyn Manson even used it in his proto-metal tune "Beautiful People". Some bands, like Guns N' Roses, made a point of *not* using it, and that was for a reason. But the way that it was used provided some guidance as to whether bands were hard rock or metal.

Hard rock bands, or more specifically, party rock bands like Dokken or Winger, would draw out the word, as in *"Heeeeyyyy!"* Meanwhile, metal bands enunciated it in such a way that it was short, quick and punchy; almost taking you by surprise the first time you heard it. Almost like the way you would yell at your dog if it tried to grab your sandwich off of the coffee table while you were watching TV.

The tonal quality also varied. Use in a metal context was deeper, sharper, and more baritone without being too bassy. Almost like a platoon of Marines responding in unison. It sounded thick and authoritative, so much so you could almost picture your favourite headbanger's face inflecting that '*eh*' sound* with squinted eyes and mouth wide open to expose both top and bottom rows of teeth. Like every live and sweaty shot of Rob Halford featured in Hit Parader. And maybe Nikki Sixx too. But he was faking it. Stephen Pearcy wasn't, because his facial expression in those pictures always showed more of a seductive pucker. That *"I'm-so-banging-you-after-this-music-thing-is-over"* smirk.

Out of curiosity, I went through my CD collection to do some research on the use of *"Hey!"* to see if my theory stands up.

Because my collection is in alphabetical order, I started at 'A' and worked my way through, taking out every hard rock and metal CD that I either a) knew contained the *"Hey!"* gang vocal in any capacity, or b) took out CDs that I suspected may contain the *"Hey!"* gang vocal.

It's a simple matter of course that German heavy metal juggernaut Accept would make use of this device. It's there at 1:15 of "Balls to the Wall". A bit long, but that Teutonic cadence makes up for it. As I listen, I

---

* *This descriptive has absolutely nothing to do with my being Canadian, by the w-eh.*

realize that a potential problem with this exercise may be bias. Because as I hear this, just above the perfect crunch of the riffing, I think that Accept may have made *"Hey!"* an exclusive metal device. It's hard to believe that it doesn't appear on *Restless & Wild* or *Metal Heart*, even as the faux-Gregorian monk chant is heard towards the end of the "Metal Heart" title track at 4:12. *Metal Heart*'s last track, "Bound to Fail", does contain something akin to *"Hey!"* in the choruses, but it's inaudible. Same concept I suppose though.

On we go to Bon Jovi's *New Jersey*. This version of *"Hey!"* during the extended intro of album opener "Lay Your Hands On Me" is an example of *"Hey!"* being used in a faux-metal way, with that faux-aggression that Bon Jovi was so good at conveying. I haven't heard this record for a long time, and something about it makes me bristle. Everything is so drenched in reverb and delay that it reminds me how terrifically obtuse the 80s could be. But at the end of the day, I have to hand it to Jon Bon. There's no denying that he was in complete control at the height of his powers, and that motherfucker knew how to capitalize on his strengths better than anybody. Still does.

As a kid, I came for the aural saccharine of "Bad Medicine" on *New Jersey* like everyone else did, but I hung around a little longer for stuff like "Homebound Train" and "Ride Cowboy Ride" after the hype subsided.

Motley Crue's *Shout at the Devil* may offer the most perfect example of how *"Hey!"* should be used in a metal capacity two minutes and thirty-five seconds into the brilliant fake-metal anthem "Looks That Kill". The positioning of the *"Hey!"* is spot-on, inserted post-guitar solo after two run-throughs of the main riff. Whoever was responsible for this (Tom Werman?) is a genius. It's so perfectly executed that every time I hear it I can't resist mouthing it, twenty-seven years after I bought *Shout at the Devil*. Superb.

I figured that Mr. Ronnie James Dio must have benefitted from use of the *"Hey!"* device on his solo stuff, and I'm correct. Right off the hop in opening track "Stand Up and Shout" from *Holy Diver*, a Pink Floydian "Another Brick in the Wall" type *"Hey!"* is heard at 2:26. Not as baritone as most metal examples, but nonetheless effective. As I listen to the rest of the track I remember how much Vinny Appice's clackety snare drum fills annoyed me as a teenager.

Montreal thrash metal band Eudoxis use *"Hey!"* at the end of each chorus in "Metal Fix", with the first one coming at 1:15 and the most effective one ending the track. If it weren't for the crappy production, this example might be in the same ballpark with the one in "Looks That Kill".

Helloween's use of *"Hey!"* on their "Ride the Lightning" rip-off "Gorgar" is the polar opposite of the Bon Jovi example. Short, crisp, no reverb, and has a really creepy, distant effect that reminds me of Nazis. Especially the first one at 1:26. There's definitely a correlation between the workmanlike quality of good German heavy metal and militarism.

In looking through my Lizzy Borden CDs, I'm inclined to think that *"Hey!"* must appear at least once somewhere on 1986 release *Menace to Society*. "Notorious" contains an upfront *"Hail Caesar!"*, gang vocal in the chorus. For some reason, the vocal sounds like it's being shouted by a bunch of older men, not the spandex-clad mile-high haired young chaps who grace the *Menace to Society* cover. Album closing track "Menace to Society" also contains some gang vocal backups in the song's bridge in the general vein of what *"Hey!"* stands for though, but that's as close as they come. Vinny Appice could really use a drum lesson or two from Borden skinsman Joey Scott Harges. The guy is incredible.

At 0:32 in "Crazy Nights", Minoru Niihara and his mates in Loudness sneak a barely noticeable *"Hey!"* into the first verse, getting some points for unorthodoxy. The "Crazy Nights" choruses are rife with gang vocal chants, a peculiar facsimile of *"Hey!"* repeated thrice that is actually *M! - Z! - A!*. Apparently MZA has no underlying meaning. It was just part of the guide vocal Niihara used in pre-production when they were recording the demos for *Thunder in the East*. Apparently they couldn't come up with anything else after the rest of the lyrics were done, so he and producer Max Norman decided to keep the MZA bit. It's hard to believe that they couldn't come up with something more relevant than fucking *MZA*, and perplexing that they didn't just default to *"Hey! Hey! Hey!"*.

If I had any Manowar CDs in my collection, I would kick my own ass. But I would also suspect that they would contain a *"Hey!"* or two. Being the heavy metal loin-clothed alpha males that they were, they *had* to have used *"Hey!"* somewhere in their catalogue. But I have no idea because I'll never own a Manowar CD. I may have a couple of cheesy records in my collection, but a band that uses song titles like "All Men Play on 10" will never be a part of it.

Queensryche have all kinds of gang vocals happening on their second record *The Warning*, and they're all derivatives of *"Hey!"*. At 1:59 of "Warning", you hear what sounds like *"Yeah!"*, and at the song's conclusion at 4:19 it sounds like the band is partaking in a Ju-Jitsu drill, vocalizing four exclamations that sound like *"Huh!"*.

The Sunset Strip approach to the use of the *"Hey!"* device is exemplified by Ratt on "You Think You're Tough" at 0:53 and 1:57. There's nothing metal about these. The *"Hey!"* is drawn out and sassy. As in, *"Heeeyyyy"*. And I'm not saying this in a way to suggest inferiority or anything, because the approach works well within the context it's used in. I really like that Ratt EP. Except the bass mix in "Back for More", which was wisely improved before the song's release on *Out of the Cellar*. If you can track down a copy of the EP, listen closely to the bass line in "Back for More". There's one recurring note in the bass line that sounds funny because it pops up in the verses in a way that's way overstated.

And lastly, though it's not specifically a *"Hey!"* gang vocal, Tesla takes the metal rationale and puts their own personal spin on it at 2:29 of "Action Talks" from their *Bust a Nut* record. One of my personal favourites. I recommend having a listen.

So, it would appear that the *"Hey!"* exercise underscores the observation that the way in which certain musical elements are *deployed*, not *defined*, can help to determine whether a band is really metal or not. But this can only provide a basis for contemplation. There are so many factors to ponder, and it's only after they're all considered within the scope of the band's complete body of work that an opinion can be formulated.

Look at a band like Led Zeppelin. Some people say that "Communication Breakdown" is a heavy metal song, and that Zeppelin is even a heavy metal band. But this is far from accurate. If we take a step back and consider Zeppelin's complete body of work spanning their entire career, where their creative forces drew influence from, and where their finest, purest moments in musical achievement lie (and there were many), they can't possibly be considered a heavy metal band any more than "Communication Breakdown" can be called a heavy metal song. Sure, the guitar on that track is played in a muted staccato picking style and it's loud and raucous (for its time), but that's really as far as it goes. I suppose that the heavy metal tag may have been applied prematurely back then because a) people didn't have Zeppelin's entire body of work as a reference point, b) heavy metal itself was still neophytic as a genre, and c) people arrived at lazy, reactive conclusions to summarize something that was new, aggressive, and quite possibly a bit alarming back in 1969.

But they're still doing it today.

✸ Fifteen ✸
Hard Rock is Dead, Long Live Hard Rock

AC/DC was never any more a heavy metal band than Led Zeppelin was, but I think in AC/DC's case a lot of the potential confusion comes from that 'dark' period they had, around the time *Highway To Hell* and *Black in Black* were regularly referencing hell and Satan. Sure, Jimmy Page was a Crowley enthusiast. But other than some vague album cover imagery on Led Zeppelin IV they weren't as overt about it as AC/DC was, even if it didn't mean anything. Does it ever though? Even if you're King Diamond or Venom, does it really mean anything?

Back in Black featured the same bloozy shitkickery that *Highway to Hell* did but it had a very macabre, very distant and dissociative feel about it. A bit like KISS' *Destroyer* did. Of course, the loss of singer Bon Scott figured into this premise. But it always struck me how much the record really seemed to give the impression that the band was indifferent to the attentions of the listener, polarized against the jokey extroversion of Scott and previous AC/DC records. *Back in Black* was aloof and malevolent, and all business. That's how I heard it as a young kid anyway. The dark imagery only framed the blackness that stirred within the musical output.

That record was so dark that it actually frightened me a little bit as a kid. But as Black Sabbath and the *Friday the 13th* horror film franchise would teach us, fear is really just interest we haven't exploited yet.

My *Back in Black* apprehension was further enhanced in my impressionable mind after I read a letter someone submitted to *Hit Parader* sometime around 1982, claiming that *Back in Black* contained satanic messages that were audible only when you spun the record backwards. According to this letter, there were two backward masked messages on *Back in Black* – "Satan has me prisoner! Free me! Free me!" and "Satan helped me and he saved my life. Hail Satan! Hail Satan!". Of course, I spun the record backwards over the spots during the "Hell's Bells" and "Back in Black" tracks where the messages supposedly were. After the first spin I froze, eyebrows raised. Then I did it again. And again. In pushing the record back against the stylus of our already sub-par quality record player enough times to eventually damage it beyond repair, I contemplated the remote possibility that AC/DC was in league with Satan. Horrors!

As with all of these scientifically unfounded intangibles, validity ultimately hinges on the individual's interest in believing, because ambiguity makes it optional. And I believed the backwards masking was there and real at that time, but only because I *wanted* to believe it. It was all part of that glorious fantasy of listening to music as a kid. Of course, the messages were unintentional if they were even there at all, but the power of taboo and suggestibility made the experience so much more tantalizing.

Not like an immense record such as *Back in Black* needed it however. If Satan does exist, I would imagine his voice sounds exactly the same as Brian Johnson's singing voice on *Back in Black* and *For Those About To Rock*. One of the things I overlooked and took for granted about *Back in Black* was the quality of Johnson's vocal on this record, and subsequent releases *For Those About To Rock* and *Flick of the Switch*. *Back in Black*, unfortunately, is one of those classic records that you only really hear on a superficial, desensitized level because it's ingrained so bloody deeply into your psyche that you actually have to really concentrate while listening, to hear what it *really* sounds like. In doing this recently, the first thing I noticed about it was that Johnson's voice was abrasive in a good way. A whiskey-soaked quasi-falsetto that was perfectly suited for the dark, moody overtones of *Back in Black*. I took that for granted back in 1980 as I ice-skated along to "Shoot to Thrill" while it blared from the speakers of the Espanola Arena during public skating afternoons.

Unfortunately, the second thing I was reminded of in listening to *Back in Black* today was that "You Shook Me All Night Long" plays about 489 times a day per channel in the average classic rock radio market. To this day, I avoid the song like the plague. In fact, I would be inclined to say that the song ranks third on my list of *Songs I Never Ever Need To Hear Again*:

1) "Takin' Care of Business" by Bachman Turner Overdrive
2) "Rock & Roll" by Led Zeppelin
3) "You Shook Me All Night Long" by AC/DC
4) "Rock n' Roll All Nite" by KISS
5) "Livin' on a Prayer" by Bon Jovi

While it may be out of context here, BTO's "Takin' Care of Business" tops any list of songs I can't listen to for whatever reason because it's actually the most grating and stupid song I may have ever heard. This is only because "Takin' Care of Business" is actually meant to be taken seriously. With other grating and stupid songs, like say, "I Want To Be A Cowboy" by Boys Don't Cry, the stupidity is overtly implied.

"Tainted Love" by Soft Cell is also on my list of *Songs I Never Ever Need To Hear Again*, but again out of context in this grouping. Ditto any song George Thorogood ever recorded.

Let's face it. Nobody's concerned about the artistic development of AC/DC. Nobody buys their records in anticipation of them having written their "Stairway To Heaven". Quite the contrary, in fact. Like every AC/DC fan, I expect them to consistently deliver that special brand of bluesy, misogynistic 4\4 time rock and roll until Angus Young can no longer run across the stage for fear of shattering one of his hips. And while they may be approaching that point now, I praise AC/DC for sticking to what they know and not getting caught up in the latest soup-du-jour trend in an attempt to stay current or sell records.

I always thought AC/DC's *Flick of the Switch* was a great record. It didn't even really render a single, but that's probably why I liked it so much. It just seemed like it came out at exactly the right time in 1983, and was positioned in exactly the right space - just far enough away from *Back in Black*'s juggernaut success, and enough before 80s-drenched *Fly on the Wall*. It was raw, dirty hard rock augmented by still relatively new guy Johnson's impossibly sandpaper-shrill vocals. The production is simple and unpolished, perfectly suited to the musical message. AC/DC's identity has always been rooted in the band's simple open-space rhythms that enable that same tribal vibe that made The White Stripes so popular. Not flashy or stylistic, just keeping solid time with a great backbeat and zero frills. Less can indeed be more.

Flick of the Switch is one of those straight-ahead rock and roll groove records that you put on when you're getting ready to get monumentally blasted with your buddies. It's a severely underrated record having suffered the comparison to *Back in Black*, but this is perfectly fine with me. I actually prefer these types of releases. Hearing other people overplay this record probably would have put me off it (see Pearl Jam's *Vs*). *Flick of the Switch* didn't sound like it was written for airplay, or for anyone in particular, and as a result it may have been AC/DC's last really great record.

And if we're talking about under appreciated, under-the-radar records that are perfectly placed among a series of otherwise successful rock records, Van Halen's *Women and Children First* has to be mentioned.

Roth-era Van Halen is fucking *special*. In 1980, Van Halen was the perfect rock band. Not too commercial, not rebellious just for rebellion's sake. Not too heavy, but harnessed much power. Not too good-looking (David Lee Roth had an image to keep up), not too ugly. Not too intellectual, but plenty clever. Not super glitzy, but unmatched in showmanship. Van Halen was all things to all people back then.

Only David Lee Roth would be able to get away with poofy opening lines like *"We're getting funny in the back of my car"* from "Feel Your Love Tonight", or schmaltzy phrasings like *'sastify'* in the place of 'satisfy' at the end of "Ice Cream Man". I never so much as made a face when I heard Roth's bizarre Tarzan mimicry at the beginning of "Everybody Wants Some!", because it just seemed like it fit. It just sounded cool. That's what Roth did, because that's what Roth *was*. He always pulled it off because it was natural and he wasn't trying too hard. And when you step back to take a look at the ensuing hair band movement that Roth and Van Halen spawned, including bands like Poison and BulletBoys, it's easy to put everything into perspective. Van Halen and the Sunset Strip hair bands both deployed that same vaudevillian flamboyance, but only Van Halen did it without making us cringe.

Edward Van Halen was the fastest and most creative guitar player in all of rock in his day. He was responsible for all kinds of six-string firsts, like the "Eruption", "Cathedral", and "Spanish Fly" solos. But he was also responsible for other little subtleties like rubbing the palm of his right hand on the strings to create the "Atomic Punk" intro riff. Seemingly insignificant things like dragging his pick over the guitar strings behind the tuning nut at 0:17 of "Runnin' with the Devil". Some little things nobody else did, some big things nobody else could do, and all kinds of things that no one else thought to do. But most important of all, Ed's playing featured all of this stuff *and* had dimension and warmth. Sharp edges, round shapes, and a richness you'll probably never hear again. The guy is a genius.

Women and Children First came to me when I needed it most. It wasn't too heavy and wasn't too soft. Just a brilliantly dirty rock and roll record. It gave me the impression that it was largely unedited, the way that *Exile on Main Street* and other records of this ilk were. *Women and Children First* was made on the tail end of a period when good rock records had a feeling of warmth to them, as Van Halen's first five records all did. It's organic, dynamic, and loosely cobbled together, and at its heart is an ethos that makes you want to crack a bottle of Jack and throw away the cap.

Above all, the aspect that makes *Women and Children First* so special is that it marks the beginning of the end of Roth-era Van Halen. The album represents the creative nexus of ringleader Roth's rock and roll lechery juxtaposed against Edward's distinct virtuosity, captured just before the ego friction resulting from this synergy disrupts the band's balance on follow up record *Fair Warning*.

Great records like *Women and Children First* are made a little bit more magical because of the fact that they embody a unique purity and legitimacy that isn't found in today's hard rock records. The purest form of the hard rock genre has expired, and it's been completely played out. Its context has been exhausted, and no newness with any lasting value can come of it. It has enjoyed a finite, natural life cycle with a start and a finish. It has certainly run its course. There can be no mistaking that while the spirit of pure hard rock may still live on through the spinning of the old records, anything new put forth for consideration can only be a rehashed version of something that's already been done.

I'm talking about prime hard rock here, bands like Deep Purple and Led Zeppelin. Then AC/DC, Aerosmith, Van Halen, and Guns N' Roses. I'm not necessarily talking about the broader 'classic rock' genre. I hate that term anyway because it sounds so stale and convenient, and in this case it's not accurate because classic rock proper is amorphous enough to span bands like Supertramp and The Guess Who.

So - new hard rock doesn't matter for a couple of reasons.

The first one is that the hard rock landscape is based on a finite premise. Things have already been done and established over time, and positions have been occupied. Most of what follows afterwards is also-ran. When we pan out to observe the entire scope, we see the gradual continuum of popular music and the periodic creation of genres and sub-genres vacillating across time. '*Rock and Roll*' can be considered as an enduring and perpetual zeitgeist when it's contemplated as a form of conceptual spirituality for people, but the bricks-and-mortar of a sub-genre's unique identity are limited to finite moments in time. They're created, they exist, and we move forward. What were The Beatles, The Rolling Stones, Led Zeppelin, and every other pioneering monolith of their time, can never exist again in the rock and roll construct. They Christopher Columbused their position in the annals of rock. They emerged first and made their mark, and they'll always serve as a measuring stick for future efforts whether anyone likes it or not. They invented the unique identity that we have come to know and celebrate them for today, and they can't be matched. They can be copied *ad nauseam*, but they're never duplicated. From the pundit's mocking point of view, Whitesnake can be a wayward Zeppelin replicant, and Robert Plant himself can refer to David Coverdale as David Coverversion. Regardless of anyone's opinion, we all understand the hierarchy.

Ideally, the substance provided by these classic hard rock bands is used to expand upon and develop new ideas taken to new places along the continuum via *influence*. It does occur, and new genres are created. If we're talking about the all-encompassing arc of rock and roll, it regularly morphs into subsets that are sometimes interesting, sometimes not. The more commercially viable and less interesting subsets move across the continuum in lockstep with popular trends. These days they have a much shorter lifespan than ever before.

As such, I'm reluctant to include these types of music under the rock umbrella in the same way that HMV might. They're more a front-loaded, commodified 'product' that has little to do with the overarching concept of rock. They have more to do with consumption, disposability, and the business aspect of music. *Women and Children First* was as far from product as it could have possibly been. We all know that the record business obviously trivializes rock, much in the same way that Ashlee Simpson does when she wears an Iron Maiden t-shirt to be 'ironic'. Tragic and vile, and quite honestly makes me throw up in my mouth a little bit.

Some rock subsets are created with more legitimacy, and there are some great bands out there at the vanguard of the latest machinations of rock. But it would seem that the further underground and more independent they are, the more interesting, original, and gratifying their work is. This is a segue into the second reason why real hard rock is dead.

Commercialization of something as feral as hard rock just isn't possible, and it'll always be met with square-peg-through-round-hole results. The best example of this concept was when Elvis was to appear on television from the waist up because his hip gyrations were considered vulgar. Back then, rock was neophytic and mysterious. It was a forbidden pleasure, something that tapped directly into primal tendency. Rock represented a means of manifesting the collective *id*, that basic idea taking hold in 1951 and still existing today, albeit in more convoluted permutations.

Attaching a business construct to this idea is watering it down and sapping it of its strength. Censorship has conceded considerably and self-expression has obviously flourished since Elvis made the girls scream and think impure thoughts way back when, but the signed artist is still a caged lion. Artists are at their most pure when the trappings of commercialization don't dilute them because unsigned, underground bands have that organic ferocity that's compromised by any involvement of money. The term "rock and roll business" is an oxymoron.

Any new rock band has these two strikes against them right off the hop. We've watched our fair share of artists wither and quite literally die at the hands of the industry machine over the decades. We've also seen a cyclical 'retro' movement that has typically taken between fifteen to twenty years, but lately with the proliferation of technology, population, and an increasing insatiability for stimulus consumption, one full retro revolution can be as little as three to five years. The machine moves a lot more swiftly that it did when album rock was relevant and appreciated, and the prevalence of musical ADD in our society only allows for negligible shelf lives for most new bands.

While its culture does continue to bubble and simmer healthily underground, hard rock does re-emerge on the scene every now and again. Upstart hard rock bands are afforded a small window of opportunity whenever the retro iron gets hot in their genre, usually when their progenitors reunite and tour the world. In today's times, the perpetuation of any identity or impact these new bands have is stifled after their first record. Or in Velvet Revolver's case their second record, based largely on the heft of their top-hatted leader's previous outfit. This is because any new hard rock band is doomed to fail, formulaic approach or not, based on the premise that it cannot thrive creatively after it's been recognized for what it is, based on our compulsion to compare and categorize. We all do it. *"Hey, I just heard this band, they're great. They sound like a cross between ___ and ___".*

Even given this argument, a few really good hard rock bands have stood out among a rash of less-worthy peers over the last few years. Most aren't really around anymore in any significant capacity though. Hurricane Party/Roadstar (now called Heaven's Basement) succumbed to the syrupy-AOR-ballads-equal-airplay formula after a brilliant debut EP. Silvertide was choked with legality issues. Jet continued their Icarus-like swoop and flew just a little too close to the Beatles/Oasis sun with their second record. The Darkness imploded, with some members forming an outfit called Stone Gods (I'm still not sure exactly what The Darkness really was, satire or otherwise). A band just about to enter their flameout phase is Australian hard rock band Airbourne, a Rose Tattoo clone that features a single with a riff so close to Priest's "You Got Another Thing Comin'" that I'm not sure how they've avoided a lawsuit thus far. Active hard rockers Broken Teeth (a combination of Dangerous Toys and Dirty Looks alum) and Vains of Jenna (a young, poorly-named third rate version of Guns N' Roses) understand their roles and simply exist within their confines. Wolfmother is still around, though it's really just original lead singer Andrew Stockdale and some hired guns he picked up after sacking the other original members.

Other peripheral contemporaries come to mind that fall into the post-Zeppelin scheme of things. While they were quirky and peculiar in a more indie-ish way and lacked the requisite tight slacks swagger and Jack-swilling misogyny of prototypical hard rock, The White Stripes, or more specifically Jack White, deployed *feel*. And feel is the single most important ingredient of a legitimate hard rock record. Very few Johnny-come-lately bands can make that claim. White's *Elephant* album, which featured filthy stripped-back blues songs like "Ball & Biscuit", and whereupon he used only antiquated pre-1960s recording gear and a duct-taped 8-track tape machine, harkens back to the days of *Zeppelin I*. But even then, the path has already been forged and heavily traversed, and you can't compare the two in any term of equality.

A lot of bands that are billed as 'hard rock' these days really aren't. They don't fit in to the immediate Stones-cum-Aerosmith-cum-GN'R genealogy of pure hard rock, because they descend more from post-Grunge ancestry. Chad Kroeger, Nickelback leader and resident pincushion of emo-rock, has admitted to studying hit songs for years in an attempt to capitalize on success before Nickelback made it big. With no disrespect to Kroeger (he already gets enough of it, poor chap), this is a symptom of the state that popular music at large is in today. It's contrived and doomed to live in a shadow of comparison against the original model. Kroeger is a huge fan of *Back in Black*, and interestingly enough Mutt Lange, the producer of that record, was at the production helm for Nickelback's *Dark Horse* record. But as a self-described student of music, Kroeger most likely has the wherewithal to understand that the magic of a colossal record like *Back in Black* can't be recreated. Angus Young didn't have an '*Angus Young Signature XRS-2000*' effects pedal back then. The output was pure and gimmick free.

The fact that AC/DC has had success with their latest release, *Black Ice*, is because they're recognized as originals. They're the Grand Poobahs of pure hard rock. They wrote, and rightfully own, their own recipe. The simple fact that you can't say that about many active bands these days supersedes the content on the release and any commercialization it's been subjected to. And nostalgic fans will always shell out for it. AC/DC need not break any significant ground on their latest record, just because of their position in the hierarchy. We've seen that *Back in Black* broke all the ground necessary.

By their own admission, and despite all the hype surrounding Brendan O'Brien being at the controls for *Black Ice*, Angus *et al* have essentially released the same album over and over again since the 80s. And that's fine in AC/DC's case. Because *they're AC/DC*. They're a brand-established institution. As I mentioned earlier, people don't want AC/DC to grow and develop artistically. They occupy a specific segment and serve a certain purpose as is. Buying an AC/DC record is a very linear notion. It's like going to Taco Bell. You're going there because you're *not* going to McDonald's or Burger King. You have a very distinct craving to satisfy, and you know that there's only one thing that will do the trick.

I'll admit that as a hard rock fan of many years, selfish nostalgic impulses quietly implore me to root for these retro hard rock movements to endure. Maybe even try to see things in them that may or may not be there. Because in a way, it's depressing to know that these new bands can never represent anything beyond themselves in the genre. They're making music that won't matter in twenty years. Anything they do will ultimately be considered either as plagiarism or homage.

I still do indulge, but I have to enjoy newer hard rock for what it is, in the exact same way that I would enjoy Schwarzenegger in *Last Action Hero*. Anybody who knows anything about rock and roll knows that all this new stuff – Black Veil Brides, Bullet, New Device, Hell City Glamours, whatever – as good as it might be, it's all redux. It's representational fun, and not anything that's catalytic in any way. Guns N' Roses were the last *real* rock and roll band, and that will most likely never change. Time marches on, and because today's hard rock acts are merely navigating paths that were already forged by their heroes, or previously by themselves, they'll always be destined to live in that long, nostalgic shadow of the past.

✴ Sixteen ✴
The Pointlessness of Debate

Alison and I used to play a game to kill time during longish road trips in the car. The rules for the game went more or less like this: using the standard six channel radio console that every car had in 2001, one person would select a channel, all of which were already programmed to rock stations. The other person would identify the band or artist and then anticipate whether that artist would be more important than the other artists that would be heard on the remaining five channels. For example, if the band selected was say, The Rolling Stones, odds would be that the Stones would be considered more important when compared to bands on the other channels. Then we would go through the other channels to see if the selector was correct; if indeed the Stones *were* more important than the artists on the other channels by comparing them directly. Rules were instituted, amended, or jettisoned randomly in loose fashion, but the overall supposition of the game remained - that some artists could be considered more important than others.

Or could they? The channel selection part and the guessing about who might be on the other channels were formality. The crux of the exercise was really the discussion that was generated through artist comparison. Which bands would be more important than others, and why? Where exactly do The Rolling Stones rank in the grand musical scheme of things? Are they directly underneath or on equal footing with

The Beatles? Where does David Bowie fit in? Radiohead? Nirvana? Is Aerosmith more important than AC/DC? Who tops this hierarchy as the most important artist of all time?

The real answer to all of this, much to the chagrin of rock historians everywhere, is that there really is no answer. Just like there's no winner or loser in the radio game. Only dialogue based on personal perceptions. Debate is circular and pointless.

For the purposes of the game (intended to be nothing more than a time-killer focused on meaningful discussion and not argumentative debate), if someone selected The Beatles it would be considered a safe bet just because a huge number of renowned artists that followed cite them as an influence. It would seem a logical conclusion that most everything can be traced back to The Beatles almost in a musically genealogical sort of way. But even then, main Beatles-influencer Elvis Presley looms large. And Chuck Berry. Et cetera, et cetera.

The consideration of *importance* in rock is as aloof as the genre it strains to evaluate. Loads of evaluative criteria come to mind but few can be used with any legitimacy. For example, record sales can't mean anything if you're going to assess artist importance with even a modicum of good conscience, if for no other reason that Gene Simmons is good enough to remind us on a daily basis that KISS has more gold records in America than any other recording artist.

By the same token, some would consider chart positioning and occupancy duration as a measure of importance. While this method provides a certain scientific irrefutability of a band's popularity, it doesn't speak to a band's substance any more than record sales do. Besides, I can't be counted on to recite how many weeks any given Zeppelin record has been in the charts. Although, I am aware that Pink Floyd's *Dark Side of the Moon* pulled off a ridiculous 741-week residency in the Billboard Top 200.

If we care to look beyond record sales and charting stats, we can consider the breadth of an artist's footprint within the genre by contemplating the amount of influence an artist commands. Pink Floyd has obviously cast a long and influential shadow, and the record sales are reflective of that. But record sales and chart positioning are just peripheral achievements relative to what really makes a band important. To what degree did an artist contribute to a genre, or change the course of musical history by going so far as to actually create one? How did their music shape the landscape in terms of what would follow? How substantial and meaningful was an artist's volume of work as part of the bigger picture? These are the real questions that provide clarity on the relevance and importance of an artist.

There will never be an ultimate and omnipotent authority on this topic. Not even Gene Simmons. Contemplation of what's even germane and what's not in popular music can almost run parallel to the basic tenets of organized religion. This is because the greatest power of music is that it exists within spiritual contexts. Music has the ability to shape emotion and feeling at our deepest cores. It stirs our animating principles as beings. It proves indelible when interwoven with significant personal experiences. So it's understandable that people can tend to be a bit territorial about their musical devotion.

There will always be discourse. Whether or not it's purposeful is another story.

The advent of technology affords unlimited capability to speak our minds. Given the luxury of keyboard anonymity, most YouTube enthusiasts I've observed leave comments the same way that dogs piss. Not to contribute intelligently, but rather just to mark territory. You know the ones. They argue back and forth calling each other 'fucktard' over whether Joe Satriani is a better guitar player than Steve Vai. The unfortunate evolution of bathroom stall wisdom in the Information Age.

Radio stations and print & electronic media 'Top 100 of All Time' rankings are really just foolishness with zero redeeming worth outside of their entertainment value. They don't mean anything, because they can't. They're compiled for mass public consumption via the public. And because subjectivity is a sociological imperative, there can't be a truly definitive measure of, say, who the *best* drummer of *all time* is. Measuring actual musicianship as a technical skill may lend itself to a more definitive consensus, but even as obviously and remarkably skilled as Rush's Neil Peart may be, there will never be a universal consensus that he is in fact *the best drummer ever*. It's still music we're talking about, and personal musical passion will always usurp any credence the science of technical measurement may have in this discourse.

In any musical context there will be *great*, but there can never be a *greatest*. There's simply no justifiable criterion by which to measure that, and too much piousness involved to respect the criterion if it did exist. But really, is there even a need for one? The answer is no. There can be a *favourite*, and I suspect that this is what people would endeavour to say when the word *greatest* is instead used.

Every individual's considerations are intangible, but they carry weight only to the edges of said individual's own personal truths. In a democratic society this is elementary. The kicker is that these intangibles are presumably, or at least ideally, driven by logical and informed personal opinion.

All things considered, it can only be good enough to be open-minded and to recognize the importance of informed opinion in musical discourse. Because in the end, though not sadly nor happily, the pointlessness of debate will perpetually continue to swirl in the wind. And none of it will ever really mean anything.

⛥ Seventeen ⛥
The Church of Axl

W. Axl Rose is the consummate anti-hero.

I've had a love / hate relationship with Rose since 1987. I suppose this is largely due to the fact that when I used to think I finally pinned him down and understood him for trying so desperately not to be understood, he would just take me in the opposite direction again. It would be easy to write Rose off as an eccentric, self-absorbed, embittered asshole, but there's a lot more to the story if you're really paying attention.

Axl Rose's various proclivities, bizarre as some of them may seem, should be contemplated in a separate context from the quality of his musical output. Unless you consider the quality of the music to be a result of some form of mental deviation or even pathology, in the same way that Vincent Van Gogh's artistic genius was a by-product of his madness. Some have made this connection in the past with musical artists like Kurt Cobain, Syd Barrett, and others, and without making direct and unnecessary comparisons, the same theory may apply in Rose's case.

Since *Appetite for Destruction* came out in 1987, Axl Rose has occupied a unique space, partially due to the fact that he was the de facto leader of a band that proved they existed on a much higher plane than did their Sunset Strip hair metal brethren, and were considered by many, myself included, as capable of being the next Rolling Stones. That's a bold goddamn statement, but Guns could back it up. Looking back on what made Guns N' Roses a special band in their original member heyday, it might be easier to consider what they *weren't* doing rather than what they were.

Guns N' Roses was formed in 1985 smack dab in the middle of Hollywood's Sunset Strip, during a glam metal movement that had already launched the likes of Ratt, Dokken, Quiet Riot, and Motley Crue during its first wave with Poison, Warrant, and Great White on deck for the second onslaught. Guns may have gained their footing on the Strip, but it was clear by the following year that they didn't belong. Slash has said in the past that a large part of Guns N' Roses' fame can be attributed to the fact that the band was simply "in the right place at the right time". He was being overly modest, but he was right.

It was primarily Van Halen that initiated the 'metal lite' infrastructure of the Sunset Strip scene. They were the only other real rock and roll band on the Strip previous to Guns during the entire movement. Van Halen touched off a frenzy for all things longhaired and hard rock sounding.

As they began to assemble a following, the Gunners distanced themselves from most of the pack with powerful and innately talented performances, with a look and attitude that was more Sex Pistols than Slaughter. Even when you make a more apples-to-apples comparison between Guns N' Roses and grittier, less glammy Strip bands like Jetboy (whose singer Mickey Finn wore a mohawk), it was clear that Guns stood alone. They were a bunch of anti-glam dirtbags who gravitated to each other via repulsion from the Aqua Net set. So when Slash says 'right place right time', it only means that they were fortunate enough to be able to use the Sunset Strip hotbed as a starting point to catapult themselves onto the world stage. *Appetite for Destruction* was a great record with more musicianship and promise than its contemporaries, boasting riffs like the "Nighttrain" intro and arrangements featuring the "Sweet Child O' Mine" breakdown, but it wasn't completely demonstrative of Guns N' Roses at the height of their musical powers. That moment would come with the release of *GN'R Lies*.

Appetite for Destruction didn't really sell for almost a year after it was initially released in 1987, because at that time people didn't necessarily recognize the band for what they really were. Guns had certainly distanced themselves from the Poisons and the Warrants of West Hollywood with their image and live performances, and despite having some great songs in "Mr. Brownstone", "Welcome to the Jungle", and "It's So Easy", they weren't yet completely distinguishable from other Sunset Strip bands like Faster Pussycat, Junkyard, and Johnny Crash (Guns keyboardist Dizzy Reed and original drummer Steven Adler's replacement Matt Sorum were both Johnny Crash alumni). Soon-to-be-anthem "Sweet Child O' Mine" was intentionally buried on side two by Geffen A&R guru Tom Zutaut to maintain Guns N' Roses' reputation as a dirty rock and roll band first and as intuitive musicians second. This move was indicative of Zutaut's genius because we ate right out of his hand.

Personally, as a new Guns N' Roses fan in 1987 after having seen the "Welcome to the Jungle" video on the MuchMusic *Power Hour*, I bought *Appetite for Destruction* on the strength of that song and the video. After giving side two of my *Appetite* cassette the standard perusal, I went right back to side one and just rewound it continually, almost treating the record like it was an EP – "Welcome to the Jungle", then "It's So Easy", to "Nightrain", into "Out Ta Get Me", and finishing with "Mr. Brownstone". With a lineup like that, I couldn't sit through "Anything Goes" and "Think About You" to get back to side one. I would always hit the stop then rewind buttons on my lousy little boom box right after those last four sneering notes rang out from Slash's Les Paul at the end of "Mr. Brownstone". Da da, da *daaa*....

Superhits "Paradise City" and "Sweet Child O' Mine" were eventually 'discovered' by the world via MTV (and I guess MuchMusic), and Guns N' Roses elevated themselves beyond the Sunset Strip scene, but it wasn't really until *GN'R Lies* came out that we would come to know Guns' real depth. The *Lies* album itself is an awkwardly cobbled together amalgam of two EPs; the previously released 1986 "indie" EP *Live ?!#@ Like a Suicide* forming side one, and with four new songs making up side two. *GN'R Lies* and *Appetite for Destruction* are polarized in that with *Lies*, the real magic comes from side two. The four songs on it are all acoustically rendered, and they unveil that coveted facet of substance and feel that every hair metal Sunset Strip outfit lacked. The same one that great bands like the Stones seemed to keep tucked in their back pocket so naturally.

The real evidence of this is in "Patience". Guitarist Izzy Stradlin came to the band with this song and while it's a good one, the tangible difference really lies in how it's transmuted in the band's warm, folksy delivery, particularly through Slash's blues inflections. The performance is a clear indication of Guns N' Roses' musical import. This is especially significant when you consider the fact that this would have been the band's *ballad moment*, that crystallizing rite of passage for every hair band of this period. Guns N' Roses may have been spawned in this hair metal movement, but "Patience" was evidence that they never belonged in it.

When we consider the more notable ballads of the period, they all subscribe to a common interchangeable formula. Poison's "Every Rose Has Its Thorn", Slaughter's "Fly to the Angels", Warrant's "Heaven", Motley Crue's "Home Sweet Home", and Skid Row's "I Remember You" all used that acoustic intro with the schlock power chord chorus approach. Most every band popular and lesser known alike all did it, but what's funny is that it didn't really need to be done.

The other day I was watching a YouTube clip of a Tora Tora live performance of their ballad "Phantom Rider" that looked like it was shot just a few years ago. It was intriguing because while "Phantom Rider" follows the formula to the letter, in this case with the big crashing electric guitar power chord coming after the first chorus, I thought about what this song would sound like if it was completely stripped down and played as a strictly acoustic arrangement with no manufactured crescendos.

The setting for this video was one of those smaller bars in the midwestern U.S. like Jaxx or whatever. The crowd was ample enough. When the song started, people were yelling like it was the second fucking coming of Christ. They sang every word, before and after that unnecessary power chord. This song meant something to them. I wondered if it could have maybe meant a bit more to more people had it been conveyed in a more natural, less formulaically governed way.

I smiled to myself when I remembered playing "Phantom Rider" in my university dorm back in 1989 on my student loan-funded Nakamichi stereo for a (metal-hating) girl I was dating at the time. She listened intently from the beginning, and then as soon as that crashing C#5 / D5 / D#5 / E5 distorted electric guitar chord sequence leapt out of the speakers, she asked me to turn it down. She said, *"I liked it up until that part"*.

If we're being honest, "Patience" isn't necessarily a superior musical composition to "Phantom Rider". What makes it great is how the song is conveyed. Guns N' Roses knew better than to deploy that shallow format and forge their own path their own way per their own musical pedigree. But the most important thing about "Patience", the ultimate game-changer in this song - and what would establish Axl Rose and Guns N' Roses as a musical force - was the *whistling*.

Think about that for a second. Who had the balls to try something like that at that time in hard rock circles? As malevolent and bent on destruction as the Guns gang was, they pulled off something that you might expect from Pat Boone - something you'd never, ever expect on a hard rock record in 1988. But Rose's pairing of brazen legitimacy and musical sensibility allowed him to carry it out in such a way that made it special and believable. People *got* that, and it changed things. And whaddya know? Lo and behold, whistling appears two years later on Scorpions' ballad, "Wind of Change".

Equally intriguing for me was the concept of Axl Rose as a potential modern day tragic hero - channelling the ghosts of rock and roll past in our collective rock consciousness, strapped in and barrelling toward an inevitable demise of his own making, all the while imploring those who thought they saw glimpses of themselves in his gloriously chaotic story (like, of course, me) to hop aboard and join his revolt. I have to admit that as a young fan I accepted that invitation from a distance, all the while introspectively measuring my own propensity to 'use my illusions', drawing parallels that would nonetheless remain benign and securely sheltered in the back of my teenage mind.

Typically, I categorically like or dislike things and people as a general rule. No greys. With Rose, I was a fence sitter for a long time. I loved some of the music, loathed some of the music. Most of the good stuff is obvious - "November Rain", "Patience", "Sweet Child O' Mine", "Estranged". Even the cover tunes are ameliorated. "Live and Let Die" realizes previously unrealized power in the Guns canon.

On this particular topic, cover songs are a great example of how Guns N' Roses embodied musical greatness in comparison to their L.A. peers. Any metalhead worth his or her salt will know that Lizzy Borden also covered Paul McCartney's "Live and Let Die" on their 1985 *Murderous Metal Road Show* live release. Though I do consider myself a Borden fan, the comparison between the two versions doesn't even warrant consideration, and I'm sure even Lizzy himself would admit it.

With Rose's unique facility in creating vocal ad-libs and melodic harmonies that augment already great compositions, he takes the songs to another equally worthwhile and sometimes even better place, as heard in the acoustically-rendered bootleg of the Stones' "Jumpin' Jack Flash". My favourite Guns cover is probably a little-known Black Sabbath song from *Technical Ecstasy* record called "It's Alright". I love it because while the original is an obscure Sabbath throwaway, Rose performs the song on Guns' *Live Era* record as a vocal-and-piano-only version of how you would think the song should have come across all along. The guy is a musical King Midas. What really sets him apart is his vision to recognize possibility in things.

Rose's artistic yang to this yin is self-indulgence like "My World" and the other unnecessary, cacophonous nonsense that cluttered the *Illusions* records. The uncomfortably awkward, point-blank intensity of his open book psychosis is unsettling to witness. The fleeting glimpses Rose offers in "Don't Cry" and "Don't Damn Me" are digestible, but they're more like the showing of a Band-Aided wound as opposed to him picking off his sociopathic scabs and throwing them at you. As such, his histrionics can carve such a deep swath that indifference is ratcheted up to acute irritation.

I recognize the fact that Axl Rose's voice is one of the most powerful in the history of rock and roll, and that his range and use of an even, controlled vibrato technique is letter-perfect. He sings in various tonal colorations and timbres, all distinctly recognizable as unique Axl-isms. If singing voices were knives, Rose's would be a machete. If you listen to the bootlegs of him appearing with Tom Petty on "Free Fallin'" and with Bruce Springsteen on "Come Together", you tend to feel kinda sorry for those guys from a vocal perspective. Petty had a sneering, badass singing voice on stuff like "Refugee" and anything pre- *Full Moon Fever*, and The Boss was obviously no slouch either, but when you hear them singing side-by-side with Rose in a neutral element like the MTV Awards, it's clear that he just flat out crushes them by a significant margin.

And yet on the other hand, I've heard his voice sound painfully screechy and fragile as well. I was always interested by the fact that, knowing how much of a vested interest Rose has in anything with the Guns N' Roses name on it, the "Patience" live track that appeared on *Live Era* is a version that actually garnered his approval given the poor quality of the vocal track and the presumably kajillions of recorded versions of that song to choose from. It's real deal to be sure, even very remotely reminiscent of Jagger's jangly, vulnerable vocal on *Exile on Main Street's* "Sweet Virginia" insofar as it gives the same raw stripped-down, *tortured-artist-suffering-for-his-art* impression, just unfortunately without coming across nearly as vibey. Regardless, its inclusion on the record is most likely by design on Rose's part, just another peculiar contribution to his bid to be considered as ultimately quixotic.

I have to admit that after passing on the opportunity to sample countless *Chinese Democracy* leaks in previous years, I eventually broke down and listened to a couple of the bootleg tracks before the record finally came out. This was more or less because I questioned whether it would actually be released, because I do have a personal philosophy that applies to this sort of thing.

If I respect an artist and consider myself a fan of theirs, I believe that I'm obliged to support them by paying for the entertainment they provide me as their fan. It's fair and equitable, and I'm just old-fashioned like that. I've dabbled in all those Napster-clone downloading sites in the past to obtain one-off songs by one-hit wonder bands, the ones that had one song that I liked but the rest of the album didn't warrant my spending $17.99 on it because the remainder of the songs weren't my cup of tea. Like Autograph's "Turn Up The Radio". I would have never bought that whole record. It was hypocritical, but my outlook was that if I was a fan of the song not the band, I didn't see the harm in accessing the odd tune or two for free back then. I do now.

These file-sharing sites were also virus-sharing sites, not to mention the question of quality and even content of the file you were downloading. Often a file that carried the name of the song you were looking for wasn't that song at all. There were decoys that contained that dickhead imitating Bill Clinton in an endless loop. Or, the downloaded song might cut off halfway though, might sound like shit, et cetera. My personal favourite of all of these pitfalls were the downloads that contained high-pitched squealing sounds after the first thirty seconds or so of the song, these music files being deftly inserted into the internet piracy petri dish by the record company in an effort to bid me a sharp *fuck you* for stealing from them, and rightfully so. I actually thought this was a clever strategy and a well-deserved touché. Hey, you gotta give credit where credit is due.

When iTunes finally came along, I used it to sample entire records to determine if I liked them. Now I use Grooveshark to listen to the whole song, or record, and then just buy the songs I wanted for 99 cents or go ahead and buy the CD if I liked at least half of the record and the artist. Easy, and everybody's happy. I've never been to those sites that allow you to download full albums, despite people continuing to extol the virtues of these things. I know a guy who is a blatant pirate who downloads whole albums, the album art, liner notes, all of it. It kinda makes me a bit sick to be honest, because it almost carries that implication that he gets a charge out of the sticking it to the man thing, which actually supersedes the point of obtaining the music just because you happen to like it. It goes back to the fan loyalty thing for me, but also rather than take the time to download an entire record with artwork and all the rest of it. If you like it, just buy the bloody record!

But back to the *Chinese Democracy* leaks.

At the time I had previously read all kinds of commentary about these songs from all kinds of sources, but there was always one common denominator – they sounded grand. And I can say that the songs were indeed that - *grand*. If anyone was looking for the natural succession to *Appetite For Destruction* or even to the *Use Your Illusions* records, they needn't have looked there. To really enjoy these songs, you need to consider them as separate entities in and of themselves, having little to do with old Guns N' Roses, and really nothing at all to do with *Appetite*.

I understand that this is difficult, as a key cornerstone of Axl Rose worship is rooted in the jackhammering swagger of *Appetite for Destruction*. And I can tell you that I do *looooove* that record. But when it finally came out, the *Chinese Democracy* album dared the listener to consider Rose as an upper-echelon songwriter, on a higher level than as attained by anything previously output, including "November Rain". All sorts of new elements introduced themselves, including trip-hop beats accompanied by flamenco guitar. This new stuff was truly epic, demonstrating that Rose possesses a legitimate understanding of melody in composition, swelling crescendos, quieted subtlety, and wry cleverness. The music was powerful, vital, and absolutely relevant. In fact, it actually changed my mind about the possibilities in potential for musical growth and artistic progression. I would previously long for my favourite artists to just rewrite their best records over and over again, out of my own selfishness and skepticism that they could navigate with any success into any other musical oeuvre. But Rose did so quite successfully on *Chinese Democracy*. And as such, I don't think he should have called this new incarnation Guns N' Roses.

Here's why. I think about what the product of an original-lineup, modern-day Guns would sound like, considering the important variables in the progression of that group (minus drug-addled Steven Adler) and assuming Slash and maybe Stradlin would be the only other meaningful songwriting contributors in addition to Rose's material.

Yes, I do know that bassist Duff McKagan was lauded by some folks as a formidable songwriter. I never saw it. Listen to his first solo record if you need proof of that. The most compelling thing about Duff back then was how much longer he would last before his pancreas finally exploded through that ghastly black mesh shirt that barely covered his bloated torso every night (Duff is back in incredible shape these days though, and he sounds more and more like the intelligent human being I'm sure he was before he regularly drank and drugged himself into the stratosphere previously).

Anyway, we know that Scott Weiland was a competent purveyor of melody, and in Velvet Revolver he likely built upon Slash's riff foundations for the two VR records with the remaining band members as secondary contributors. But as much as I like the VR records, the second more than the first, they simply didn't measure up to the material on *Chinese Democracy*. Not even close.

And I'm not talking about the curious first-single selection "Chinese Democracy". I'm talking about songs like "There Was A Time", "Prostitute", and "Better". Pinheads will argue that Rose took ten-plus years to come up with the material, and blah blah blah. But as much as I do love Slash, as a guitar player and a genuinely organic musician the likes of which is rarely seen today for playing the hell out of the pentatonic scale but with brilliant note selection, I think we all know who the most prolific songwriter in the Guns gang was.

Thus, Rose could and should have easily housed this new project under a separate name. Hell, he could have even called it something as unimaginative as AXL or whatever, thereby inadvertently keeping the Guns brand alive in order to avoid the risk of a freefall into obscurity. But, it would seem that in his megalomaniacal style Rose recognized himself as the nucleus and thus sole and rightful proprietor of the Guns N' Roses namesake and this new musical direction is the natural path that this entity would have taken under his leadership. With or without Slash and the remainder of his former peers.

A real Guns N' Roses fan shouldn't have been surprised by the trip-hop beats and other never-before-heard-on-a-GN'R-record elements. You had to know that anything was possible after 1993's *The Spaghetti Incident?* featured a remake of 50s song "Since I Don't Have You" and a cover version of Charles Manson's "Look At Your Game, Girl". What is considered germane at any given time is completely up to Rose. That's simply the way it is in Axl World, and it doesn't appear this is about to change any time soon. I'll admit that when he forged out on his own in the mid-to-late 90's, I anticipated a plunge into nebulousness that he wouldn't ever recover from, a consideration that was validated at the time by his tragic performance on the MTV Video Awards in 2002.

I remember reading about the GN'R developments post-*Illusions*, most likely both real and fabricated. That Rose wanted to take the band in a Nine Inch Nails industrial direction. That Moby was involved in the production of the new record. That Rose was going to learn how to play lead guitar in a bid to replace Slash after he left. Not to mention that airport incident in the late 90s where he took on a cop in a baggage inspection dispute that earned him some time in the cooler. All of these things were bizarre and weirdly interesting to me at the time. Coupled with all the nonsense that was common knowledge about Rose not showing up at gigs and all of his other unsavoury behaviour, I didn't have a lot of faith in this new Guns thing. I had already written it off.

But since I had happened across Guns N' Roses at a point in my life where they, in particular Rose, were able to make an indelible impression on me, I still felt a marginal sense of community and remote loyalty. Back then Axl was the illustrious and colourful tip of the spear. He was the omnipresent ally to a surging, rebellious high school kid, a delectably malevolent Pied Piper beckoning to an impetuous teenager. I wasn't an impressionable kid anymore, but I still felt an oblique allegiance and I kept a bemused eye on the headlines, few and far between as they were.

When it came time for Rose to re-emerge by appearing on the MTV Video Awards in 2002, I was watching. And after what I saw I wished I hadn't.

It was like a scene from a Paul Thomas Anderson movie. I felt gravely deflated by that performance, like having watched the home team get royally shitkicked by the visitors. I was disappointed on a larger scale, because I felt like Guns N' Roses was a little part of who I was at my core, and it was a like a sign of the times that the party was emphatically over. I remember feeling a little bit like I had just seen the dreaded man behind the curtain. Like something that I had believed in was now without validity, and that it had wizened right before my eyes.

When Guns N' Roses booked a stop in Toronto later that year, I bought a ticket as a skeptic. I didn't know what I was going to witness, but I did know that I had to witness it. In person this time. I expected the worst, despite having read recent show reviews that claimed Rose was in decent if not good voice and that the show was worth seeing.

On the night of the show at the Air Canada Centre, in typical Rose fashion, the band came on late. The good news was that the crowd was distracted for a while by a cheeky little game the camera crew were playing. They trained their cameras on certain members of the female contingent in an attempt to have them bare some flesh for the rest of the crowd, who could see them on the huge video monitors above the stage. Four or five women started things off sheepishly with some weak faux-flashes. But, predictably, the spark that was needed to start this fire eventually came with one enthusiast yanking her top right up for a full naked ta-tas shot. Now it was on. The skin ante was upped each time the camera went back to a previous flasher. Soon things developed into a competition that saw a bit more than just a pair of tits exposed. These camera chaps, equal parts scoundrel and genius, had obviously carried out this exercise before. I didn't know what was more amusing, the flashing or the inadvertent anthropological experiment that had just been carried out.

Because the previous Guns N' Roses show in Vancouver that was scheduled a few days before had been cancelled at the last minute and a riot had ensued, I suspected the same might result in Toronto. It had been over an hour since the band was expected to come on, and that very tangible *Lord of the Flies* pack-mentality tension was in the air. It seemed as though the first chairs were about to fly just as the house lights came down. You could almost hear a collective sigh of relief exhaled from the members of law enforcement on hand alongside that opening delayed E note of "Welcome To The Jungle".

Whoever was playing the intro that night of the three guitarist troika comprising Fortus, Finck, and Buckethead, was only playing that first note of the six that make up that distinctive opening "Jungle" riff, over and over, letting the note delay teasingly while the crowd squealed in anticipation. I smiled to myself when I considered the acute irony of this fact.

The show itself was much better than I had expected. I knew that the musicians would all be crack. But they were almost too good. The songs came off sounding like a perfectly note-for-note rendered version of the real thing from a tribute band. The performance shone with a veneer that the original Guns N' Roses would have never mustered if they tried. It was apparent to me at this point that there would be a new way. A departure from the raw, fanciful sloppiness of the *Illusions*-era Guns crew. Each band member was extremely talented in their own right. The most gifted of them most likely being

Buckethead, who began his solo spot with a nunchakus demonstration followed by a robot-dance routine and eventually, a very impressive guitar solo.

I didn't *want* to like this because it felt mildly like blasphemy. But I have to admit it was highly entertaining. Buckethead sure as hell was no Slash, and vice versa, and this production I had just witnessed definitely was not the Guns N' Roses I knew at all.

Rose himself was much more gregarious than I had expected. He interacted quite a lot with the crowd, making jokes, odd cracks about Lars Ulrich, and even engaging in that ol' heartstring-puller of donning the sweater of the local pro hockey franchise for a song or two during the encore of the show[6]. He hit ninety-eight percent of the notes, not quite getting up to the highest registers of "You Could Be Mine" and "Welcome to the Jungle", but he sounded a hell of a lot better than he did during the MTV debacle. The new cornrows lid and the peculiar fact that he was wearing several layers of shirts even after his trademark myriad costume changes took some getting used to, but the bottom line was that I was actually proud of him for pulling it off. He kinda seemed like a shadow of his former self from the Guns glory days after that night, but this was easily overlooked and even expected. It made his public figure more palpable somehow. He was no longer invulnerable, and it made him less distant.

After that show Rose and company went on to play rock star mecca Madison Square Garden and by all accounts, killed. Unfortunately, Rose failed to appear for the Philly show and promoter Clear Channel pulled the plug on the remainder of the tour. I had read that he commented that there was no way he could duplicate the success of the MSG show, so there was no point going on. I also heard that he refused to leave his hotel room because he was watching an NBA game on TV, and that he travelled with his own personal therapist who literally had to talk him into going on every night to perform. Not sure if any of this stuff was true or not.

---

[6] *Around this time I had seen a picture of Axl allegedly taken in some Los Angeles club wearing a Toronto Maple Leafs jersey. For rizzle.*

No Sleep 'til Sudbury

I saw Guns N' Roses again in Toronto in 2006. Rose looked quite a lot better. Thinner, and with actual eyebrows. More normal looking. And this time, there was no fucking around singing-wise. Each and every note was hit with authority. Rose even held them a little longer as if to send a bit of a message to the non-believers. I was happy to see him back on top of his game.

On the whole, I try to give the guy some latitude with the bizarre behaviour thing. I just sidestep it when it has the potential to impact me personally. That last Toronto show I was at intentionally started at 11pm, getting me back home at 3am and having to be up for work the next day just three hours later. Not good. This forced me to impose a firm self-governing policy that would prevent me from ever attending another GN'R show on a school night, which I unfortunately upheld two months ago when the band came through town on a Tuesday night.

Regardless of all of this, I am rooting for Axl Rose. That sociological imperative defined by the sadistic pleasure we take in witnessing public failure, the more gruesome and salacious the better, has reared its head in his direction often enough. It's like David Lee Roth said – *"Dare to raise your head above the crowd, and somebody's bound to throw a rock at it."* As I write this I'm reminded of all of those disarming t-shirts that Rose wore on the *Illusions* tours that carried messages like "Charlie Don't Surf!" and "Nobody Knows I'm A Lesbian" (my personal favourite, even had one of my own). One particular shirt he often wore stands out in my mind as an ironic self-prophesy check against his own self-aggrandizement. It read, "Kill Your Idols". Axl Rose was, is, and always will be his own worst enemy. And inherently, I think he knows this.

The depth and breadth of the concept of W. Axl Rose is profound. I say *the concept* of, because at the end of the day I don't know the guy. Like anyone else, I can go on what I glean from the mass media and what he puts out there for me to consider. But the legitimate, visceral, and *real* connection, as it always has been for music fans and their favourite artists since the dawn of popular music, is through the music itself, and the perception of the message it delivers.

While I'm positive that Rose is extremely cognizant of image creation, maintenance, and spin, his message delivery is still met with extremism, because he has developed such a sizeable spectrum for the concept of himself through his inexplicable conduct. Reactions and responses will always be polarized, and The Church of Axl will almost certainly continue to enjoy economy of scale in this sense, as people will forever be interested whether we empathize because we think we understand his myriad troubles and can relate, or because we scathingly loathe his unfathomable disingenuousness and dismiss him as an unworthy, spoiled crybaby.

The contradictions are many and certainties few. Nevertheless, Rose is wise enough, creative enough, and resilient enough to have the last sardonic laugh. And my money's on him.

✡ Eighteen ✡
Jammed
~

Now, the bet isn't against Slash, and it doesn't have to be. Slash exists on the other side of the coin, almost like Van Halen and Van Hagar. Just like it would be best if Guns N' Roses never got back together again, it's also best that Slash and Axl exist in their own mediums. I picked up Slash's new record, and I have to admit that it's better than I thought it would be. On the surface it would be easy to perceive this as a Santana-inspired wankfest. But Slash, by virtue of his organic rock instincts, is able to turn out a record that succeeds in areas you might not think it would.

His track with Adam Levine from Maroon 5 is outstanding. In fact, it's a perfect blend of the separate musical dimensions that Levine and Slash occupy. After listening to the Levine track "Gotten" it sounds more like Slash is building synergistic Frankensteins with less likely collaborators that turn out to actually be really great songs. "Gotten" comes from the same place that "Fall to Pieces" does but by using Levine as a foil, Slash can allow himself the guilty pleasure of a song that's more beautiful than it is dark and malevolent.

Most of the songs seem to be trade offs, like the Kid Rock tune. Kid gets the Uncle Cracker sounding verses and chorus; Slash gets the extended solos and the obligatory dirty abridging riffs. It works, and it's nice to see that it works. Slash actually comes across as an instinctual genius for taking the idiosyncratic elements of guys like Lemmy and Ian Astbury and serving up platforms for them to project from. The perfect example of this is the last track on the record, "We're All Gonna Die" featuring Iggy Pop. Slash harnesses that beautiful idiocy of Pop's that made dumb songs like "Lust For Life" so enduring, by encouraging vintage Iggy-isms like *"I'm gonna pee on the ground"*. It's only because Slash understands this stuff that it works, from Adam Levine and Iggy to Kid Rock and Avenged Sevenfold. The songs are actually good songs, not just vehicles designed to get Slash back into the public eye.

The Myles Kennedy material on Slash's record is just fucking *golden*. I like how Kennedy borrows *ever* so slightly from Axl at 0:31 in "Back From Cali". And "Starlight" is the song that Guns plagiarists put their fists through walls over and cry tears of despair after hearing because it's not fair that they didn't write it between now and when "Sweet Child" came out. Kennedy sounds a lot like Robert Mason, and this tune sounds like something from the band he was in with blues guitar genius Audley Freed, Cry of Love. It's money. Slash's pairing with Kennedy mines the same gems as he did with singer Eric Dover on his first solo record with "Beggars and Hangers On". Slash needs to lock himself in a room with Kennedy and come out only after they write an album's worth of this stuff.

I read that Slash imagined certain people singing the songs he was writing as he wrote them. When I hear the Ozzy song, I listen to the riff and wonder if he was thinking Black Sabbath, which would make sense for Slash. It comes across sounding more like Ozzy's late period stuff, like "Back on Earth". I was expecting something a bit darker. The darkness comes through in the lyrics though I guess, with cheeky lines like *"a loaded gun jammed by a rose"*. Zing. Wonder who that's about.

As for Slash getting back together with Axl, they probably will but I really hope they don't. It just wouldn't be right. Guns N' Roses Proper went as far as it could. While it lasted it was undistilled and glorious, and this is the principle that made them great. There's a beauty in that intense volatility of what was GN'R that would be cheapened by a money-grab reunion. It could only make a mockery of that legacy.

Nineteen
Canuck Metal

Ah, Canadian metal.

Until just recently Rush may have been the most widely known Canadian "metal" act, even if it was just through lazy, lackadaisical association. Rush was another band that was never technically *heavy metal* at any point of their career. It's a moot point anyway, since the instantly but deservedly world-famous Anvil may now hold that distinction. Famous at least at the time of writing.

Back in the early 80s, Anvil was on my radar even before Iron Maiden, Judas Priest, or any other NWOBHM bands. Listening back to their 1982 *Metal on Metal* record now, it's clear that it was definitely on par with anything that bands like Tygers of Pan Tang or Angel Witch were putting out at the time. If you didn't know any better, you might even think that Anvil *was* part of the British metal invasion. Most of the songwriting and instrumentation on *Metal on Metal* is more than vaguely correlated to the two first Maiden records, but the Canadian giveaway is radio hit Hail Mary "Stop Me". I always thought that Anvil rhythm guitarist Dave Allison's vocal on "Stop Me" sounded like an extra-wasted Ace Frehley circa 1978, singing in a wonky English accent. Come to think of it, *Metal on Metal* is pretty much exactly how KISS would have sounded had they been a NWOBHM band.

I have to admit that *Metal on Metal* intimidated me a bit back then. It was heavy, but unlike Iron Maiden it wasn't cut with a colourful mascot or imagery of any sort. It was just four mean-looking dudes on the back cover. Listening to *Metal on Metal* at that age was kinda like drinking booze without mix, in the sense that there was no image to temper the heaviness of the music. They did have an image I guess, but that image was lead guitarist and vocalist Steve 'Lips' Kudlow running around on stage in a leather bondage get-up making maniacal faces and playing his guitar with a big dildo like a fucking mental case. Because we only had a few channels on the telly at that time, I didn't find out about any of that stuff until much later. In 1982, I had this record and nothing else. And hearing songs like "666" without having a fantastical Eddie-type character to overlay the darkness of the song against, I didn't stick around. Unfortunately, I was a sucker for the optics back then.

What I didn't know back in 1982 was that Anvil was influencing bands like Metallica, Anthrax, Slayer, and people like Slash from Guns N' Roses. The bad news is that Anvil would fail in their bid to join these bands in the upper echelons of fame. But the *good* news is that one of their old roadies from the 80s, Sacha Gervasi, would go on to become a film student in Europe and decide that it would be a good idea to shoot a documentary of the band's crummy plight called *The Story of Anvil*.

As good documentaries do, *The Story of Anvil* strips away artifice and humanizes the central characters in unsavoury ways. Ways you may not like. Previous documentaries (*Metal: A Headbanger's Journey*) and mockumentaries (*FUBAR, Spinal Tap*) alike have nothing on this movie. The photo inclusion of Lips' full frontal nudity to start the movie is an allegorical indication of the cringe-worthy, painful-to-watch raw exposure that Lips and his band (and heavy metal as subtext) would be subject to in the film.

Most of my friends saw the movie before I did and asked me for my thoughts on it. Because almost all of my friends are more or less repulsed by heavy metal, as I watched *The Story of Anvil* I considered how diametrically differently a metalhead would experience this movie in relation to someone who wasn't a heavy metal fan. When I saw the opening scenes of Anvil playing live in Japan in 1984, with the guitar players lined up beside each other, hair flying, headbanging to and fro in unison to the pounding beat and the "Metal on Metal" riff blasting from the amps, it was electrifying. The hair on the back of my neck stood on end. This stuff was a very special and personal totem for me. And for most of my friends, it was hilariously stupid.

I have to confess that I had a hard time watching this movie. It challenged my personal constitution as it relates to self-image because it forced me to deal with the fact that a considerable portion of *real* heavy metal fans are not like me at all. I've used the term *metalhead* in self-reference in passing as a matter of convenience, but I've never really considered myself a real metalhead in the same context that people like those two gentlemen in the movie singing Anvil songs to each other *a capella* might. As much as this clip is senseless contribution to an unfortunate yet very prevalent stereotype, I still felt guilty for being some kind of shape-shifting phony.

My hangup in high school used to be trying to prove to people that you can be a heavy metal fan beyond the obvious stereotype (read: *literate*), but that stemmed from personal identity crisis issues of my own. I loved the metal but vehemently dodged the stigma. I didn't know what that made me, and I still may not know. This movie plays up that stigma in horrifying detail. And it ain't pretty, man. The primary reason I felt a bit uncomfortable watching *The Story of Anvil* is because it's a staid reminder of a hard lesson I avoided learning for a long time about not giving a fuck about what other people think.

This very premise drives the beautiful ugliness of this movie. Lips and his bandmate, Anvil co-founder Robb Reiner, want what every headbanging outcast wants – not to have to give a fuck, and acceptance while not having to give a fuck, *but not for not giving a fuck*. I have to admit that Anvil deserves immediate props just for letting this movie be released to the public with such a mortifying scope of exposure. The movie itself, however, is befitting of the real respect they're due for staying true to themselves throughout their career and for being resilient enough to be who they really are, even to this day.

While Anvil finally does appear to be 'famous' at the end of the movie it almost seems to be in more of a manufactured, placated way. When I finished watching the movie I considered *The Story of Anvil*'s popularity among non-metal fans potentially being soup-du-jour fodder for cred-hungry hipsters. Or worse, popular for the same reasons people watch those shows about hoarders and interventions on A&E - they derive morbid pleasure from seeing other people at their lowest points.

Regardless, 'making it' seemed to be the prime objective of Lips and Reiner, so for them to watch the beginning of *The Story of Anvil* was either the next best thing to making it, or a flurry of blindingly painful roundhouse kicks to the pills. Slash, Lars Ulrich, Lemmy, and Scott Ian from Anthrax, all world famous rock stars in their own right, offer some pretty mind-bending Anvil accolades in the commentary they provide on the band. Ulrich goes as far as saying that Robb Reiner was considered to be the best metal drummer out there in the early 80s. Slayer's Tom Araya says that Anvil was 'thrash' one year before The Big Four[7]. I was hoping this wouldn't serve as a kick in the nuts for Lips and Reiner more than panacea for all of the heartbreak they've endured over the years. Because this segment, mind-boggling as it initially is, instantly deconstructs the basic concept of idolatry and demonstrates just how ridiculously frustrating and senseless it can be. These huge rock stars are saying these really heavy things about Lips, and later on in the movie Lips himself is shown running after guys like Tommy Aldridge backstage at a festival in Europe and calling them his heroes, with the giddy excitement of a starry-eyed kid. It's absurd.

This absurdity reminded me of a recent visit to a friend's cottage up north, a few years before *The Story of Anvil* was released. We were sitting around drinking one night and I was chatting with one of the locals from town about guitars. He happened to mention that he had received lessons from Dave Allison, *"a guy who used to play in some band called Anvil in the 80s"*. Intrigued, I started asking questions about how he knew Allison. He and a few other people around the table proceeded

---

[7] *Considering that three of the Big Four bands are represented in the movie, it instantly makes me wonder what happened when Gervasi approached Megadeth founder Dave Mustaine for his input.*

to share stories about how Allison, nicknamed "Squirrelly" back in his Anvil days and now shortened to "Squirrel" by the locals, lived in some cottage or something not far from town. According to them, he had a reputation for more or less being the town drunk. Their stories focused on Allison's tendency to pass out with a lit cigarette, once resulting in the loss of all of the guitars he owned during his Anvil days.

I was mildly thrilled that they knew Dave Allison, the original guitarist from Anvil, but in their eyes he was just some sloppy old boozer. This was intriguing to me partially because when you look at old pictures of Anvil from when Allison was in the band, he was actually the coolest looking guy in the group. And to Anvil fans in the 80s he was very highly revered, especially among the female contingent. I questioned what these people would have thought of him had they any idea who Anvil was, or if they had seen him in full rock star mode in front of a stadium full of screaming fans in 1984. The answer was probably not much more, as such is the plight of the headbanger. Most people just don't give a fuck. But headbangers don't give an even *bigger* fuck in response. At least on the surface anyway, per the rules of Outcast 101. And as it turned out Dave Allison, despite his modern-day short grey hair, glasses and beer gut, was still not giving a fuck with booze and lit cigarettes in a cottage down the road just a few minutes away.

Anyway, among all of the incredible things that are said about Anvil during this commentary, there seems to be some uncertainty as to why Anvil didn't 'make it' the same way Metallica and other bands did. The comments held that the band had the entire package - they were influential, talented, driven, et cetera. Enter our wise old friend Lemmy Kilmister, who says: *"You just have to be in the right place at the right time. That's the whole thing"*.

Bingo.

I like Lemmy, but Motorhead ain't exactly lighting the world on fire with its musical virtuosity or its matinee idol pin-up looks. As I mentioned earlier, Slash has also attributed the fame of Guns N' Roses to the same 'right place, right time' idea. Seems to me even Father Van Halen once responded to an acknowledgement of his guitar godliness by saying that there were better guitar players than he slogging it out in small clubs right now, which will never be discovered or recognized for their abilities on any great scale. You can't deny that Slash and Edward are extraordinarily talented, but despite talent, hard work, networking, image, and so on, timing is still ultimately *everything* - it's the X factor that encapsulates all of the perceived success variables, and maneuvers them and the band through that glut of club circuit gigging, word of mouth exposure, media enablers, management deals, major label record contract availability, and other factors that all need to line up precisely for a band to make it. It either happens or it doesn't. It can't be controlled.

In the DVD bonus features section of *The Story of Anvil*, the Anvil accolades continue during an extended interview feature with Ulrich. He had some really interesting things to say, in addition to stuff like the fact that Robb Reiner was asked to join Ozzy's band in the 80s. Didn't know that. Ulrich impressed me with his knowledge of obscure Canadian rock bands like Streetheart, and I thought his explanation of the rationale behind the *Kerrang!* phenomenon that resulted from the Geoff Barton-driven British music press hype machine was bang-on. I also loved his bit about Anvil not selling out, and that a few bands had radically changed what they were doing to 'make it' but fell flat, looking bad and losing respect in the process. Ulrich shies away from naming names, but I'd be willing to bet that two of the bands he was talking about were Raven and Celtic Frost.

Anyway, the most interesting bit came at the very end of the interview. Gervasi elicited a response from Ulrich that he didn't expect when he asked Ulrich what he would say to Anvil if they were there. Ulrich said he would shower them with compliments, buy them their beverage of choice, and hope that they wouldn't roll their eyes too much when he told them how great he thought they were. Gervasi got up and went over to Ulrich and sincerely thanked him for saying that and gave him a hug, saying that Lips would be genuinely moved to hear what he just said, because having stumbled around through the dark for fifteen years it would mean quite a lot to them. Ulrich seemed surprised and touched by Gervasi's emotion.

This was my favourite part of *The Story of Anvil*. It's a great example of why I'll always rent the DVD when I want to see a film. The behind-the-scenes pieces aren't technically part of the movie, but they provide added scope that the movie couldn't be expected to provide on its own. In *The Story of Anvil*, the bonus features inadvertently supply the most meaningful moment of the movie. Ulrich's exchange with Gervasi most effectively validates the *fait accompli* of Lips and Anvil actually having achieved success with the only goal that actually mattered. Not to mention validation of the fact that 'fame' is an artificial, nonsensical concept that really means very little.

Now back to Rush. While some may argue (and let's face it, someone is always going to argue, no matter what point is made) that Rush is a progressive rock band. But, in their beginnings and at their height, they were a hard rock band. Their 80s output contained an increased amount of synthesizer and a diminished amount of guitar (much to the chagrin of sole guitarist Alex Lifeson), but their early stuff was pure hard rock. Not heavy metal, but definitely hard rock. I only know this based on what I've seen and heard peripherally through radio or otherwise. Perhaps ironically, I've never been a Rush follower. For a Canadian hard rock and metal fan of my vintage to not be a Rush fan has perplexed even myself at times. It seems illogical. The band's technical and musical sophistication is immense, and the reach of their influence is such that I know enough about them to be a fan. But I never was.

I'm making a point of avoiding saying that I'm not a fan in present tense, because I feel like I should be. Not only is Rush's music prolific, but the guys in the band also seem to be decent people and proud Canadian ambassadors. They've involved themselves in Canadian parody institutions like Bob & Doug MacKenzie and The Trailer Park Boys (Axl Rose is also a big fan of TTPB, most likely via the influence of Canuck Sebastian Bach). A friend who plays guitar once told me that when he cleaned pools one summer, bassist and lead singer Geddy Lee was one of his weekly customers. By the end of the summer, Geddy had invited him into his basement to jam Rush songs.

Jesus. How could I not be a fan of this band?

It's for a couple of reasons. My music fan formative years were converse to hard rock bands that achieved their zenith in the 70s, like Deep Purple, Black Sabbath, and Rush. KISS is an exception, and they actually shed some additional light on my non-interest in Rush. As I mentioned in the second chapter, KISS was branded to include kids as fan acquisition targets in their juggernaut marketing campaign in the late 70s. They yanked me in with their image and kept me sated with flash. With blood. Fire. Action figures. Other bands didn't operate in this way, at least not to KISS' degree. And sadly but truly, I just wasn't as captivated. My vulnerability to image was fully exploited by Nikki Sixx and Blackie Lawless. As brilliant as Geddy Lee was as a musician, I wasn't sold.

Sloss was a Rush fan though. He had a vinyl copy of 2112 that I perused one night while we were listening to music in his bedroom back in our grade nine days. The visual was mildly interesting, but I remember thinking that it was no *Shout at the Devil*. The songs had mystical names like "Xanadu", and it seemed a bit too intellectually involved to me at the time. I also surmised that the band's technical precision, represented in large part by drummer Neil Peart (who may well have sold his soul to Beelzebub in exchange for his incomprehensible drumming ability), was too crisp and refined for my teenage rebel phase. If it was evident that Rush was a great band because of their musical heroics and focus on achievement through superior ability and high-mindedness, I had no time for that. Those bands were the enemy. I was more interested in bands singing songs about banging promiscuous chicks and general havoc. Not songs about Syrinxian temples and red barchettas. I didn't even know what a barchetta was in 1983. Actually, I still don't. But the difference is that now I care a lot more.

So after feeling a bit nonplussed by Rush's bookish image, I dismissed them and never looked back. It's almost like I programmed myself to dislike Rush just out of spite. Every time I heard Geddy's falsetto warblings come through the car radio speakers, I would automatically select another radio station. I made excuses saying that their songs were too intellectually highbrow. Or that Geddy's voice was too shrill (it kinda can be sometimes though). Regardless, the span of Rush's popularity was massive and omnipotent. Which made me dislike them even more in some peculiar way.

Lately I've been considering my position as a non-fan, and I have yet to admit to myself that it would be worthwhile or prudent to buy one or two of Rush's classic records. Maybe *Hemispheres,* or *A Farewell to Kings.* The fact that I know the names of these albums and that they're classics, though never once having listened to them, is centric to the frustrating quandary that is my relationship with Rush. I know that sooner or later, as a hard rock and metal fan, and maybe even as a fellow Canadian, I'll have to bury my silly self-imposed hatchet and recognize them for what they truly are. Even if I don't become a real Rush fan, I could never deny the fact that the band have realized some incredible achievements over the course of their career, the likes of which any band could be genuinely proud of. Canadian or otherwise.

I know it may sound stupid or even insecure to make loaded statements about national distinction like this. But it can be hard to avoid as a landlocked neighbour of the United States of America. As a Canadian, it's easy to demur in the shadow of the United States and to contribute to pre-established stereotyping. Particularly if you let mass media draw your conclusions for you.

In my opinion, the main difference between Canada and the U.S.A. is that America is distinctly and proudly insular, while Canada is more globally minded, particularly where America is concerned. Canada is consistently aware of America's presence and influence in every aspect and we quietly defer, whether or not we care to admit it. Canadians don't seem to know what they have because of the disparity between our two nations relative to national identity.

By way of history, America's radical assertion of New World nationality was very clearly spelled out in their *Declaration of Independence,* and Canada was much slower to cut ties with British imperialism.

America itself defined what America was and was not. Canada languished within the British Commonwealth, through tenuous relations between English Canadians and French Canadians. All beneath the foreboding hyper-nationalistic cultural heft of The United States of America, who were right next door.

American influence is immense, particularly in Canada. I've always been interested in the fact that American awareness is engrained in the collective Canadian psyche from the get-go not only via media outlets, but also in our schools. American history is prevalent in Canadian educational curriculum, but based on what I've gathered from conversations with Americans I've known, Canadian history is more like Canadian mystery in the States.

As an acquiescent Canadian, I admit that I have been preoccupied by how Canada is perceived by Americans in my conversations with them. I visit the States a few times every year and I've had plenty of conversations with plenty of Americans from most parts of the country. Americans are an overtly proud and extremely patriotic people, and I've always respected that. But, societal cross-sections are the same in the U.S. as they are in Canada – intellectual sophistication and values vary across populations, Canadian, American, or otherwise. I know that stereotypes exist mainly to define conclusive logic for people with lazy minds. I also know that it would be extremely stupid to throw the stereotyping blanket on every American to portray them as being self-important, obnoxious, war-mongering vanity cases, just as much as it would to paint every Canadian as bungling, donut-eating lumberjack hosers. The stereotyping surrounding intense American patriotism is most likely left over from eras when American Imperialism and Manifest Destiny were actually embraced as matters of course. Not really so long ago. Residue from these movements still resonates within Western civilization. I can't speak for Mexico, but it's certainly the case in Canada.

As imperialistic and potentially diabolical as Americans may seem to some, Canadians still revere Americans. Canada needs America. America may covet some of our material resources, like water, but we need their *culture*. Canadian music tells us so. The other day I was reading about one of those dreaded Top 100 song lists, this list being the *Top 100 Canadian Singles*, as voted for by more than 800 Canadian music industry types. Canadian reliance on America was defined in this exercise by the fact that the song that was voted to be the best Canadian single of all time was none other than The Guess Who's "American Woman". Irony rarely gets thicker than that. Number fourteen was "New Orleans is Sinking" by The Tragically Hip, one of Canada's most patriotic bands.

And yet I'm not familiar with one single American song that references Canada. Not one. Quite the contrary, in fact. Americans delight in writing songs about America. In a metal context, back in high school I listened to Lizzy Borden's "American Metal" and pondered Canada's unrequited cultural obsession with America. In the "American Metal" vocal outro starting at 5:07, Borden ad-libs about international heavy metal. He mentions, in this order, first something inaudible that sounds like New Zealand (or Cleveland, but that makes even less sense), then Germany, France, Japan, Australia, Russia, and then, after a slight pause, trumpets – A-MERICA! Regardless of the fact that Lizzy Borden can hardly be considered a paragon of international cultural influence, this is a stupid assemblage of countries anyway. If we're talking about heavy metal representation, how do you overlook the U.K., responsible for introducing the world to such metal giants as Iron Maiden, Judas Priest, and Black Sabbath, and really, heavy metal in particular? It was also peculiar to me that Canada was not mentioned in this little rap if you're naming France and Russia. WTF? Maybe Borden is actually saying 'Canada' when I think he's saying 'New Zealand' and I owe him an apology. Or, maybe I placed way too much focus on such trivialities as a kid with not much else to think about in my snoozy little town.

If you asked Megadeth's Dave Mustaine for his version of an international metal rap, he may be more inclined to include Canada. This is because he's a big fan of Canadian 80s metal band Sword, a highly underrated group from just south of Montreal. Sword is one of those fantastic little-known unplucked gems barely marketed by their little-known record label (Aquarius) that you wouldn't know about unless you somehow happened to come across them by chance, as I did. They opened up for Alice Cooper in 1986, bringing them to little ol' Sudbury Arena along the way.

The opening act slot can be an unforgiving one. For the most part no one cares about you because they're at the show to see the headliner. Most folks don't even show up to the concert until after 8:30, knowing the headliner typically comes on at 8:45 (hi Axl). The irony is that, while the headliner deploys opening acts to 'warm up' their crowd (ideally without stealing the show), the opening band is to use this opportunity to create a fan base with a limited amount of tools. In all the shows I've seen since 1984, I've only encountered two opening acts that compelled me enough with their performance and their songs to actually go out and buy the record they were touring. One of them was Silvertide, a hard rock band from Philadelphia who opened for Van Hagar in 2004. The other was Sword. I'm not counting Metal Church, because while I did get buy their 1986 release *The Dark* as a result of seeing them live with Metallica headlining, technically the opener on that show's three band-bill was Canadian act Kick Axe. And I already had Metal Church's debut record.

The Sword / Alice Cooper show was in February 1987, but I only know that after having searched an Alice Cooper tour date listing archives website. However, on the site it appears that the Sudbury stop is mistakenly listed as being a Toronto show – there are two entries for the February 26 show at Toronto's Maple Leaf Gardens. I emailed the site's Webmaster to advise of this clerical error. Not sure if I'll get a thank you or invective for that [8].

Until I noticed the date duplication, I wondered if this was the same approach Maiden took with the omission of their Sudbury stop in December 1984 from their official World Slavery Tour tourbook. I'm not sure if Maiden's reason for the omission may have been because Sudbury was a late addition to a tour that ordinarily took the band to

---

[8] *Turns out I got a nice thank you email for my trouble, with the possibility of getting a ticket stub from the show if the Webmaster can track one down. It pays to be a good citizen.*

larger venues. Maybe the Sudbury gig was a last minute one-off show, who knows. Because electronic archiving seems to be available for most bands, I investigated other shows I know took place around that time to see if the Sudbury dates are listed. Black Sabbath appeared in Sudbury during the 1981 Mob Rules and 1983 Born Again tours and they both appear. The Metallica 1986 Sudbury show appears as well, but has the wrong date.

Anyway, Alice and Sword was my third concert, after the Iron Maiden and Twisted Sister show in 1984 and the Metallica, Metal Church and Kick Axe show a while later. I was getting to know the score a bit at this point. Because Alice is more of a mainstream act I went to this show with some non-metal friends, Johnny being the exception. Metal was probably his music of choice but like me, he was an atypical metalhead because he didn't oppose other types of music that were polarizing, like say Depeche Mode. I should say he wasn't a metalhead at all, even though he absolutely loved Metal Church, Randy Rhoads, and Metallica. He didn't seem to care so much about the awareness of defining social roles as the rest of us did. As such, he moved in varied social circles that spanned a number of age groups. This was most likely because people were interested in his tendency to evade socially categorization in a town where categorization provided security and comfort. I'd like to say he was wise beyond his years, but I think he just didn't care. Or maybe I'm making some of this up in my head several years later because I wanted him to be that way.

So Johnny and I and some guys from the non-metal crowd drank a bunch of beers and went to see Alice Cooper. As I mentioned previously, Sudbury Arena was dry back then. I personally didn't need any more booze when we got to the show anyway. I was drunk off my ass already. The beauty of shows at the Sudbury Arena was the general admission concept across the board, regardless of who the act may have been. You could get as close as you wanted to the stage if you were one of those assholes who pushed your way through the crowd until you got there. I wasn't, but that night I *was* that asshole that decided it would be a good idea to go ahead and urinate on the floor so I didn't lose the spot

I did have in the crowd. It didn't seem like a big deal at the time. A few people noticed and just kind of moved back so as not to be splashed. I'm still surprised that I didn't take at least one punch in the head for that.

That was during Alice's portion of the show. We did arrive early enough to see most of Sword's opening set, and they were incredible. Great singer, crushing guitar sound, and well-written songs that were brilliantly performed. They had that compelling spark that you don't see often, the one that makes you want to learn more about the band. And I did, even in my inebriation. After Alice wrapped up his set, which was more interesting from a visual point of view with the extremely cool guillotine and *run-a-woman-through-with-an-epee* illusory routines, someone drove us back to Johnny's house. We needed to finish the rest of the precious beer that we had paid someone who was older than us to get from the beer store. Couldn't waste 'em. And I was so impressed with Sword that night that I pledged to seek out their record the next day. Right before I puked in Johnny's kitchen sink and made my way home.

There were loads of other Canadian hard rock and heavy metal bands on the scene in the 80s, and Toronto seemed to be the epicentre of the movement. It was a backwater Sunset Strip of sorts, but it did have some cool venues. There was The Gasworks, Larry's Hideaway, Rock N' Roll Heaven, and a few others. I kept tabs on the scene from northern Ontario as best I could via a magazine called *Metallion*, which was almost like a Canuck version of *Kerrang!*. When Sebastian Bach recently opened for Axl and Guns in Toronto a few years ago, he was going goddamn nuclear during his set between songs talking about how he used to take the Yonge subway line down to the Wellesley stop to get to The Gasworks back in the day. This must have been sometime around 1984, when he dabbled with local band Kid Wikkid and then Madam X before he went on to join Skid Row. Someone once told me that just after Bach moved to Toronto from Peterborough (while he was still known as Sebastian Bierk), he lived in an apartment above the *Sam The Record Man* flagship store on Yonge. Apparently, he used to loiter in the store all day to the point where they used to kick him out for being a nuisance. Not sure if that's true or not.

Following the Canadian metal scene in the 80s through print media was worthwhile, but seeing and hearing it in motion on Toronto's MuchMusic was where it was really at. MuchMusic was made available to Espy folk in 1985, and part of the free preview was the *Power Hour*, a segment featuring only hard rock and heavy metal hosted by one young J.D. Roberts, these days more popular known as John Roberts of CBS and CNN fame. When he was *Power Hour* J.D., Roberts used to wear a leather jacket with these huge chains on it. While the jacket was a prop for the segment, if Roberts didn't enjoy his time hosting the show then I was definitely fooled. Back then Roberts *was* the MuchMusic *Power Hour*. He hosted it first, and no one did the show better than he did after his departure. Not even Laurie Brown, who did her last show drunk and lifted her top on live TV. Shortly after I had first noticed that mulleted rocker J.D. Roberts had metamorphosed into debonair New York CBS anchorman John Roberts, I couldn't reconcile the duality. This is because I typically default to that lazy cognition that leads me to believe that people should look and act exactly as they did when I left them years before. Regardless, I can't help but wonder if John Roberts still rocks out to Thor in the privacy of his own home.

While the Canadian Radio-Television and Telecommunications Commission insisted behind the scenes that he do so based on Canadian content guidelines, J.D. played plenty of Canadian metal on the *Power Hour*. Of course, that meant lots of videos from Rush, Triumph, and Helix. But some lesser-known Canadian outfits could also be seen, like Montreal thrash metal outfit Eudoxis and their video for a song called "Metal Fix".

I thought the vid was interesting, but it didn't make me rush out to buy the record in the same way that Cinderella's "Shake Me" did. It was lo-fi and just seemed...*meh*. At the time, it was like a second-rate version of Slayer circa 1983 – leather and spikes, and the same brand of thrash that *Show No Mercy* deployed. Right down to the lead guitar tone, style, and countless harmonic whammy bar dive-bombs. Singer Liev Arnesen was compelling and terrifying at the same time. He looked somewhat out of place, and more than a little bit like Grace Slick with blond hair. When I watch the video now on YouTube, I love it. It's genius by indie standards. The song is fantastic, and the video is shot perfectly to capture the band in all of their majestic, beautiful stupidity. It brilliantly underscores that one golden aspect that makes heavy metal so wonderful, and one of my favourite things in the world.

Bands like Eudoxis were not well known. Sometimes I wonder though if this might be the best thing that could have happened to them. The band actually stuck it out in various permutations until 1993, but I, like a lot of others, only know them only for "Metal Fix". And this is a good thing. I prefer not to be privy to a band's 'Fat Elvis' period. I don't need to know about that stuff. It only besmirches the legacy of an artist. Quick flameouts for obscure bands are almost akin to that fascination felt for dead rock stars that got away from us before their mortality could be exploited. As distasteful as it may sound, the best thing that could have ever happened to Kurt Cobain's legacy was death. With one quick pull of the trigger, he permanently flash-froze his status as a musical deity, and eternally disarmed a legion of critics who sat in wait licking their lips in anticipation of rendering him limb from musical limb the very minute he would be vulnerable to the public's favour. Because every artist very much unfortunately is, whether we care to recognize it or not.

There was a plethora of bands in addition to Eudoxis that occupied the position directly below the mighty Anvil in the Toronto 80s metal scene food chain, and I liked them best when they were there. Of Jade, Razor, Blind Vengeance and so many others, my favourite of all of these bands was Hateful Snake. They were another group I would have never known about had I not serendipitously taped the video by accident from the *Power Hour*. Their song "Are You Ready" was nothing special at all. In fact it was sub-standard if we're being honest. But there was something charismatic in the way that singer Brian Simpson delivered the whole package in the video. He came across as self-deprecating but cool at the same time, and he rose just above that FUBAR-type metalhead ethos. I still watch the "Are You Ready" video from time to time and I still get a huge charge out of it. I remember thinking as a highly impressionable sixteen-year-old how cool it would have been to hang out with that guy. What would he be doing in 2011? Still most likely in the Toronto area, hopefully not living a life similar to Squirrel's. I looked him up on the 'net, but nothing. Hell, I'd like to chat the guy up. He's got to be on Facebook.

One other Canadian band that was in the mix around this time yet not from Toronto was speed metal band Exciter, who formed in Ottawa in 1978. They actually signed a deal with metal impresario Jon Zazula and Megaforce Records a few years and rubbed shoulders with bands like Mercyful Fate and Anthrax. I was mildly intrigued by the feature of their *Violence & Force* record in the Megaforce lineup alongside Metallica's *Kill 'Em All* and *Ride The Lightning*, though maybe slightly off put by the peculiar socio-political messages the album cover conveyed. Have a look and you'll see what I mean.

I was going through a drum fascination phase at this time, and because Exciter drummer Dan Beehler was also the singer I bought the next record, 1985's *Long Live the Loud*. I liked Beehler's voice, and because it seemed he was the de facto leader of the band as the singer, his drumming was featured more prominently on Exciter's records. Up until I heard "I Am the Beast" from *Long Live the Loud*, my favourite drum tracks at the time were from KISS' *Creatures of the Night*.

I used to try to mimic drum parts with these black drumsticks I bought at Wally's and an assemblage of anything I could hit with these sticks that would remain stationary. My first drum kit was some ice cream and margarine tubs secured in the footrest of an old black recliner. The lids weren't up to the task though, and they couldn't withstand more than a couple of hits without giving way to Wally's overpriced sticks. I eventually got frustrated and used to just sit on my bed balancing my pillow on my right thigh as the snare (and thigh protector) to play along with KISS anthem and drumming tour de force "I Love It Loud", hitting an imaginary hi-hat with my right hand and stomping out the kick beats with my right foot. Very much to Mom's chagrin. After I had that song worked out, I figured I would raise the bar a bit with Exciter's "I Am the Beast". After trying to keep up with the much quicker beat and crazy fills, I gave up after hitting myself in the face with the sticks a few too many times.

In my nostalgic assessment of Canadian 80s metal, I would be remiss if I didn't mention the Metal Queen herself, Lee Aaron. In the 80s, Americans had Lita Ford, but Canadians had Lee Aaron. And this was just another reason to be a proud Canadian really. I liked that Aaron, born Karen Lynn Greening, was primarily a much better singer than everyone else out there that she would inevitably be compared with at the time. She was also hotter than any of her metal peers, including Ford and even Warlock's Doro Pesch. So much for being a Canadian apologist, eh?

Aaron manufactured a J.D. Roberts move of her own around the mid-90s when she categorically dropped the rocker chick gig and began singing jazz. She always seemed like an intelligent observer of the scene, having begun subtly and gradually metamorphosing away from her Metal Queen persona when it was time. She played the sex card to her advantage in a less obvious and vulgar way, craftily and learned after having been coerced by her manager into a 1982 topless spread in *Oui* magazine to bolster the career in the early days. I developed a new appreciation for Aaron after her jazz transition, partly because of her talent as an artist but mostly because she actually has her head on straight enough to stay ahead of the curve and avoid being painted with the one-trick-pony brush, unlike so many of her metal contemporaries. The essence of events like Rocklahoma and the prospect of seeing Karen Greening revert back to Metal Queen Lee Aaron employ that same melancholic cheapening device that guides the televangelist to the hooker's trick pad. We all know it shouldn't be done, but the tabooed exhilaration that comes from guilty pleasure will always be a temptation. Good for Karen for not giving in. And good for me for wanting her to do the right thing.

No Sleep 'til Sudbury

Okay, you can't make this stuff up.

Well, you can, but I didn't. This is just one of those crazy things.

One quick preamble here before I get into that crazy thing. I reconnected with my old Espy pal Bryan Sloss in late 2008. We have lunch or dinner together regularly, and shortly after we regained contact with each other his wife invited me as a surprise guest to his 40th birthday party, which I humbly accepted. I thought was a fantastic gesture and I was honoured to be there.

So Sloss and I were at the Kool Haus in downtown Toronto to see Slash two nights ago, while I'm in the middle of writing this chapter. The opening band is on, and we're standing in the general admission crowd having a beer. I looked over at Sloss to say something, and in the fluorescent purple-lit crowd standing directly beside Sloss, is someone who looks remarkably and quite coincidentally like...Lips!

I almost pissed my goddamn pants.

Immediately I say to Sloss in a mild panic, *"Dude, is that Lips?"*

He looks over. *"Holy fuck. I think it is"*.

This goes on for three or four minutes. The crappy purple fluorescent lighting is screwing with my perception, but a) I don't want to creep Lips out by continuing to leer at him like a weirdo, and b), I don't want to start a fight by leering like a weirdo at some guy who really looks like Lips. I'm a bit nervous as a result of occupying the same space as the man who growls "Metal on Metal" through my Paradigm Phantoms, but I still don't trust my cognition enough to walk over.

The anxious leering continues until Sloss taps on the shoulder of the woman who was with this individual and says in her ear, *"Excuse me, but is that Lips?"*

After a brief pause, she nods affirmatively. I didn't have to hear the question. The nod lifts my eyebrows and makes my mouth uncontrollably form a circular shape not unlike Mr. Bill's. In the most perfectly serendipitous way and in the most ideal setting, I'm about to meet Steve "Lips" Kudlow, leader of Anvil.

After most of the geekery is worked out of my system, I'm able to have a brief chat with Lips. As if to qualify myself as a legitimate metal fan, the first thing I tell him is that I bought *Metal on Metal* when I was thirteen, and that I still listen to it today. These two pieces of information are absolutely true. I rediscovered the "Metal on Metal" title track a few years ago to a degree that made Alison familiar enough with it to sing along in the car when it played. She likes "Metal on Metal", but she would never admit it [9].

Next I tell Lips that I'm not going to bother him, but that I just wanted to say that I saw the movie and that I was happy for him that he got to do it. I told him I had a lot of respect for him and wished him the best of luck, because he genuinely deserved it. He responded very meekly with a humble smile, the same one that he wore during those points in the movie when it seemed as though things would finally go his way. Man, I was happy to be able to talk to this guy. My hope was that my words could somehow fortify, even in some small way, the greater affirmations that came as a result of the Anvil documentary.

I asked him if it would be okay to get a picture with him. He graciously agreed with a big smile. I stood beside him after giving Sloss my cell phone for the snap, and that awkward pre-flash posing that I loathe so intensely lasted into its second lifetime before Sloss said the flash wasn't working. Christ. Poor Lips. During the downtime I ask him if he's playing lately, and he says yes. When I ask where, he plaintively says with a smile, *"Here"*. He's very shy, and maybe even a bit intimidated. I notice that he's wearing a t-shirt under his leather jacket that says, "I'm huge in Japan". Perfect.

As we're talking, it strikes me as a bit odd that no one else at this show seems to know who Lips is. We're posing for pictures so a couple of people are looking, but they have furled brows. Considering the demograph and musical taste of the crowd, I'm intrigued and disappointed at the same time. We use Sloss' phone instead to get the picture and Lips is smiling that classic, wonderfully goofy smile that I remember from the "Mad Dog" video on MuchMusic all those years ago. I take

---

[9] *She also secretly likes Rainbow's "Man on the Silver Mountain", despite the fact that she says she thinks it's gay. But I know she's lying.*

one of Sloss with Lips and we thank him about fourteen times each before wishing him well.

While Sloss and I are giggling like schoolgirls over the happenstance a few moments afterwards, I consider the impossibility of the situation on a greater scale. As we ate overpriced raw fish with our chopsticks at the King Street sushi restaurant we were at before the show and chatted about our careers in real estate and telecommunications, I joked to Sloss that we were a long way from the home we came from. But, after having reunited with him through Facebook twenty five years later, seeing a Slash show together, and at that show, bumping into the subject of this chapter of a book I'm writing about my small town heavy metal youth, it occurred to me that maybe I was a bit closer to home than I thought.

✸ Twenty ✸
I Don't Trust People Who Don't Drink

I understand alcoholism. I absolutely understand and appreciate the constructs that can make alcoholism a reality. Because quite honestly, life just seems so much easier when you're drunk. When I'm drinking, aside from all of the obvious improvements in mood and gregariousness, my mind operates on a completely different plane.

I have mild compulsions in everyday life just like everyone else. Nothing too serious. I might be overly concerned about food waste avoidance. Might feel pangs of guilt when I lose money. No big deal. A bigger compulsion of mine involves the passing of time and the premise that I should always be taking full advantage of every moment because I only have a finite amount of it in this mortal coil. That one gets the best of me sometimes. The inevitability of death.

But this concern, along with every other one I might have, are summarily wiped away by booze.

I should state very clearly at this point that I don't drink with the express intention of alleviating these quirks. It's not like I'm desperately suffering from some disorder or anything. I drink because it's fun. Any preoccupation alleviation is just a nice residual benefit. I don't even drink that much anymore really. I'm at that stage in my life where I'm starting to value Sundays without hangovers more than getting wrecked and staying up until six in the morning acting like a jackass. I can't deal with the hangovers anymore.

When I am drinking though, I do forget all about the passage of time and any associated trappings of guilt it may burden me with. I live in the moment, and I don't worry about anything. Everything is a continuous stream of happy goodness. This is the allure of alcohol, and the brass ring of the alcoholic. It's an artificial escape mechanism.

Like most other kids away at university, I drank like a motherfucker in my early twenties. Because my grandfather may or may not have been an alcoholic, Mom used to hit the panic button periodically when things got out of hand a bit. She had a pretty good sense of humour about all of it, but it's probably a good thing I didn't ever share the true degree of stupidity that was achieved back then.

My decision to live in dorm while attending university is probably the greatest one I've ever made. I may have actually learned more in dorm than I did in class. Dorm was like the inadvertent sociology course that I didn't sign up for. Sure, having to share an immediate living space with twenty-three other guys and a building with two hundred-plus other guys and girls had its shortcomings sometimes. But the perks outweighed all of those shortcomings by a long shot.

I have reams of wonderfully ridiculous and mildly frightening stories. People being hung out of windows by their ankles ten stories from the ground. Recliner chairs, guitars, oven doors, and all kinds of other items being thrown out of those same windows. People drinking their own vomit in talent contests. People purposely urinating and defecating in their pants to win drinking games. And, like a common thread that ran through my entire dorm career, more nakedness than I ever could have ever imagined. There weren't really any rules, and the average age was twenty. Damn good times.

I met all kinds of characters from all kinds of places when I lived in dorm, from Scarborough to Serbia. One year I hung out with a guy that used to pass out with his eyes open, which was more than a little bit creepy. There were whispers that his dad was an alcoholic. When I saw him last, he seemed destined for the same fate. I'm not sure what ever happened to him, though. I've looked around cyberspace and there's no trace of him. It's entirely possible that he may have died. It makes me think about the people I knew at school that pushed the alcohol envelope way too far, beyond the point of cool, fun, or any romantic affectation you could possibly cull from the experience. One of those people had become a full-blown alcoholic and was removed from school to receive treatment, and another one killed himself one night driving drunk over summer break.

Sometimes those years feel like one big blurry sojourn. I met Alison in dorm during those years. She lived on the 4th floor, and I lived on the 11th. We've talked about all the capers. Still do. One day recently we had a discussion, without sounding too dramatic, about how many times we may have looked death directly in the eye after enjoying too much of the drink. Every drinking enthusiast has at least two of these episodes from their drinking days, times when they've put themselves at a very specific and absolutely realistic risk of death while intoxicated. Ironically, a number of these are most likely unknown to the drinker based on the level of inebriation, but there should be a couple that are easily remembered based on the outcome. Some of those maybe even being grave enough to instantly sober the drinker up. I always think about the time when Garvey and I decided to go swimming after the bar one night at that resort we worked at. I took a running dive head first into the shallow end, in my drunkenness mistaking it for the deep end. When the lower half of my face smashed against the bottom of the pool it straightened me out instantly, and I often consider the outcome had I dove in at just a slightly different angle. Maybe a spinal, maybe complete paralysis. Maybe worse. This is grim stuff, so it's important to end these discussions on a positive note. This is easy to do because there's a plethora of hilarious drinking stories too. Like the one where I tried to get out of bed and go to the bathroom to throw up but in doing so, I fell off my dorm bed that was more than five feet off the ground.

The dorm rooms were small, and it was common practice to put your bed up on stacks of milk crates like bunk beds to make extra space. It was one of those nights where the room was spinning and I was lying motionless just trying not to move, wanting drastically for it to be over. One of those nights where if you even just move your pinky finger, it's over. Lest I moved even just one iota there would be immediate spewing. After thinking about it for a while I decided that the spewing was probably inevitable, so my new goal was just to not throw up in my bed. And subsequently on the sleeping female who happened to be sharing it with me.

I spent a lot of time laying there thinking about how I was going to pull this off discreetly. In my attempt to put my head over the edge of the bed and get it over with, I slipped and fell off. Threw up in the air on the way down. I landed first, on my back. And in exactly the same way that the Acme anvil had landed so precisely and perfectly square on Wile E. Coyote's head again and again at the hands of the Roadrunner in *The Bugs Bunny & Tweety Show* cartoons, the cursed vomit also landed, right on my face. I elected to not move and just stay put on the floor after this happened. When I woke up there in that same position in the morning I discovered that my guest had departed, without waking me for some reason.

I've also told the story about the time when I was waiting in line to get into a bar in Cancun and had to pee very urgently. I thought I was being clever by urinating into an empty drink cup I inserted up the pant leg of my shorts so as not to lose my place in the line. This line was tremendously lengthy, and before long I had to repeat the procedure. No worries. Worked like a charm the first time, no one was the wiser. Unfortunately, the second time I attempted the manoeuvre I was too gonged to realize that the cup wasn't positioned effectively. I had completely pissed my shorts, just in time to be admitted into the bar. Cheers.

The tricky thing about booze is that everyone reacts to it differently. There are happy drunks, sad drunks, angry drunks, and downright psychotic, Jekyll-and-Hyde blackout drunks. And while that may make for some less than savoury scenarios sometimes, it's fine. It's fine because the bottom line is that people show their cards when they're drunk. You get to see the most realistic version of who people really are during those times. I know it's slightly counter-intuitive, but I tend not to trust people who don't drink for this reason.

The difference between an alcoholic and a recreational drinker is the aspect of control. In most cases, an individual's personal constitution allows for them to avoid getting into too much trouble with booze. I vividly remember one specific period of time when I was twenty-four or so, and I had started to navigate that dubious area of extra-curricular drinking territory. That drinking out of the bottle area. The one where heavy drinking at non-typical drinking times, like early afternoon Sundays, occurs. During that period, I stuck my head into that area and took a really good, hard, honest look around.

But these exercises are really just simple exploratory forays for most average people like me. To become an alcoholic just seemed so unrealistic, even at that time. But it's in this specific area that drinkers complete their transition into alcoholics. Where they begin that metamorphosis into a full-blown abuser, and where they relinquish control over the drink to the drink itself. It's the alternate direction in that catalytic fork in the road, less travelled and initially much romanticized. It's clear that most alcoholics have not so easily exorcised demons that walk them down this path hand in deathly cold hand, the same psychological demons that obscure clear perspective and personal constitution.

The reason I'm going on about all of this is because I just finished reading Ozzy's autobiography. If half of the stories in this book are true, Ozzy Osbourne is one of the most durable and insanely prolific alcoholics of all time. I like reading autobiographies, because in most cases they give you a truer sense of what the subject of the work is really all about. When I learned that Ozzy was writing a book, I felt like I needed to put on a helmet before opening it. I had hoped it would contain the proper tellings of all of those stories of debauchery made legend over the years – the bat biting, the dove biting, the Alamo incident, the ant-snorting with Nikki Sixx, and on and on. And it certainly did.

Turns out that Ozzy was even more of a fucked up headcase than I had imagined. There are a lot of really funny stories in this book. One of my favourite parts is when Ozzy talks about the period when Black Sabbath were just getting started and had just recorded their first album. They were in Zurich playing crappy bars and trying to avoid girls from which they might catch diseases. Two dirty hookers lure them back to their apartment with free dope, despite Geezer Butler's wishes. Ozzy wants to go and convinces Geezer that if either of the girls tries anything during the dope smoking that he'll "kick her up the arse", and they would leave. Geezer eventually agrees, and they go back to the apartment. It's dark, Blind Faith is playing on the stereo, and everyone gets right into the weed. After a while, Ozzy says he hears this deep voice moan, *"Oi Ozzy, time to put the boot in"*, and Ozzy starts laughing so hysterically that he's crying, after peering through the darkness and clouds of smoke to see Geezer laying on his back with his eyes closed and a look of pain on his face while this sketchy hooker is straddling him.

Of course, fame and money would eventually give young Ozzy licence to really rip it up on a completely different level. In addition to the more popular tales I was already familiar with, there were many more in the book that illustrate just how much of an absolute lunatic Ozzy was. He talks about waking up on the median of a major highway with cars whizzing by in either direction after chugging a huge bowl of sake with Tommy Lee, and how he met one of his neighbours in the local pub and invited him back to Chez Osbourne for a drink. After his guest passed out, Ozzy took off his clothes and threw them into the fireplace.

The most compelling aspect of the book is how likeable Ozzy is throughout, even at his lowest points. You can't not like this guy. The book is written in the same creed by which Ozzy seems to live his life – what you see is what you get, disgusting warts and all. He tells his stories with such earnest that I actually ended up feeling sorry for him after I finished the book. It reads like he was just some jackass delinquent who fell into a river of gold in the opportunity to play with guys who were much more musically skilled than he was (guitarist Tony Iommi was asked to join Jethro Tull and accepted while the nucleus of what would eventually be Black Sabbath was still forming, but left to rejoin Sabbath after only a few days). Ozzy was never really a gifted singer, and more or less just got by as a result of someone else's intervention or perseverance (hi Sharon). He obviously didn't drink just for kicks. Ozzy drank himself into oblivion nightly because he was never comfortable in his own skin. The demons were rife and powerful.

Reading this book made me consider the expansive dichotomy between the glamorous and grotesque sides of the substance abuse coin and the inevitable price to be paid for the unbelievable stories, hilarious antics, and artificial idolatry power. At that level, and in situations like Ozzy's, the glamour always gives way to that ugly after school special image of a Lindsay Lohan-type character passed out in a strange bathroom, head buried in a dirty toilet. Not to mention the Icarus-like tragedy in how effectively alcohol helps to break down social barriers and generate popularity, albeit under phony pretences. It's all fake. The real depravity comes when you consider the level of self-loathing required to continually put oneself in such a desperate position, and that lots of people out there actually think it's cool. Not because of the guilty pleasure we take as a society in watching people publicly fail, but because they can or want to relate.

Hypocrisy is palpable. Most of us are weak and we have our crosses to bear in various capacities. My friends and I would have never dreamed of going to a party without booze after age fifteen, and until we were well into our thirties. If you look at it that way, the reliance on alcohol was substantial. Not enough that ultimate control was compromised at any time, or that a physical dependency was developed or anything like that. But there was a social dependency that couldn't be denied. The booze is a coping mechanism whether or not we want to admit it.

Ozzy does admit it, in pathetic detail and with absolute humility. He was an extreme example, an out-of-control, raging behemoth of an alcoholic who theoretically should be in the ground today. For all of his adventures, Ozzy Osbourne is probably one of the luckier alcoholics in the history of all of alcoholism if not for just surviving his travails.

But he's also got a brand new whiz-kid guitar player and he's still half-decently thriving in his career these days. He's in decent shape. Posture notwithstanding, he looks fine. He somehow managed to avoid developing that pockmarked gin-blossom nose of the aging drunkard. He shakes, but he claims the tremoring is hereditary and not associated to his substance abuse. Sure, he mumbles a bit when he talks and his singing is weak. But for a guy in his sixties who allegedly did acid every day for five straight years at one point, what do you want?

In situations like Ozzy's, people most often expect a corpse if not just to remain in keeping with the morbidly attractive dead-rock-star tragic romanticism theme that alcohol so commonly imbues. Ozzy clearly looked the Grim Reaper directly in the eye more than once or twice, but he ended up having his cake and eating it too. Then he threw it up and ate it again.

⛧ Twenty One ⛧
Dreaming of a Black (Sabbath) Christmas

Speaking of Ozzy and drinking, it's Christmas vacation and I'm on a major Black Sabbath kick at the moment, for three reasons I'm not particularly proud of.

The first reason is that as a fan of 80s hard rock and heavy metal, I appreciate the genealogy of its history. But it wasn't until I got older that I would actually respect it. I realize that Black Sabbath was essentially the root foundation of the heavy metal family tree. But in my teenage metal fandom, I didn't really give a fuck about respect for structure, and I just wasn't particularly fond of 'older people's music'. Bands that had already enjoyed the apex of their career before 1980 or so were someone else's imprint. I couldn't form a connection to these groups as a kid because I felt like I wasn't on the same wavelength. Stupid really, as I would later find out that some of the truly great hard rock and metal actually happened *before* the genre really took flight in the mid 80s. In fact, the gross majority of it did.

The second reason that prevented me from really getting into Black Sabbath back then was one of my high school friends, Kelly. He was a Sabbath lunatic in the 80s. He had every cassette, even one called *Live At Last* that wasn't available in Espanola or Sudbury. He picked it up on a family trip to Nova Scotia or something. He basically worshipped the band. Whenever we listened to music together he always went into the Black Sabbath sales routine, but this routine actually worked in reverse. His incessant promotion of the band polarized me against them. I didn't like when people tried to push things on me back then. Still don't, as a matter of fact. Sabbath was sacrosanct to Kelly, so they couldn't be to me.

The third reason was Black Sabbath's material itself. My younger, more cognitively underdeveloped mind was for the most part, more interested in Occam's Razor-ish concepts - simple strategies resulting in immediate gratification. I preferred the standard 3:05 length song with the basic variants of riff/verse/chorus/solo/bridge/chorus structure. I wasn't into Led Zeppelin's brand of extended jam solo rock, and I immediately lumped Sabbath in with them, particularly because of the meandering hippy-trippyness of Sabbath's material on their debut record, *Black Sabbath*. I prematurely concluded that guitarist Tony Iommi and the rest of Sabbath were boring old stoners that belonged more to the generation before mine. And of course, I was a tool of the marketing gestalt that realized big money could be made by selling image and production ahead of music per my unfortunate KISS programming a few years earlier. I was myopic. I craved more easily digested compositions whose structures tidily came in under four minutes.

I did have a few Sabbath CDs in my collection before I got onto this big kick. I had *Black Sabbath*, but I don't remember how or why I had it. It's a helluva debut, but considering that (a) it goes against my 'greatest hit' rationale by featuring three of Sabbath's most well-known tunes ("Black Sabbath", "The Wizard", and "N.I.B.") out of a total of only five[*] tracks, meaning it was sixty percent a greatest hits album, and (b) it

---

[*] The *Black Sabbath* album, as would the subsequent three Sabbath albums, features 'sub-songs' - one formal track would be comprised of miscellany that featured anywhere from two to four song parts, which was apparently meant to lead the listener to believe that there was more material on an album than there actually was. This pretzel logic was likely chemically manufactured.

wasn't there as a result of my buying the CD versions of all of my favourite high school metal cassettes, it's unlikely that I bought it. Someone must have left it behind one night.

I also had *Black Sabbath Vol. 4*, but I know why. I bought this CD because I liked the "Supernaut" cover version featured on the Sabbath tribute record *Nativity in Black*, and I was curious to hear the original version.

Technical Ecstasy was purchased for the same reason. I picked it up after I heard Axl's version of "It's Alright" on Guns' *Live Era* record. I loved the performance of the song and knowing it wasn't a Guns tune, I wondered where it came from. I recognized the composer's name, Bill Ward, in the *Live Era* liner notes as being Black Sabbath's drummer and looked for it on all of the Sabbath records. I found it on *Technical Ecstasy* while flipping through the Sabbath bin at Sam the Record Man on Yonge Street, but I was disappointed upon hearing it. Ward not only wrote the song but performed it as well, however not nearly as interestingly as Rose had. The rest of the record didn't do anything for me and I shelved it.

Sabbath Bloody Sabbath was also in the collection. I bought that to hear the original version of the songs Metallica covered in their Sabbath medley on *Garage, Inc.*. I had a perfunctory interest in the original versions, being more enamoured with Metallica at the time. I should also admit that I found the name and the cover of *Sabbath Bloody Sabbath* pretty compelling, stemming back from the times when I used to hang out in Kelly's room listening to music.

For the record, I also had *Mob Rules* and *Heaven and Hell* on CD, *Live Evil* on vinyl, and *Born Again* on cassette. But none of these really count as *real* Black Sabbath albums, in the same way that post-David Lee Roth Van Halen records aren't *really* Van Halen records.

So - one night recently I'm scanning my CD collection looking for something to listen to, and I mull over *Black Sabbath Vol. 4*. I generally listen to music based on my mood. This in turn is largely dictated by the weather, what day it is, and what time it is, in that order. As I said previously, I make direct and perhaps unfortunate correlations between music and environment. I say unfortunate because it's a compulsion (another one!), and one that can be somewhat limiting.

Here's an example. Any of Joni Mitchell's first eight records are equated with sunshine in my mind (Mitchell lost me after *Hejira*), and I really only listen to them on weekend mornings if the sun is shining. Conversely Van Halen's *Women and Children First,* the hard rock equivalent of the Stones' *Sticky Fingers*, is one of the penultimate Saturday night records in my collection. And I would never listen to *Women and Children First* or *Sticky Fingers* in the morning. Unless maybe I was still drunk from the night before.

At this point in my translucent appreciation of Black Sabbath I was at least given to the obvious - that Black Sabbath was dark and moody. It was nighttime when I looked through the collection, so logic dictated Sabbath might be a good fit. I threw in *Black Sabbath Vol. 4*, and I liked it. I put on *Sabbath Bloody Sabbath* next. It occurred to me at this point that these were both very good records; substantial, atmospheric, nicely balanced between light and shade, and mostly defiant of categorization.

It also occurred to me at that moment that I needed to obtain the remainder of Black Sabbath's first eight records so that I could get more properly acquainted with a band that I had overlooked up to this point. And I would spend my Christmas holiday doing it. Because nothing says Christmas quite like Black Sabbath.

Of course, it wouldn't be necessary to include 1975 greatest hits album *We Sold our Soul for Rock and Roll* in this grouping. It *would* be necessary however to include 1978's *Never Say Die!*, even though I know it most likely sucks. It was written during the Black Sabbath deterioration period that saw Ozzy's first departure from the band, and is widely purported to be Sabbath's weakest Ozzy record. It would also be Ozzy's last album with Black Sabbath, as he left following the nightly upstaging they received from a very young Van Halen while touring the *Never Say Die!* album. My curiosity is mildly piqued when I learn that it was recorded at Sounds Interchange Studio in Toronto.

Buying *Never Say Die!* despite its quality would be necessary because without it, a proper assessment of the entire Ozzy-era Sabbath collection and an understanding of what Black Sabbath was really about wouldn't be completely possible. Familiarizing myself with each record from a band's entire catalogue tells me a story about the band that reaches beyond any of their individual works. Before artists and their music were rendered so disposable, they had careers that typically spanned at least four or five records. It's interesting to retrospectively observe the artist's career by listening to each of their albums in succession, examining each one as individual building blocks. Making sense of how they progressed along their life span. Evaluating their contributions and their position within a genre with the intention of trying to interpret what the artist was saying.

The feel of each of an artist's albums, when positioned against one another, adds dimension to the consideration of the band's efforts through their career. Contextual questions are raised, like why this direction was taken over that, and how significantly the band's music may have been impacted by external factors like drugs, Yoko types, and so on. This leaves the listener with a more meaningful understanding and hopefully, an appreciation of the band.

Interpretation can take several forms and get pretty granular. Like wondering why Tony Iommi or *Sabotage* producer Mike Butcher chose not to eliminate the popping sounds coming from Iommi's guitar pickups heard on most of the record, particularly on "Thrill Of It All". But these are representations of the joys of really *listening* to music – that added cognitive element that comes from hearing songs from the inside out.

So, all of the Ozzy-era Sabbath CDs are purchased on eBay and on their way now. Merry Christmas to me. The band's sixth album, *Sabotage,* shows up in my mailbox first. I notice a couple of things right away. First, that it's a pirated CD-R with weak-ass DeskJet-printer artwork in the liner. And that Sabotage is spelled 'Sabbotage' on the CD itself in two places. Megalomania is spelled 'Meglomania' on the CD and back liner by whoever the pinhead was that put this product together. Lesson learned on my part for trying to get CDs on the cheap. The CD quality is actually up to snuff however, and the content is damn good.

So good that as the other CDs come in, I just keep playing *Sabotage* over and over again.

Album opener "Hole in the Sky" is plodding, pioneering heavy metal with a simple but effective melodic chorus. It ends abruptly and goes right into track two, instrumental "Don't Start (Too Late)". Because there's no pause in between songs, I wonder if this is a result of this crappy bootlegged copy I stupidly bought. No pause again into "Symptom of the Universe". I would find out a bit later that this was intentional after I went out and picked up a copy of the actual Warner Bros release. In addition to the typo issues, the song order was wrong on the bootleg, with "The Writ" being track seven and "Am I Going Insane (Radio)" track eight.

Anyhow, the brief instrumental interlude between two crunchy metal songs, as on other Black Sabbath records, may seem pointless and awkward to the listener who's looking for a linear metal album with eight or nine skull crushers. But on the whole, these interludes do add volume and texture to the overall album. For 80s metalheads like myself who cut their teeth on the KISS-cum-Motley Crue slick n' simple hard rock and metal starter kit, any arrangements that deviated from the basic template where unnecessary. As mentioned, my third reason for avoiding Sabbath as my younger, more foolish self.

The sequencing approach of inserting instrumentals in the number two slot would be admonished in the 80s. The new formula would have the band's first single as either track two or three, with the first song being an aggressive number possibly with the interlude on the front of it. Plenty of 80s bands followed this format on their records – Def Leppard's *Pyromania*, Winger's debut album, Cinderella's *Night Songs*, Motley's *Shout at the Devil*, the BulletBoys' debut, Ratt's *Out of the Cellar*, and loads of others[*].

---

[*] *As mentioned earlier, 1987's* Appetite for Destruction *deviated from this formula at the specific behest of Geffen A&R rep and general Guns endorser Tom Zutaut, as he attempted to first demonstrate the band's grit by loading up side one with "It's So Easy" and "Nighttrain", and 'hiding' "Sweet Child O' Mine" on side two. Guess it worked.*

One of the beautiful aspects of listening to albums by Sabbath, Zeppelin, Aerosmith, and other 70s bands is that album sequencing wasn't yet overtly prone to formulaic commercial strategies.

I can't decide if Iommi's guitar tone in "Symptom of the Universe" is sparingly cool or frustratingly lo-fi. In the spirit of the times during which the record was produced, I should be inclined to go with the former. I just can't help but wonder how much more powerful the song would sound if Iommi had borrowed Accept's Wolf Hoffmann's gear for the guitar track. I know there would be a chronological impossibility involved with this, but I don't care.

The funky breakdown that ends "Symptom of the Universe" is another example of the unorthodox writing style that gave Sabbath's records an enjoyable insouciance. It breaks convention by not looping back into the song's main riff as a typical interlude might, but instead it just fades out. As I listen, I wonder what I was thinking when I was overlooking this stuff.

While it would happen more than once over the course of my listening to *Sabotage*, I notice first on "Symptom of the Universe" that Ozzy's vocal delivery is vital, raw, and desperate, particularly at 1:51 during the second chorus. Ozzy's never really been known to be a real *singer*, but I have to say that the ferocity of this vocal is one of the elements that gives *Sabotage* real teeth. I realize at this point that an interesting subtext of this familiarization with Black Sabbath is that it will inadvertently provide a new and proper frame of reference on the quality of Ozzy's solo career. Considering the artistic merit of *The Ultimate Sin*, I decide not to go there.

One of the main focal points on *Sabotage* comes next in the instantly attractive "Megalomania". Its first segment is brooding and atmospheric, and it offsets Ozzy's initial mystic soothsayer against his more regular loutish routine in the second segment of the song, wherein he feels it necessary to growl *"suck me!"* in between two of the verses. Despite clocking in at almost 10 minutes in length, it's never boring at any point. The fact that it's basically two songs fused together makes me wonder what the motivation was in doing so. The band could have had so much more material by taking one song's myriad riffs and creating four or five separate songs. Metallica and Megadeth both did the same on their early records (possibly a result of Sabbath's influence), and Dave Mustaine has speculated in interviews that he regretted it.

"Thrill of it All" continues with the conflation pattern. It melds an initial plodding riff with an up-tempo bridge and then introduces another grinding main riff for a few verses. Then into a piano passage, and then into a soaring synthesizer line, during which Ozzy excises the "oh yeah, *oh yeah*" vocal melody directly from The Beatles' "I've Got A Feeling". Four distinctly different pieces, but it does work. The progressive format is nimble and fast moving, and free of the protracted righteousness that prog rock usually typifies.

I hear where Ozzy's "Diary of a Madman" track came from when I hear "Supertzar". This is a really special record. Hearing the "Supertzar" track at this point of the *Sabotage* listening experience reminds the listener that Black Sabbath is malevolent, audacious, and impervious. And that they will not be fucked with. *Sabotage* is money.

"Am I Going Insane" deploys the same florid synthesizer that "Thrill of it All" does, but with varying results. The composition seems formulaic and it doesn't quite fit on this record. I see much more clearly now that Metallica were astute students of Black Sabbath early in their career. In addition to the use of brief acoustic intros into crushing riffs to manipulate mood and the use of twenty-six different riffs per song approach, Metallica may have also borrowed the insane-laughter-as-coda from "Am I Going Insane" for their own "Master of Puppets" track.

The best song on *Sabotage* is buried at the end of the record in "The Writ". Seems like Sabbath most likely sought to end the LP sides with the two epics, "Megalomania" and "The Writ". Not only is "The Writ" the best song on *Sabotage*, it may even be my favourite Sabbath song. At this point, I've listened to the song so many times that I've noticed the presence of faint, errant reversed cymbal washes in the bass breakdown at 2:16 in the left channel and 2:19 in the right.

Ozzy's spirited vocal in the opening verses is mildly shocking and very compelling, delivered perfectly with equal parts insolence and fragility. The vocal delivery is so cool that I almost didn't want to know what the actual lyrics were, for fear of them not measuring up to my expectations and diminishing the quality of the song in my mind.

Turns out the lyrics are as impressive as Ozzy's singing. Bless the World Wide Web for providing this information in the matter of a few seconds of Googling. I would have parted with one or more of my fingers for this technology as a teenager.

After the song morphs into a passage that was quite possibly lifted by Tom G. Warrior of Celtic Frost for "Circle of Tyrants", there's an acoustic interlude in "The Writ" that reminds me a lot of Alice Cooper's "Only Women Bleed". There's a lot of content jammed into this one song. I appreciate the diversity, but I don't know that it's necessary to jump back and forth between all these passages the way Sabbath does, or if they should have just stuck with the main song structures and developed whole songs from the other bits. As with most of the other songs on *Sabotage*, the elaborate song-within-a-song structure in "The Writ" kinda gives the impression that Sabbath shoots off all the fireworks at the same time.

When I'm finally finished with *Sabotage*, I start at the beginning of the Ozzy-era collection with the intention of working my way through the entire collection. Starting with 1970's *Black Sabbath*.

The first song, "Black Sabbath", I've obviously heard many times before. I had heard about the "devil's tritone" (also known as the much cooler-sounding *Diabolus in Musica*). These are the three notes that make up the core of this song. Apparently religious folk used to be quite nervous about these three notes being played in succession for fear of Satan being conjured up. For real.

The song gets the record off to a good start and sets a tone commensurate with the intended Sabbath vibe and the creepy album cover. I'd also previously heard the next song, "The Wizard". It's probably the most listenable of the Black Sabbath greatest hits and maybe the most peculiar. The lyrics describe an individual that walks around town with "twinkling bells" who doesn't talk, who *"just keeps walking, spreading his magic"*. Geezer has said it's about Gandalf from Lord of the Rings, but that's probably bullshit. I would think that it's more representative of Black Sabbath's superhuman drug use, most likely a thinly veiled description of their drug dealer.

With the exception of "N.I.B.", the rest of the record meanders through Iommi's several lead breaks and extended stoner jams. It occurs to me that this was what turned me away from Sabbath all those years ago. The last cluster of songs just seems like an extended, confused Led Zeppelin recitation. I'm glad when it's over. Onward to *Paranoid*.

Paranoid is considered by many to be Black Sabbath's best record. I already know all about "War Pigs" and "Fairies Wear Boots". I'm wondering what the "Luke's Wall" and "Jack the Stripper" annotations represented, as they seem to have been overlooked on subsequent greatest hits packages. I don't need to hear "Iron Man" or "Paranoid" ever again. I had heard "Electric Funeral" playing in the background during my high school years and I was mildly interested by the spooky minor-key riff, but at this point it doesn't possess the same lustre that it did back then. And Bill Ward's stifled drum fill at 3:05 makes my eyes squint. He redeems himself afterwards with a tasteful snare rim and kick drum shuffle riff on "Hand of Doom". The interlude that begins at 3:38 in "Hand of Doom" is also pretty cool, but it gives the impression it was carelessly cobbled together when I hear it choppily segue back into the main piece. The drum solo in unnecessary instrumental "Rat Salad" makes me wonder if Ward wishes he could go back and replay it. It's weird, because he's obviously a talented, hard-working player, but he's left exposed sometimes by awkward filler.

The most compelling song on *Paranoid* is "Planet Caravan". It's ethereal and intimate, like some strange audible secret. It's polarizing because it's one of those songs that seems out of place and maybe even pointless, but it grips me with its plaintiveness. Ozzy's Leslie-speakered vocal line gives the song a melancholic fragility that makes it really attractive. It makes use of the same vulnerable earnest that Neil

Young's "Needle and the Damage Done" does, making me want to listen to it over and over. It sounds the way Kubrick's *2001 Space Odyssey* looks - detached, solemn, and anonymous. Less is again so much more.

I've always loved that coughing delay effect that opens "Sweet Leaf" and the *Master of Reality* album. As a youngster I overlooked the marijuana connotation related to the harsh toke-induced cough, and it kind of relaxes the greatest hits stigma surrounding the track briefly as I reconsider it.

The opening riff of "After Forever" has a slight mid-period Beatles flourish to it, contrasting notably with the verses, in which Ozzy lazily sings along Iommi's riff without bothering to offer a vocal melody to complement the riff. I remember reading somewhere that this was something Iommi disliked and was happy to have put behind him with the arrival of Ronnie James Dio following Ozzy's departure.

Celtic-inflected instrumental "Embryo", in all of its thirty seconds, raises questions. It makes me wonder about the motivation behind its inclusion on an album that already contains one instrumental ("Orchid"), and only eight songs including these two.

The real consideration here though is Tony Iommi's contribution as a virtual riff machine. He seems capable of churning out enough material for a whole other (instrumental-free) record. This is supplanted by the Sabbath logic of having a small number of songs on an album, and by Sabbath's own admission that they tried to make it look like they had more songs than they actually did by adding thirty-second instrumentals and extended jams featuring as many as four titles representing a single track on the record (*Black Sabbath*'s "Wasp"/"Behind the Wall of Sleep"/"Bassically"/"N.I.B."). I'm sure that fans found this just as cool as Sabbath's other countercultural representations though. Black Sabbath's popularity is attributed to their anti-conventionalist unorthodoxy as much as it is to their music, even if it's via something as innocuous as song titling.

I have to admit that despite any greatest hit marginality "Children of the Grave" may have suffered, the song is bloody powerful. It ascends from Butler's galloping bass riff like an airliner taking flight and continues to bludgeon throughout. It's here that the listener gets the clearest glimpse into the heavy metal future Sabbath so clearly created. The hard rock and metal acts that would follow were all vaccinated by the "Children of the Grave" needle.

Meanwhile, "Orchid" seems bland and listless, and "Lord of This World" is churned out per the typical Sabbath formula. "Solitude" borrows from the "Planet Caravan" motif. It provides a welcome juxtaposition with what sounds like a synthesized flute against the rest of the record. Not sure why it's noted as being 8:08 minutes in length on the liner. It's actually 4:49 with ten seconds or so of silence at the end of the track before "Into the Void" begins.

The intro riff for "Into the Void" sounds a bit like the theme from the *Inspector Gadget* cartoon. The song is essentially a re-rendering of "Electric Funeral", right down to the up tempo break. And these liner run times are completely wrong. The song goes for just over six minutes, but the liner indicates that it's three minutes and eight seconds long. This is important only because I elect to hear the entire record before taking a bathroom break to rid myself of all the eggnog I consumed earlier. With the exception of "Children of the Grave" and that intro to "After Forever", *Master of Reality*, like "Lord of this World", is a passable, average work. Meh.

Clearly much has changed for the band by the time *Black Sabbath Vol. 4* is released. What makes this record fantastic is an inverse correlation, one similar to the dynamic that makes the attractive girl who has no idea she is attractive even more so. The band exudes a newfound swagger on most of the tracks. A sophistication that wasn't present among the glib naiveté of *Master of Reality*. But therein lies the rub - for all of their effort toward a brighter, more engaging foray into the rock and roll mainstream, they unwittingly produce more viscerally haunting moments that they had on each of their previous secular doomy-gloomy albums. And seemingly without even trying. This is the beauty of *Black Sabbath Vol. 4*.

"Wheels of Confusion" begins with a forlorn riff that breaks down into a shuffling boogie, by way of a pummelling middle eight and back to the main piece. The rhythm guitar of flanker instrumental "The Straightener" roars over an acoustic 12-bar blues derivative. The fuzzbox guitar in "Tomorrow's Dream" reminds me that for all of his accomplishments in riff creation, Iommi didn't really have a distinctive sound or tone that separated him from his peers in the way that Slash, the great Edward Van, or most of the players of the next generation would. This fact is kind of moot considering the experimental landscape Sabbath found itself in around this time, pharmaceutically and otherwise. Of course this isn't to say that Iommi's playing style wasn't instantly recognizable, especially his shrill and frenzied lead technique.

The earnest "Changes" provides *Black Sabbath Vol. 4*'s first uneasy moment, partly through its barren delivery and lilting piano line. But that's what makes the record so good. A song seemingly steeped in triteness actually asserts itself as the complete opposite. Rather than sounding weak the orchestral swells are given to a quiet, brooding power, particularly in their final measure. Whether or not those last three piano chords in "Changes" were specifically designed to be as eerily emotive as they were, they would nonetheless serve as a template for a genuinely melancholic musical device that could be replicated but very rarely matched. I had heard this song before, but I have a newfound appreciation for the fact that its power endures to this day.

The pointlessness of "FX" challenges me to consider even the most infinitesimal shred of depth or intellectual exercise I may be missing, but all I'm left with is that the digital delay effect must have been cutting edge back in 1972. I'm sure it was even more fascinating with a head full of coke.

Speaking of chemical adventures, "Supernaut" positions Ozzy endeavouring to touch the sky, amongst a middle eight featuring Santana-inspired Latin percussion that disappears as abruptly as it appeared. Touch the sky indeed, as Ozzy clarifies what the title of the next track, "Snowblind", represents by whispering '*cocaine!*' at the end of the main verses like he's trying to give me a hint based on what the song is about. I feel pity for Ozzy at this moment for some reason.

Bill Ward has said in interviews that "Snowblind" was actually the name chosen for this album until the record company suits intervened at the last minute with probably the weakest name possible for this record. Bill Ward has also said that he almost had his ass kicked out of the band for repeatedly fucking up the drum parts on "Cornucopia" and being sent home because he was too blasted to be a meaningful contributor to the song. Good thing Ozzy only had to worry about singing.

The next eerie delight on this record comes next with "Laguna Sunrise", though more pensive than haunting. The repeated flamenco-ish guitar line is creepily reminiscent of those Pink Floyd acoustic passages that freak you out when you listen to them lying in bed in the dark, as I admit I have done. Try it.

"St. Vitus' Dance" sounds like a lost track from Bowie's *The Man Who Sold the World* sessions. Album closer "Under the Sun" features the archetypal ominous metal riff, macabre and loping, possibly the creepiest I have ever heard. It would be immediately successful when transposed as a soundtrack against any horror movie action sequence of your choosing. Picture that little puppet man from *Saw* driving his tricycle with this playing in the background and you might wet yourself.

"Every Day Comes and Goes" is a throwaway track tacked on to "Under the Sun", almost like a bonus akin to the free Graty you get if you purchase the Slap Chop in the next 15 minutes.

Regardless, *Black Sabbath Vol. 4* is a very strong record. I'm thinking at this point that the ascension Sabbath has achieved can't possibly be maintained, and that it will likely result in a death spiral with *Never Say Die!*. Any album that features an exclamation mark in the title just can't be taken seriously.

But Sabbath was certainly coming into their own with *Sabbath Bloody Sabbath*. The venomous lyrics on the title track are spat out by Ozzy via a trebly vocal line that has great feel, but could use either more bottom end or an adjustment of key for poor Oz.

The queasy riff for "A National Acrobat" is both peculiar and attractive in a sinister way, which is essentially the cornerstone of Sabbath's allure. The song veers this way and that though a series of tempo changes in keeping with Sabbath's *an-album's-worth-of-material-jammed-into-one-song* approach. Instrumental "Fluff" doesn't sound malevolent or ominous enough to make any kind of impact. It's aptly named and up to this point, the instrumental interludes were usually a nice balance of a bit more shade than light. "Fluff" inverts this balance though and comes across as being airy and mellifluous. And at 4:10 it's way too long.

"Sabbra Cadabra" recalls the Metallica cover in my mind. The lyrics counter the song's title, but they belie Sabbath's development away from gloomy gothic imagery and progressing toward a more commercially accessible hard rock act. This is complete with a honky-tonk piano line and Ozzy ad-libbing what sounds like percussive vocal scratching at around 4:33. Some remnants of Scary Sabbath riffing remain in the verses, though only vaguely.

It's at this very point that you can literally witness Sabbath's actual metamorphosis from dark, bludgeoning plodder into savvy streamlined rock outfit, not unlike an inverted Incredible Hulk transformation. Sabbath was now clearly developing a slickness that propelled them into the upper reaches of their career arc with a cohesion that was first evidenced on *Black Sabbath Vol. 4*.

As far as the individual songs go, the unsettling synthesizer on weirdly interesting "Who Are You?" defies convention. It stands in bold contrast with the more AOR smoothness of the upbeat and almost-formulaic "Looking For Today". "Spiral Architect"'s acoustic intro very vaguely namechecks Randy Rhoads in my mind at the instant of that first chord change. Portions of the remainder of the song, particularly the string-swelled bridge, provide a glimpse of Ozzy's later solo work, specifically "S.A.T.O". from *Diary of a Madman*.

And now, on to *Technical Ecstasy*. I suspect that things are about to get interesting from the career arc perspective.

✸ Twenty Two ✸
Fear and Consumption

After going through the *Technical Ecstasy* album once, it's clear that it was a failed experiment in changing the band's direction. Gone are any signs of the doom-laden Black Sabbath of old. That version of Sabbath was traded wholesale for a stadium rock star troupe.

The liner notes of the Gimcastle *Technical Ecstasy* re-release I got on eBay contains some chat from someone named Hugh Gilmour. Not sure if should I know who he is. The notes talk about *Technical Ecstasy*'s resemblance to Queen's *A Night at the Opera*. I'm skeptical about this and I haven't even heard most of that record. Turns out the only real Queen connection is the yellow leather suit that Iommi is wearing in his sleeve photo, bare-chested and moustachioed a la Freddie Mercury.

The first song, "Back Street Kids", reminds me of Scorps' *Lovedrive*. The chorus is sneering, and a Styx-esque synthesizer break after the second chorus affirms that Sabbath had firmly entrenched themselves in the AOR trappings of the 70s.

"You Won't Change Me" starts out more like classic Black Sabbath but comes across as reluctant. Weak lyrics and a third-rate Beatles bridge weigh it down. Iommi's lead playing sounds more than ever like a cross between Keith Richards' shrill "Sympathy for the Devil" lead and any given Vinnie Vincent frenzied note salad solo.

Billy Ward's "It's Alright" is really poor. When Axl did this song live as a segue into "November Rain" during Guns N' Roses' heyday, I have to wonder what his motivation was. Did he a) do it with an ironic, mocking intention, b) see something in the song and attempt to shape it into something prolific (which he successfully did), or c) was he drawn to the song because of its bizarre nature as an unorthodox Sabbath composition with Elton John piano styling? The answer is most likely d) all of the above. As if he was trying to redeem himself, Ward starts "Gypsy" off with a cracking good drum riff, maybe the best on any Sabbath record I've heard up to this point. Then a synthesized guitar takes the song to the land of Prism and ELO.

"All Moving Parts Stand Still" is clumsy. I've heard the verse passages in another song before, quite possibly Motley Crue's "Louder than Hell". It almost seems like there's an ardent attempt to steer clear of any perceived darkness on this record, as everything is so shiny and bright. "Rock N Roll Doctor" deploys the full gamut of 70s rock clichés complete with cowbell, early period Rush guitar riff, and hackneyed piano line close.

"Dirty Women" suffers in the same way that "You Won't Change Me" does, by virtue of being a passable effort had they been recorded by a band other than Black Sabbath. This whole record would be a decent effort if Foghat had released it. At its core, *Technical Ecstasy* is something that Sabbath tried to pass off as rightful participants in a 70s rock landscape, not naturally purvey as an extremely capable hard rock outfit the way they did a year earlier on *Sabotage*.

It's hard to believe that "She's Gone" was even approved for release to the general public. It would be easy to make light of how truly awful this song is, but what's more interesting is how polarized it is by other more mellow Sabbath songs by virtue of variance in apathy. It compels me to digress a bit.

That old showbiz saying 'always leave 'em wanting more' defines the *more is less* maxim. This rationale can be applied to emotional experience. When an artist demonstrates apathy in the form of a song, a painting, or a written work, there's an interest generated based on the premise that being prompted to feel *too much* can be perceived as emotional exploitation or manipulation. Resistance is formed, emotional response is subverted, and the art is romanticized and individually internalized. And less becomes more.

In my second year of university, a ruffled, longhaired musician who we would later call 'Ike' moved into my dorm halfway through the school year. We hung out a lot. He taught me how to play guitar on an old Yamaha twelve-string acoustic that I traded a pair of speakers for with another guy from our dorm. But he also taught me a lot about music in general.

Ike introduced me to the musical world that I had previously eschewed for no particularly good reason. That world that included artists like The Beatles, The Rolling Stones, and Neil Young. Up until that point the only non-metal recording I had in my collection was Pink Floyd's "Astronomy Domine", and that was just because I liked Voivod's version.

Ike and I would sit around drinking Wiser's rye, playing acoustic guitar along to The Beatles' *White Album*, and boldly philosophize in the way that drunken university students with inflated senses of how clever they are often do. We discussed a sociological theory that we called *The Principle of Least Interest*, which postulated that when two people are in a relationship, the strength of attraction one person feels for the other is driven by how much that attraction is reciprocated. More specifically, if the person you're involved with doesn't seem to like you as much as you like them, your attraction will increase in equal proportion to their indifference. This of course will diminish their interest in you, again in balanced proportion, resulting in several incidents of embarrassing public behaviour, ultimately repelling you from one another. Except for the inevitable subsequent boozy late night hookups.

It seemed as though our relationships had been governed by this principle up to this point in our 20-year-old lives, and Glenn Close and Michael Douglas even seemingly validated the principle's existence in *Fatal Attraction* just a few years later. Whether or not the principle is psychologically endearing or even healthy is beside the point (because I know it isn't). It goes without saying that I've since grown beyond the limits of the principle as it applies to relationships. But while the principle itself was more engrossing to me as a drunken young sociologist, the gist of it remains valid where the concept of apathy is concerned.

Whether we admit it or not, apathy is attractive. It's attractive because it engages mystery and uncertainty as its primary devices, and uncertainty opposes the obvious. The obvious is boring. We're intrigued by indifference because it can imply vulnerability and a lack of control, even if you're not psychologically imbalanced. Easy conclusions are non-stimulating and dull. Mystery is naturally stimulating. Take the Loch Ness Monster for example. It's intriguing to consider that a seemingly prehistoric beast has defied scientific convention and subsists in the murky depths of the Loch Ness. But, if it did in fact exist and was discovered, any intrigue it previously carried would gradually fade. It might be *interesting* for a finite period, but the *intrigue* is gone. We would move on. The possibility of extraterrestrial life is a similar consideration. People love this stuff, because it's implied to be outside the limits of convention. But what we really love about it is the offer of perceiving it in *our own way*.

Let's face it. Human beings are really just the most highly evolved species on the planet. I say *just* because we don't think of ourselves as animals as much as we probably should. Despite our refined social mores (in most parts of the world at least), we're still intrinsically just as territorial as any other animal. Our more highly evolved new mammalian brains allow us the luxury of being able to achieve and appreciate civility.

But we still have base tendencies, including self-preservation and a necessity to satisfy our urges. With respect to the unknown, the key variable is that missing piece that we can contemplate and assimilate in a way that's best for us *as individuals* – making sense of things to best serve our individual selves and our consumption tendencies.

Though I wasn't completely dialled in to his music I always respected Marilyn Manson's insight, particularly when he said in

Michael Moore's *Bowling For Columbine* that fear and consumption are western society's main behavioural drivers. It's absolutely true. And naturally, things are most interesting to us when we can't consume them, or *have* them.

This is the difference between Black Sabbath's "Planet Caravan" and "She's Gone". "Planet Caravan" is cold, distant ethera, and "She's Gone" just lays it all out on the table in a heap of overblown sentimentality. In doing so, "She's Gone" willingly gives itself to you while "Planet Caravan" is more elusive, creating a host of alternate and intriguing possibilities. Songs like "Planet Caravan" use emotion against *you* and songs like "She's Gone" use emotion against *itself*. And if you believe in this rationale, the best songs lure us with apathetic content. But they'll never let you get close enough to them to completely *have* them.

Sadly, the most remarkable thing about *Technical Ecstasy* is that it marks the dubious point of Black Sabbath's transformation from heavy metal monolith into just another rock band. I wonder if Sabbath devotees from back then felt the same way about this transformation that Metallica fans did when Hetfield and the boys cut their hair and played a promotional gig in Tuktoyaktuk with Veruca Salt.

At this point, I'm kinda worried about loading *Never Say Die!* into my player.

The song "Never Say Die" is the only one I know from this record. I heard the Ozzy *Speak of the Devil* live version, but it was usually just playing in the background whenever I heard it. This Black Sabbath version features a considerably thinner vocal from Oz, and as Simon Cowell would say, the song sounds too big for him. At the end of the song, someone adds a very baritone *"ne-ver saaay diiieee"*, suitably capping off a decidedly crap vocal performance on the leadoff track.

Something has happened to Iommi's guitar sound. It sounds super compressed and slightly buried in the mix. The lyrics for "Johnny Blade" suck. "Junior's Eyes" sounds like Black Sabbath covering someone else's material. All of the Sabbath earmarks have gone. This is particularly problematic when you consider that Iommi's killer riffs were a substantial factor in Sabbath's success. The problem is that for a prolific band like Black Sabbath, casting off a key aspect of what makes you who you are is an enormous gamble that results in a loss more times than it does a win.

"A Hard Road" is stolen from Cheap Trick who stole it from The Beatles. The lyrics in "Shock Wave" are particularly lousy. It occurs to me that one of the most unfortunate differences between *Never Say Die!* and *Sabotage* is the steep decline in lyrical quality. Ditto "Air Dance". This song sounds like something that fucking Captain & Tennille would have released. I'm actually really perplexed by this, and I wonder if that guy from Savoy Brown that temporarily filled in for Ozzy possibly had a hand in writing this stuff. Otherwise, there isn't really an explanation for such a radical departure. "Air Dance" actually finishes with a plucky jazz passage (!).

"Over To You" sounds a bit more like Sabbath, but it reflects the fatigue the band must have been feeling at this point. It's just being woefully trotted out. "Breakout"'s baleful drum intro gives the impression that the old Black Sabbath may be returning, but then a goddamn *saxophone* comes in. And the song is an instrumental! This can't be real. Christ! Someone else sings "Swinging the Chain", but I'm so dejected at this point that I don't even give a fuck who it is. The song's terrible.

I had no idea that this album would be horrible enough to make Papillion gag. I put on the dulcet tones on "Planet Caravan" and it makes me feel better.

I'm actually stunned. I sort of wish I hadn't heard *Never Say Die!*. I really wanted to like that album. As with *Technical Ecstasy*, I tried to look for the positives. Any redeemable goodness at all that might be in there. As I listen to "Planet Caravan" for a third consecutive time, I realize the irony in the fact that it contains jazz blues-ish inflections in its outro - the very thing I was complaining about with "Air Dance". But the difference between the two is *poise*. "Planet Caravan" deploys this inflection on its own terms that Sabbath makes their own, and "Air

Dance" delivers a schmaltzy, phony rendering that makes Sabbath, very unfortunately, seem like jokey bitches. It's inconceivable, really.

⁓〇

At this point I've spent the gross majority of my Christmas holidays focused on the Ozzy-era Black Sabbath albums. I've all but ignored the Beatles complete box set I received as a Christmas gift from Alison, though I'm sure Ozzy would have been flattered that I chose to forsake his idol Sir Paul McCartney's music in favour of his. I can say that the exercise was certainly worthwhile, and the discovery rich. Except the *Never Say Die!* part. The fact that I did this so long after my initial introduction to hard rock and heavy metal in 1982 is a bit troubling, mostly because it lends credence to the power of image and marketing.

Whether anyone likes it or not, the concept of hard rock and heavy metal relies very heavily on image. Even when it doesn't. A band like Metallica may have been able to avoid mainstream trappings like MTV and radio airplay for the first five years of their career and still achieve a considerable underground following. But this just defined their *anti-establishment image*, one the band vehemently maintained as they grew more popular. Image, or anti-image, shapes the identity of a band in the eyes of the fans, and this plays an undisputable role in a band's popularity.

Black Sabbath's failure to prosper in the thriving 80s metal environment was based primarily on the fact that their prevalent image was that of a 70s band. As an 80s teen, my opinion was that Black Sabbath wasn't my generation's music. My generation was heavily focused on image. The only reason Ozzy could become so relevant in the 80s and Sabbath couldn't, was because Ozzy and wife/manager/general handler Sharon Arden were more cognizant of the importance of image and the need to adapt.

Look at it this way. When Ozzy split from Black Sabbath in 1979, everyone was roughly the same age. Both parties were pretty evenly matched coming out of the gate into the new decade. If anything, Ozzy was at a threefold disadvantage based on a) his fondness for chemical adventure, b) the fact that Black Sabbath was already a firmly established brand, and c) the fact that Ozzy was such a berserk, fucked up weirdo who seemed challenged by most any social situation.

But, Ozzy surrounded himself with hip young people like flashy hotshot guitarist Randy Rhoads, who looked as cool as he sounded. Rhoads became the focal point of Ozzy's new Blizzard of Ozz band. It didn't hurt that Rhoads was a crazy virtuoso guitar player that would write blistering riffs for classic songs like "Crazy Train" and two albums worth of very solid material in *Blizzard of Ozz* and *Diary of a Madman*, but Ozzy's gimmicky image always afforded him the limelight. Ozzy shaved his head, bit the heads off of live animals, snorted ants, drank other people's piss, got arrested for urinating on the Alamo, dressed up as a woman, used an inverted cross as a prop on the *Diary of a Madman* cover, and partook in all kinds of other public lunacy. He took young up-and-comers Motley Crue and Metallica out on their first major tours.

In doing all of this, he distanced himself from the 70s Black Sabbath legacy. Hell, he even released a live album of strictly Sabbath numbers in 1982 and it went platinum. This was because the album was called *Speak of the Devil*, featuring a shirtless, menacing Ozzy wearing black eyeliner and fake teeth and with cranberry sauce falling out of his mouth. The inner sleeve contained the requisite ghoulish symbolism, and lead guitar was now handled by Brad Gillis of Night Ranger fame, another flashy young guitar player who temporarily replaced Rhoads after he died in a plane crash (RIP).

Ozzy - and Sharon - were able to dress up the musical product in an attractive sheen that appealed to the young 80s crowd. Even after Rhoads died and Gillis went back to Night Ranger, the flash remained with young, glammy, fleet-fingered Japanese rising sun bandana-laden guitarist Jake E. Lee. And after Lee departed, a nineteen-year-old buff beach blonde in Zakk Wylde (that look didn't last long for Wylde, but the 80s were over by that point).

Black Sabbath chose a much different path. They recruited thirty-seven-year-old singer Ronnie Dio in 1979. They made two great records in *Heaven and Hell* and *The Mob Rules*, but any image intrigue Sabbath may have had with the release of 1982's *Live Evil* was mitigated by the fact that the group just seemed...*older*. Geezer's nickname wasn't really helping matters either. After Dio left, Sabbath brought in thirty-eight-year old former Deep Purple vocalist Ian Gillan, and their *Born Again* album tanked. Surprise! By the time Tony Iommi brought in unknown younger singer David Donato, it was too late. Geezer and his geriatric nickname left the band and Black Sabbath was a shambles.

The kicker is that after Dio left Black Sabbath in late 1982 he struck out on his own, *with a band led by twenty-one-year-old flash guitarist Vivian Campbell*, and immediately began a long headlining stint following the release of *Holy Diver* and *The Last in Line*[*]. And Dio was even *older* than Ozzy and the guys in Sabbath![**]

Black Sabbath, Ozzy, and Dio all played the evil imagery card, but only Ozzy and Dio were able to capitalize on it. They infused it with youth, colour, and vibrancy, thus making it relevant to heavy metal's target audience in the 80s - the teenage stimulus seeker. Sabbath did not, and that potentially gleaming evil element that they could have had in their arsenal just translated into a dull, non-stimulating grey.

But even still, this only means that Black Sabbath were simply deferred somewhat. In retrospect it really only amounts to image over substance. Ozzy's music after his first two solo records with Randy Rhoads was more or less piffle, particularly through his 'mad housewife' *Ultimate Sin* phase. And, because they both relied on medieval subject matter in both image and lyrical content, the only real difference between the Dio and Black Sabbath bands was Vivian Campbell and his showy riffs and solos. And if we take a step backward to look at the big picture, this is typical of the 80s metal scene in general.

Where hair metal is concerned, at least for 80s adolescents like me, the countless Led Zeppelin and Aerosmith clones actually served a purpose in an inadvertent way. They provided a 'lite' version of the real

---

[*] Ironically, Dio's first guitarist choice before eventually going with Vivian Campbell was actually Jake E. Lee.
[**] Viv Campbell in fact told Guitar World magazine that playing in Dio was like being in a band with your dad.

stuff. It carried an almost children's chewable quality of the hard rock and heavy metal vitamins I may have been too young to fully digest as an ADD-addled teen.

Back then I was simultaneously fearful of Led Zeppelin's four symbols imagery that I saw on the jean-jackets of the kids in town who smoked. I was afraid of every one of those guys. I was also annoyed by the fact that "Dazed and Confused" took up precious time on MuchMusic's *Power Hour* when I could have been watching a Kingdom Come video instead.

When I was in university and had finally came to appreciate the substance and value of Led

Zeppelin in addition to The Stones, The Beatles, Aerosmith, and everyone else, I still passed over Black Sabbath. It makes 'discovering' these old Sabbath records kinda bittersweet. It's pleasing to realize that *Sabotage* and *Black Sabbath Vol. 4* are fantastic records that I actually really enjoy, but it's a shame I waited this long to find that out. It makes me laugh when I consider the irony of the myriad years I spent preoccupied with heavy metal without having paid any real attention to the band that was actually responsible for the genre.

Next Christmas: Rush.

Twenty Three
White Sabbath

Wolfmother is a band obviously devoted to Black Sabbath. I'm intrigued by the fact that people like Alison and one of my best pals and fellow music lover Kent Bailey really dig them, despite the fact that neither of these individuals are fans of Black Sabbath or heavy metal in particular. It's clear that Wolfmother's main thrust is incorporating Sabbathy riffs with a Zeppeliny vibe to create a modern hard rock package with retro charm.

So - partly because I'm a keen and industrious student of rock genealogy, and partly because I'm compelled to convert Alison and my pal Kent into Black Sabbath fans to satisfy my subconscious need for them to recognize me as an all-knowing musicphile, I decide to conduct a small experiment. Because experiments are fun. Particularly when my family and friends are the subjects and I am the conductor.

The experiment begins when I give Kent a CD-R labelled *The Fargin Bastridges*. I explain to him that The Fargin Bastridges are a hot new band with a retro lo-fi sound. I tell him that if he likes Wolfmother, he'll probably like this. What Kent does not know is that the music he will hear when he listens to the CD is actually Black Sabbath's *Sabotage*, and that The Fargin Bastridges is actually a phony alias under which Guns N' Roses used to book themselves in L.A. after they got big and wanted to play smaller clubs without drawing too much attention. I've provided Kent with hard rock music he's liked before, so this gesture doesn't seem out of the ordinary. Just in case, I also throw in a separate CD copy of Band of Skulls' debut *Baby Darling Doll Face Honey* for good measure. Alison has already heard Sabbath's *Sabotage* record as a result of the bazillion plays it has enjoyed at home and during our work commute, so I unfortunately cannot include her in the experiment.

My specific objective here is to prove a direct parallel between Black Sabbath and Wolfmother as I hear it. Kent has previously told me he was not at all into Sabbath, yet really likes Wolfmother. *Sabotage* doesn't contain any real Black Sabbath greatest hits that Kent may have heard, and because newer bands like The White Stripes (also a source of inspiration to Wolfmother) take strides to achieve a lo-fi sound by using old gear and recording techniques, the sound quality of the recording probably won't factor into his consideration. Regardless of the outcome, this should be an interesting exercise indeed.

A few days after I supply Kent with the CDs, I email him to ask what he thought of The Fargin Bastridges. He advises that he thinks that *"Black Sabbath fans would really like this"*, but that it's not his cup of tea. He also mentions that he thinks most of the songs *"sounded very similar"*. Also, that while Wolfmother does have a similar sound to The Fargin Bastridges, Wolfmother has *"more going on"* in their music. He claims he could clearly hear what he called *"the Sabbath sound"* in Wolfmother's music, but he politely declines The Fargin Bastridges because they sound too much like Black Sabbath.

As much as I didn't want this to be the outcome, the assessment was pretty accurate for someone who had only heard Black Sabbath less than five times. After I explain my experiment to him, he calls me a couple of expletives that I won't repeat here. He also says he's relieved that he didn't fall for it, proclaiming to everyone else that this hot new band The Fargin Bastridges was going to be the next big thing.

Though that would have been pretty funny, I'm glad and also impressed that Kent's ear saved him from any heckling. After all, I was really only attempting to validate my consideration that Black Sabbath could be considered in a new light based on my 'hypothesis' that *since a new band has gained popularity by having made distinct use of the key*

No Sleep 'til Sudbury

dynamics of an older one, the older band could be considered on the same merits that a new one would. But this didn't happen. It occurs to me at this point though, that Kent is a Led Zeppelin fan. This explains his point that there's "more going on". Amidst the Sabbath riffs, the jangle of Zeppelin acoustic guitars and percussion can be heard in Wolfmother's songs, all wrapped in the sheen of a modern-day production.

So while my attempts to have Kent see the light by inviting him to the dark side failed, my experiment still did validate my overall hypothesis that Wolfmother's music may seemingly contain new elements, but it's not new music. I still smirk when I hear Wolfmother's song "Joker & the Thief" in public settings. The focal point of the song, that opening fretboard-tapping riff that everyone loves to blare on their stereos like it's some awe-inspiring newfound revelation, is more than just obliquely similar to Iron Maiden's "Flash of the Blade" from 1984's *Powerslave*. Just a bit less than Buckcherry's "Lit Up" riff is completely lifted from Ace Frehley's "Shock Me".

I'm not knocking Andrew Stockdale and Wolfmother, because I own the debut album. I might even buy *Cosmic Egg* as well. But it's only aesthetic frameworking. I don't contemplate the band in the same light that others might in good conscience because as I mentioned previously, this stuff has all been created already. An expectation I had in The Fargin Bastridges experiment was an acknowledgement that an old band (Black Sabbath) had already established the basic constructs that a new band (Wolfmother) used as a foundation to launch their own music. And that was being kind. I suppose I got that, but initially what I couldn't quite get my head around was my perceived imbalance between the appreciation of what currently *is*, and the apparent lack of appreciation for what *was*. Listening to Wolfmother's debut record again just now, my stance remains unchanged. Actually, it may even be a bit more fortified.

If we're being honest, Wolfmother is basically Black Sabbath, with their predilection toward dark tendencies being brightened up by the shininess of borrowed Led Zeppelin groove.

Wolfmother is White Sabbath.

✡ Twenty Four ✡
So Much For Hollywood

And now, back to my old friends Iron Maiden.

My re-acquaintance with Maiden came in the late 90s when they were touring whatever album they had released at that time with singer Blaze Bayley. During this tour they played a show to a sparse crowd in Hamilton's Copps Coliseum sometime between 1997 and 1999. Dio and a great English band I'd never previously heard of called Dirty Deeds were also on the bill. The show had a strange stigma attached to it. The bands were playing in an arena setting, but Copps was cordoned off to one quarter of its size due to poor ticket sales. It felt very odd seeing Iron Maiden (and Dio, I guess) in this element. It seemed like they had been reduced somewhat. That typical star-and-fan symbiosis you typically experience at arena shows wasn't there anymore. It was weird. It was like seeing them in a moment of vulnerability, almost like when you visit someone in the hospital. They were exposed, and the encounter was quite different and a bit unsettling.

What I was seeing was Iron Maiden at their nadir. I hadn't seen Blaze Bayley previously, and I was mildly curious to see how he would measure up against predecessor Bruce Dickinson on vocally challenging tunes like "Hallowed Be Thy Name". Surely bassist and Maiden founder Steve Harris, as proud and steadfast as he was, wouldn't have replaced Dickinson with a lesser talent.

Turns out he did. As the show wore on Bayley did well, but his voice cracked on more than one occasion. As good as he may have been in any capacity, he was still a shadow of Dickinson. I felt sorry for Bayley, knowing that taskmaster Harris was most likely fuming with each bum note he sang. I walked away from that show feeling weirdly disenfranchised. I had that feeling you get when you look at recently posted Facebook pictures of old acquaintances you used to be involved with at some point in your past, and you're just kind of looking in on the situation from a vantage point that feels like it couldn't be any farther away. I assumed Iron Maiden had lived out the full trajectory of their life span and that the end was nigh.

When Dickinson and Adrian Smith returned to the Maiden fold around 2000, I was a little surprised. The old reunion cha-ching tour thing was becoming *de rigueur* after bands like KISS and Motley Crue started doing it, and I guess I should have seen a reunion coming after Smith had played on Dickinson's recent solo records. I was still a bit perplexed though. I'd figured the Maiden boys to be half-decently ethically responsible and scrupulous fellas based on what I'd known about them back when I was a rabid fanboy of the band in my teens. I mean, when KISS got back together no one was surprised. Ditto Motley. It was for money, pure and simple. The talk about family and all that crap is just that. Crap. But I do think that all of these individuals, whether we're talking about Rob Halford from Judas Priest, David Lee Roth of Van Halen, or Bruce Dickinson, have a moment of clarity some time after the dust settles. They look at where they've been, where they are, and where they're going and they say to themselves, *"Damn, I should be back there, man. I belong there"*.

What's left to be done when the reunion does occur is another story. I've always been of the opinion that by the time the reunion happens, the band is in the downward swing of their career solstice with twilight fast approaching. Bands that say they're revitalized and that they expect to reach higher highs in their career with new material are full of shit. They know it just as well as the fans do. The problem is, both the band and the fans want this to happen, but it never does. Because it just *can't*. Bands can't return to the creative headspaces they occupied when they were younger, dumber, and hornier. And fans really only want the classic material, mostly for nostalgic purposes. Nothing post-reunion will better that stuff. This is a transparent concept, and KISS' *Psycho Circus* is a superb example. Lots of bullshit hype for a bullshit record. The only example I can think of where this rule is somewhat excepted is maybe Aerosmith. And I said *maybe*.

Following the pharmaceutical tsunami that finally sank the good ship Aerosmith in 1979, the group's original members eventually found their way back to each other five years later and released *Done with Mirrors* the following year. This record didn't do it for them, but 1987's *Permanent Vacation* and 1989's *Pump* certainly did. It's important to note that Aerosmith really had two careers as a result of this success. The funny thing is that plenty of the new collection of fans attracted to the band by the aforementioned records and subsequent smash *Get a Grip* even seemed to be aware that the band had a history previous to 1984.

This is why Aerosmith is only somewhat of an exception. Aerosmith's career prior to their 1979 breakup was the purer version of Aerosmith. The dirty, gritty real-deal Aerosmith, prime influence of legions of 80s glam metal bands. Great songs like "Seasons of Wither", "Uncle Salty", and "Adam's Apple" came from that era, not to mention the plethora of greatest hits.

Metal guru Eddie Trunk once commented on his satellite radio show that despite the staggering amounts of drugs Aerosmith were doing in the seventies, the songs were fantastic and that maybe there was a correlation somewhere in there. I absolutely agree. I've never been a (hard) drug user or a proponent, but if we're being honest I think the drugs gave real licence to a reckless, unhinged Aerosmith - *the* Aerosmith in my opinion.

There's no question that the 'new' Aerosmith wrote great songs, several of which became classics in their own right. But the band morphed into a structured, polished, more commercially-viable machine with extended moving parts in the form of whip-cracking A&R men like

John Kalodner and professional songwriters like Diane Warren. The two Aerosmiths are both great bands, but they're distinctly separate from each other. There is Old Aerosmith, and there is New Aerosmith. Old Aerosmith is that slutty Jezebel that would take you upstairs to deliver the groceries at the end of a sloppy late-night boozefest. New Aerosmith was the beautiful prom queen with great-smelling hair you were proud to bring home to Mom. Both got your rocks off, but one cut through the artifice and did it on a much more primal level.

Iron Maiden's reunion situation first seemed to be vehemently focused against the *trot-out-the-glory-days-hits* reunion routine. This was something I evidenced directly during Maiden's Y2K tour to support their latest studio release *Brave New World*. The new lineup featured the return of prodigal sons Dickinson and Smith, and also Smith-replacement guitarist Janick Gers. This was interesting and a bit unorthodox, because keeping Gers in the lineup added a third lead guitar player to the band. I was ambivalent when I found this out, as I liked the fact that Maiden didn't just send Gers packing when Smith decided to come back. He seems like a pretty likeable chap, and it's a shame seeing loyal band members being blithely discarded to make room for someone for reunion tour purposes (hi Gene and Paul). Either way, I like Gers even though I'm still not quite sure what his exact application is in the band proper.

At any rate, during their Toronto stop on the *Brave New World* tour, the band sent a very clear message that there would be no greatest hits parade. This advisory was provided by Bruce Dickinson at the start of the show, in a bit of a harsh manner. I don't remember exactly what he said, but it bordered on being a lecture about how Iron Maiden would be playing their new songs from their new album only, and if you came expecting anything other that, well...bollocks to you lot then.

Dickinson seemed sort of cranky that night, directly pointing out someone who was sitting down in the front rows and saying, *"You paid your money, get out of your bloody seat!"* I snickered when I considered the ironic twist in Dickinson's dressing down of that sitting fan. If the guy did pay his money for a ticket, isn't it really within his personal liberty as to how he would like to experience the show, be it standing or sitting? I know it's unheard of to sit in the front row, but it's kinda funny.

Dickinson's bitterness could have been partially attributed to the fact that the band had just come to Toronto from Montreal, which is known for being one of the most mental rock show audiences on planet Earth. The crowds have a reputation for always being insane, so much so that the band and even Maiden manager Rod Smallwood has noted that Montreal is indeed one of the best crowds in the world to play for. That's quite a statement. Dickinson was good enough to remind us that night, after doing his call-and-response routine with the crowd that Montreal was a much louder crowd than we were. This was most likely true.

Toronto crowds, while maybe a tad more excitable and less glib than some other areas of North America, are maybe a bit more focused on the cognitive absorption of the concert experience. Particularly a reunion show. We may also be a bit more self-aware. And like it or not, it goes without saying that most fans are less willing to scream at the tops of their lungs for new songs that while are appreciated, hold very little personal meaning to them.

The mild hostility was okay with me. I did sit through most of the show, but that doesn't mean that I enjoyed it any less. Just because I'm not jumping up and down and screaming in other people's ears and dousing them with my beer like a fucking lunatic isn't at all correlated to the quality of the performance. Or my level of enjoyment of the show. People are people, and they're going to react the way they're going to react. I tend to be less extroverted as a person, so I can't be counted upon to act in any other way unless I've been drinking. I completely understand the artist's point when they say that they feed off of the crowd's energy. I get that. And as a former singer in bands that have played live gigs, I appreciate that. But it's not like I'm sitting there frowning with my arms crossed staring at my shoes or something. Or heckling the band and flipping them off like some morons do (I could never really understand that behaviour, particularly given the cost of tickets these days). I'm into the show, and my facial expression indicates that. And if you can't see my face, I'm far enough from the stage that it doesn't matter if I'm standing or sitting anyway. For the record, I do stand at most shows, mostly out of respect. And sometimes because the person in front of me is standing too and I can't see otherwise.

I sat through most of these new songs at this Iron Maiden show feeling even more like a distant observer than the last time I saw them. I was looking in on something that I used to know. Almost in a commemorative way, in recognition of the value of something that was once extremely centric in my life.

I should clarify that I didn't observe Iron Maiden circa 2000 in the same way that I had observed other bands doing their rounds during the 80s hard rock and heavy metal revival of sorts that had been taking place. When I moved down to Toronto in 1995, I made a point of seeing every band I was into during my high school years wherever possible. I suppose this was partly in an attempt to make up for all the action I missed back in Espanola. I also ate at Taco Bell every single day for two weeks straight and covered the entire menu a couple of times over when I first got here, but that's beside the point.

Judas Priest, Aerosmith, Lizzy Borden, Scorpions, Skid Row, KISS (5 times), Slayer, Whitesnake, Ozzy, Motley, Frehley solo, Alice Cooper, Guns N' Roses, Black Sabbath, Megadeth. You name 'em, I've seen 'em. The only hard rock and metal bands I missed that I wouldn't have minded seeing are Accept, Raven, and Queensryche. Maybe Tesla. The Poison summer amphitheatre tours were particularly useful to me in my efforts to catch up, because Poison would bring out a new host of old hair bands on the road with them every year. Dokken, Faster Pussycat, Slaughter, Enuff Z'Nuff, Firehouse, BulletBoys, Quiet Riot, Warrant, Winger, Ratt, and Tommy Keifer with Cinderella. The downside of this was having to see Poison five years in a row, but alas.

I always hoped for the best-case scenario when I went to see these bands. Because for one, original lineups were mixed and matched. You had guys like Winger's Reb Beach playing in Whitesnake and Quiet Riot's Carlos Cavazo and Love Hate's Jizzy Pearl playing in Ratt. Hired guns like Keri Kelli were playing in pretty much every hair band, popping up in a different one every summer. Not to mention the fact that bands like L.A. Guns would somehow splinter into two separate touring entities with key members in both acts. With all of this going on, it's hard to take this stuff seriously.

The other point of consideration is the fact that career pinnacles were several years in the rearview mirror for all of these bands. And it really showed in some cases. With hair bands in particular, a key element in the overall concept is youth in image. The unfortunate truth is that another key element of this sub-genre is rampant alcohol consumption, and as middle age sets in, these two elements no longer work symbiotically. In fact, the excessive drinking angle completely inverts itself by going from making you look cool to making you look like a sad old drunkard. I witnessed this during some of these shows. Band members were overweight, bald, sloppy wasted. And looking very old. Some of the shows were desperate, clumsy, and thick with an irony that couldn't be ignored.

Even considering the hair band landscape, I honestly could not believe how far off the rails some guys had launched themselves. I felt ambivalence - on one hand empathizing that most of these guys didn't know anything else in life, having come into rock stardom at an early age. They felt like this was all they could do. On the other hand, I wondered how anyone with even a modicum of a clue could contribute to self-parody in this way. I suspect some of these guys don't know, some don't care, and some just don't want to know and fake it. We all have our demons. And people do more humiliating things for money I suppose.

Nonetheless, as I watched these guys and their bands deal with their present circumstances during their sets, it was more of an examination out of sheer curiousity most times. I felt like I had to see them just once. And that one time was usually more than enough.

Iron Maiden's situation was much different of course. Their *milieu* was more in line with the valour and blue-collar nobility of the heavy metal genre. Like an Accept or a Dio, almost a Judas Priest. And without being a silly caricature like Manowar. Maiden always demonstrated a higher level of functioning. They had deeper substance and I took them more seriously. I respected the fact that they continued to make a go of it with new material, even though I didn't buy *Brave New World* or subsequent 2003 release *Dance of Death*.

But in 2004 when Maiden released a DVD exhaustively documenting the earliest days of the band to celebrate their upcoming 25th year anniversary of the release of their first album and their 30th year anniversary of their formation, my ears perked up. A tour followed during which they played only material from their first four albums. They re-released "The Number of the Beast" single, and it went to number three in the UK. I could see where things where going now.

In 2005 I was getting back into Iron Maiden again. I bought their next studio record, *A Matter of Life and Death*, but I'll admit that I didn't care much for it. They toured it by playing the record in its entirety, which apparently didn't go so well - towards the end of the tour they apparently added some *Number of the Beast* songs.

And then it happened.

In 2007, an announcement was made that Iron Maiden was going to be doing a massive world tour that would feature only songs from their first seven albums, and that they would use the World Slavery Tour stage show from (what I consider to be the apex of their career) the 1984 *Powerslave* era. The tour was called Somewhere Back in Time, and it was inevitable. At last Iron Maiden was coming to grips, whether Dickinson *et al* would admit it or not, with the fact that their true-blue fan base just wants to relive the old days. No one is really happy about it or proud of it. But it is what it is and there's no dismissing it. I snapped up a ticket right away. One ticket, because I like to go to these kinds of shows by myself. I have a personal philosophy about concerts, particularly concerts like this one.

There are a couple of different ways to see a concert in my opinion, depending on who the act is and what my relationship is with the band. If it's a band that I like but don't feel like I have any type of really strong connection with, like say a Tom Petty or a Bruce Springsteen, I can go to that concert with Alison and/or friends and it's considered a social event. Beers, chatter, and all the rest of it. I'm still a fan of the artist, interested in seeing and hearing the band in a live setting, in addition to all of the social interaction that comes along with a night out with friends.

But if the artist is a band that I am a substantial fan of, or was in my teenage years, I'll usually attend the show by myself. This is because it's a personal experience for me. I'm reliving a connection I felt with the band in my teenage years. On a grander scale, it's a portal through which to poke my head and peer back into my own past. An opportunity to relive a time when I recognized this band's music, in large or small part, as a contributor to the soundtrack of my teenage life. The show is an enabler by which to look at my own blueprint and gain a greater personal insight by contrasting then-and-now experiences with added perspective.

It's kind of greedy and maybe a little bit weird. But like I said earlier, I don't like to mix associations. These shows aren't a form of social entertainment for me. There can be no talking. I don't even drink at these shows because I don't want to miss anything, as a result of cognitive impairment or because I have to relieve myself.

Seeing a band you really like a second time is a different story. But there aren't a whole lot of bands I would see a second time at this point. I've more or less seen all the bands I always wanted to see except the ones I mentioned earlier, and since I wrote that I actually did manage to see Accept (and Wolf Hoffmann!) in a club in Toronto. Outside hard rock and metal, I'd love to see acoustic Neil Young if the bloody tickets weren't so impossible to get.

The Iron Maiden announcement of their recent 80s re-enactment tour was special however. This would definitely be a solo concert for me.

On March 16, 2008, I went to the Toronto show at the Air Canada Centre. Before it started I sat and looked around, considering the application Iron Maiden and heavy metal music had in my formative years. Almost like the consideration of an absent friend. I juxtaposed my consistent fondness for Maiden, which had endured for twenty-five years at that time, against my life. The places I'd been both physically, mentally, and emotionally. What I'd been able to achieve since I was an introverted fourteen-year-old longhaired headbanger from a small, dead end town. While I had invented and re-invented new versions of myself over the course of my adolescence, university years, and adulthood, metal had always been a touchstone. Albeit at some times obscured, it was always familiar and comfortable. Always a core reference point that stayed with me and provided me with the closest centre I'd ever known. And it never failed to provide me with an indescribably immense joy, and still does. I thought about how interesting it was that my first ever concert was the original version of the show I was about to see on this night twenty-four years later, and about how absolutely thrilled I was back then in December 1984. I smiled quietly to myself.

I also thought a little bit about how this situation was essentially the purest of examples of what so many people seem so preoccupied with – going back in time - and why people would want to do that. Resolution of some unresolved issue? Less responsibility? More security? Better metabolism? Not sure. When we get together now, Sloss and I often laugh about how hilarious it is that we're sitting together twenty-plus years after we last saw each other. Over the course of a lifetime you tend to leave a lot of people behind. Mostly because some of them are simply meant to be intermittent or transitory friends based on forced geographical or situational circumstance. But Sloss and I had enough important history to salvage lost years, and I was thankful to have had the opportunity to reconnect with him. He also recently started to rock the same type of hairstyle he had back in the day, which is a definite plus.

And now, once again, twenty-four years later...it's *showtime*.

I have to admit that as the house lights went down and the crowd freaked at the first word of Churchill's intro, it really did feel like 1984 again for me. My teenage obsession with Iron Maiden was very vivid at that moment. And now, as Maiden stormed the stage to kick off "Aces High" in the exact same way they did twenty-four years ago, I was completely riveted.

While I watched the band rip though "Aces High", following up with "Two Minutes to Midnight" and "The Trooper" immediately after as they did all those years ago, I felt a weird sense of vindication. I guess this could be attributed to the fact that I'd come full circle with Iron Maiden. I contemplated the entire sequence of events played out chronologically over the course of my being a fan; particularly that it more or less began and concluded with the 1984 *Powerslave* set design and theme. I say *concluded* in the place of *ended*, because that seems like a drastic word to use. But a term expressing some form of finality is necessary. I continue to be a fan, but this concert had very fittingly tied off a loose end that had been left hanging for almost a quarter of a century.

This is because Iron Maiden had been one of those *things* that I craved that seemed to be consistently just beyond my grasp growing up cold and bored in an isolated town. Yeah, I was lucky enough to see the Sudbury Maiden show in 1984, but it was a meagre representation of the full package that the world outside Sudbury would see. Stuff like that always stuck with me and didn't wash off. And this idea was a microcosm for how I would contemplate my life as a small town kid for a long time. I always felt like there was so much distance between where I was and where I should be, and I was always looking to make a reconciliation that wasn't possible or even really necessary. And I wore that feeling for quite some time. It fuelled this impetus to just outwardly *consume* and *absorb* to make up for all the stuff that I felt like I missed out on. When I finally left the north and got down to Toronto, I greedily sucked up every experience and Taco Bell combo that I couldn't have previously. In doing so, I built a new me. And now, I couldn't help but think that seeing this concert in this way was kinda like the icing on the vindication cake I had invented in my head.

Of course, this cake was really all icing with no substantial cake at its core at all. While it had ebbed considerably in the years leading up to this show, this event had summarily marked the merciful end of a foolish overcompensation neurosis I'd been carrying around most of my life. In this sense, Maiden's Somewhere Back in Time concert took on larger meaning.

I smiled wistfully during the closing chords of Iron Maiden's encore. As I smiled, I realized I wasn't trying so hard to seek any sort of joy that risked being artificial or greedily redemptive. Instead I felt more like I had finally arrived at a newfound understanding of the application that all of these experiences have had in my life. It took some time, but I get it now.

The basis of my fondness for all of this, the hard rock and heavy metal music I obsessed over and loved so dearly as a kid, hinges completely and absolutely on the opiate of the masses - nostalgia. The recalled identification of a time when there were no responsibilities, and nary a care in the world about much of anything. The emotional imprint resulting from mythologizing music comes through mythologizing childhood. And childhood and its emblems, like music, no matter the quality or substance, will always be naturally commemorated.

Cherishing music the way that I do is the closest I've ever come to possessing any semblance of a soul. No matter the musical genre, the real allure has always been the emotional draw that's involved. Even if you don't realize it, or want to realize it because the music may be overly telling of what's really inside you – anger, love, or otherwise. People want to feel redemption through the music they hold most dear, like an elementary extension of their own personal self-perception. We're always looking for answers in music, always looking for our emotional selves somewhere in there. Somewhere. And, as is typically the case, the journey will be more gratifying than the destination.

About the Author

Brent Jensen grew up in the mean streets of Espanola, ever curiously peering over the fence to see what was on the other side. He graduated from Laurentian University in Sudbury with a degree in psychology and headed down to the big city with a bag of clothes, a clock radio and a dream. Brent currently works in telecommunications management and has done freelance writing for various publications including *Perfect Sound Forever*. He lives in a suburb of Toronto, Ontario with his wife, and can be reached at nosleeptilsudbury@yahoo.ca.

www.ingramcontent.com/pod-product-compliance
Lightning Source LLC
Chambersburg PA
CBHW031944080426
42735CB00007B/254